CAPTAIN OATES

Soldier and Explorer

CAPTAIN OATES

Soldier and Explorer

Sue Limb and Patrick Cordingley

LEO COOPER
LONDON

First published in 1982 by William Batsford Ltd
Reprinted, 1982, 1983

Republished in this revised edition in 1995 by
LEO COOPER
190 Shaftesbury Avenue, London WC2H 8JL
an imprint of Pen & Sword Books Ltd,
47 Church Street,
Barnsley, South Yorkshire S70 2AS

A CIP record for this book is available from the British Library

ISBN 0 85052 472 5

Typeset by Phoenix Typesetting, Ilkley, West Yorkshire

Printed by Redwood Books Ltd, Trowbridge, Wilts.

To the memory of
Miss Violet Oates and
Professor Frank Debenham

Contents

List of Illustrations

Photographic Acknowledgements

The authors and publishers would like to thank the following individuals and organizations for permission to reproduce their photographs:

Colonel Sir Mike Ansell
Mrs Sheila Blenkinsop
The Illustrated London News Picture Library
Lieutenant-Colonel E. B. G. Oates
Oates Memorial Library & Museum, Selbourne
Popperfoto
Geraldine Prentice
Alan Rawlings
5th Royal Inniskilling Dragoon Guards
Sir Peter Scott
Scott Polar Research Institute
Major-General J. M. D. Ward-Harrison

The cover illustration showing Captain Oates walking to his death, by J. C. Dollman, the Cavalry and Guards Club.

List of Maps

My old heart beats with pride as I read of the heroism of the late Captain Oates. May his deeds be handed down to all generations of Inniskillings, as an immortal example of self-sacrifice to assist his comrades to attain their goal. I wrote a letter of condolence to his mother, and I was proud to receive the following reply:

'My grateful thanks – Caroline Oates.'

Mr George Maughan, a Balaclava veteran. A letter to the 6th (Inniskilling) Dragoons, February 1913.

At school there is a bronze bas-relief head of Oates outside the library. His nose is bright and shiny – it looks as if he's got a streaming cold. That's because we always touch his nose as we go past – in the hope that some of his courage might rub off on us.

Jonathan Ray. Eton 1974–8

Introduction

In 1962, Antarctic enthusiasts commemorated the fiftieth anniversary of Scott's death. At Cheltenham, the home town of Scott's companion Dr Edward Wilson, there was an exhibition, and Herbert Ponting's cine-film of the *Terra Nova* Expedition, *90° South*, was shown. Among the many interested townspeople who attended was Sue Limb, whose schoolgirl susceptibilities led her to an enduring fascination with the whole story. Wishing to make contact with a surviving member of the expedition, she decided on Frank Debenham, whose books she had greatly enjoyed. Debenham had been one of Scott's geologists and had later founded the Scott Polar Research Institute in Cambridge.

Christmas was near, so she made a Christmas card in the style of the *South Polar Times*, a light-hearted magazine which had been produced in Antarctica during the winter of 1911. Trembling slightly at her temerity, she posted the card (signed also by two friends for moral support) and waited for any response. If she was lucky, she thought, there might be an official note from a secretary. After all, an Emeritus Professor is a very august personage to a schoolgirl. But soon after Christmas a thick enve-lope dropped onto her doormat.

'My dear dear incredible trio,' the astonishing letter began, 'You have sent me the most delightful, the cleverest and the most understanding Christmas card I have ever received in my life . . .' He wrote of his life in Cambridge, was full of teases, and ended: 'If your parents would entrust you to Mrs Deb and me here for a few days on your next holidays we would be delighted to see you. The advantage of three Mahomets com-ing on their camels to one immobile mountain is that there is the Polar Institute where you would get closer contact with things you already know a great deal about.'

Sue had the great good fortune to become one of Debenham's 'adopted nieces', and though he was eighty, fairly deaf and almost totally incapacitated by heart disease, 'Uncle Deb' had a razor-sharp mind, a flawless memory and an endearing personality which made him an enchanting friend and an invaluable companion. He steered her youthful literary aspirations towards the idea of a biography of Captain Oates. Louis Bernacchi had attempted the task in the 1930s, but Oates's formidable mother had opposed the idea, and without access to family archives, or much military experience, Bernacchi was bound to be at a grave disadvantage.

Debenham introduced Sue to Violet Oates, the sister of Captain Oates, who was also in her eighties, though very active and alert. 'The important thing,' wrote Debenham after the first meeting, 'is that [Miss Oates] is ready to consider the idea of your someday writing a biography of her brother. I would not advise your attempting such a book until you have finished your school and other training so there's no hurry about that, but there should be no delay in finding or hearing the material, that is, making contact with certain people.

'That is so partly because those of us who knew him are becoming rather thin on the ground, but even more so because Soldier [Oates's nickname in the Antarctic] was far from being a letter writer and you will have to depend more on circumstantial evidence, what he said and did, than what he wrote down. His character will only appear from his deeds and not from his words.'

Debenham turned out to be wrong about the letters. When Violet Oates welcomed Sue into her home in Suffolk she showed her a trunkful of letters, hundreds of them, written by her brother to his mother from the time he was at Eton right up to his last letter home from the Polar Journey. No one outside the family had previously had access to these letters. Ill-spelt and scarcely punctuated, they commented drily on his experiences. Most thrilling of all, Violet Oates had secretly copied extracts from her brother's Antarctic diary just before her mother ordered it to be destroyed.

During the 1960s, others, too, did more than just encourage. Mrs Debenham, whose hospitality to Sue was overwhelming, was also full of useful background stories. Mrs Sheila Blenkinsop, Captain Oates's niece, helped over research into Victorian Putney. George Seaver, biographer of Scott, Wilson, and Bowers, produced notes of interviews which dealt with Oates. Mrs Dorothy Irving-Bell, an Antarctic enthusiast, gave countless snippets of information, and James Graham-Campbell supplied details of life at Eton. Sue's husband Roy Porter was a source of many stimulating ideas and her parents were invaluable throughout the whole enterprise, both in terms of general support and specific help such as the copying of manuscript material.

Conscious of her good fortune, the aspiring biographer pored over these manuscripts, and basked in the company of Violet Oates, an irresistibly sympathetic woman. From the manuscript sources and from conversations with Miss Oates and Professor Debenham, she produced a first draft of the book shortly before going up to Cambridge in 1965. Sadly, 'Uncle Deb' died during that Michaelmas Term, and Violet Oates in 1966.

Undergraduate work flooded in, then research, teaching and other adult commitments. The first draft of the Oates biography would require a great deal of military research and detail, as well as a thorough re-writing, before it could claim to be a respectable volume and not a piece of juvenilia. For some years it was impossible to find time for such a project: the military background in particular seemed a daunting area.

Then in the autumn of 1979, Patrick Cordingley entered the scene. He was an officer in Oates's Regiment, the 5th Royal Inniskilling Dragoon Guards, and his interest in Scott's expedition had led to his giving a series of lectures on the subject.

He proposed a collaboration to re-write the book. He would undertake all the military research and provide additional Antarctic material, and the book would be written as a joint effort.

The earlier notes from unpublished sources such as Oates's letters and his diary, and his mother's diary, together with invaluable memories of conversations with Professor Debenham and Violet Oates, formed the basis of this new book. Much extra material was brought to light in the regimental archives, from which 'Titus', as he was known by his fellow-officers, emerges as a highly individual and sardonic commentator on his age.

The 5th Royal Inniskilling Dragoon Guards is very much a family regiment with its own distinctive atmosphere, so wherever possible the writers drew on documents relating to the Inniskillings' own history: not just the Regimental Historical records, military biographies, and so on, but also people's memories. Mrs Susan Ingall, who as a toddler was dandled on Oates's knee during tea-parties in British India, recalled her colonial childhood. Mr H. E. Bennett, a bandsman who served with Oates in India told how he remembered the Drum horse bolting with him and ending up, ignominious and covered with dust, at Oates's feet. Colonel Johnnie Brooke, a fellow-officer of Oates in Egypt and India, who at ninety-seven years of age had survived Oates by seventy-five years, nevertheless remembered him, and regimental routine, with effortless clarity.

Occasionally, when the Inniskillings' own archives or living witnesses could not provide a necessary detail, the writers drew on the wealth of

3

military history relating to the era, in the form of manuscript letters and diaries as well as published sources. This military detail reveals the touchingly gallant, and often curiously absurd atmosphere of the British Army before the First World War. Recent works on Scott have provoked stormy debates about his methods and character, and his and Oates's place in history, and has shown that there is as much interest as ever in this unique event. Oates's military experience, and his Antarctic adventure show us a man who deserves to be known and valued for more than the brief, luminous moment of his death.

When the book was re-worked, help and advice came from many sources. Lieutenant-Colonel Ted Oates, and Mrs Sheila Blenkinsop, Oates's nephew and niece, made us most welcome in their homes and helped in every way possible. People who knew Oates, or lived in Egypt or India at the same time, such as Mrs Susan Ingall, Lieutenant-Colonel Johnnie Brooke, Major-General E. G. W. Harrison and Mr H. E. Bennett, deserve our thanks for their recollections. Others have provided information about the 6th (Inniskilling) Dragoons in the early part of the twentieth century, and many of them knew Oates's friends and fellow-officers. General Sir John Anderson, Colonel Sir Mike Ansell, and Major-General J. M. D. Ward-Harrison helped in this way. Our thanks also go to those who helped, encouraged and advised us because of their interest in Captain Oates: Brigadier Nick Ansell, Noel and Jean Santry, John Richardson, Noel and Gri Harrison, Roland Huntford, David Walton, Colonel Andy Evans, Jack Valette, Jonathan Ray and Karen Moseley.

Special thanks must go to Captain Jim Boardman, Secretary of the 5th Royal Inniskilling Dragoon Guards Regimental Association and Curator of the Regimental Museum, in Chester. He has given up much of his valuable time to help our researches. His secretary, too, Mrs Rita Robertshaw has been kind and helpful. Valuable letters and manuscripts have been shown to us by Alan Rawlings, R. Barden and A. McMillan. Dr Alan Rogers advised us of the medical problems facing polar travellers.

We could not have written this book without the invaluable help of two institutes. Jenny Streeter and Dr June Chatfield, curators of the Oates Memorial Library and Museum at Selborne in Hampshire, were liberal with material, advice and time, as were Harry King and Clive Holland of the Scott Polar Research Institute in Cambridge.

The staffs of the Ministry of Defence Library, Whitehall, the Royal United Services Institutes, the Public Record Office and the Royal Geographical Society have always welcomed our enquiries. An army of volunteers has contributed much hard work. Lieutenant-Colonel Noel

Harrison drew the maps and helped with the photographic work, together with Mr P. Bohanna and Wing-Commander John Hall. We owe a great debt of gratitude to Kay Warren, our indefatigable and sensitive typist. Michael Cordingley, Patrick Vigors and Brian Inglis read the manuscript and provided most useful comments. Michael Neve and Roy Porter were full of fascinating ideas, and David Cannadine was kind enough to undertake detailed historical advice.

Lieutenant-Colonel Ted Oates, Mrs Sheila Blenkinsop, Sir Peter Scott, Geraldine Prentice, Major-General J. M. D. Ward-Harrison, Colonel Sir Mike Ansell, Mr R. Barden, Captain Mark Anderson, The Oates Memorial Library and Museum, The Scott Polar Research Institute, The Illustrated London News Picture Library, the Punch Library, and Popperfoto all kindly gave permission for the use of copyright material.

Financial assistance in direct and indirect ways has come from Miss Violet Oates, the 5th Royal Inniskilling Dragoon Guards' Regimental Association (and our thanks go particularly to Major-General Henry Woods, its Chairman) and from Cox's and King's Branch of Lloyd's Bank (who once handled Oates's account).

We are indebted to Bill Waller of Batsford for all he has done to make this book possible. Our grateful thanks, above all, to our families, friends and colleagues for their heroic forbearance during the completion of this work.

SL and PAJC

London 1982

★ ★ ★

We were both surprised and gratified by the number of letters that we received after the first publication of *Captain Oates* in 1982. Some pointed out errors in the text, ranging from the incorrect spelling of place names in South Africa to the length of Captain Oates's yacht, *The Saunterer*. We have amended this edition as a result. Altering the print-size at the same time caused extra effort and we are very grateful to Miss Pixie Parker and Mr Ian MacLaren for their hard work. We would also like to thank Sir Nicholas Hewitt, Mrs Barbara Bramall and the editorial staff at Pen & Sword Books for their help and encouragement.

SL and PAJC

York 1995

1

Childhood

On St Patrick's Day, 17 March 1880, at 6.20 a.m., Lawrence Edward Grace Oates was born. On his birth certificate his father described himself as a gentleman – a word which was to define young Oates's values and behaviour throughout his life. It also meant, in practical terms, that his father William Edward Oates, did not need to earn a living. There was a substantial private income to take care of that. Instead he enjoyed a gentlemanly leisure. In his younger days he had travelled in Africa with his brother Frank, and also explored Spitzbergen. The Oates brothers, born in Leeds, both Fellows of the Royal Geographical Society, were enthusiastic naturalists and big-game hunters – and nobody, in the 1870s, would have seen any contradictions in that. For William, however, a fairly domestic destiny was in store, that of amateur artist (he often spent whole days sketching on Hampstead Heath) and Victorian *paterfamilias*. Lawrence Oates was his first son, and second child. There were two girls, Lilian Mary, a year older than Lawrence, and Violet Emily, a year younger. The benjamin of the family, Bryan, was born in 1883.

Despite his romantic good looks (complete with dashing moustache) and his many interests, the father William Oates remains a shadowy figure when compared with his formidable wife Caroline Anne (née Buckton, of Meanwood, Leeds). In some senses he seems to have played the Albert to her Victoria, the intelligent and educated consort who bowed out early leaving her a long widowhood in which to develop her powerful personality to the full. Caroline Oates was overjoyed at the birth of her first son, and went on calling him 'Baby Boy' for years – long after another baby boy had been born. There are many signs that she treasured Lawrence more than anyone else on earth, and she was to exert a most emphatic influence on him for the whole of his life, not least in the example of her own character. Though, in common with many Victorian women, she retired to bed for a couple of days every month, it was probably only a formal concession to nature. When fortune showered

7

its bitterest blows on her, she was to display a truly Roman fortitude.

Lawrence Oates – known to the rest of his family as 'Laurie' – was born at an oddly uncertain moment in the fortunes of his family and indeed his country. For England, the 1880s were a gloomy period of Irish troubles, massive unemployment, deflation and economic crisis. There were also rumblings in the wider world – from Boers in South Africa and the Mahdi and his dervishes in the Sudan – which were to affect the lives and fortunes of many British people, not least young Laurie himself. The Oates family was pre-occupied with the dreary business of house-hunting, for in 1880 William Oates was a squire who had not yet found his manor. He and his wife had both come from Yorkshire, where the Oates family had held property since the sixteenth century.[1] There was also an Essex connection, for at the time of the Domesday Book an Otes held the Manor of Gestingthorpe. The Oates were a most ancient family, for an Oates, or Otes, was on the battle-roll of Hastings.[2] But eight hundred years later, William and Caroline turned to London in search of a home for their growing family.

It was no easy matter, and for the first few years of his life, Laurie, together with brothers, sisters, servants and all the bric-à-brac of a Victorian household, was hauled from one end of England to the other. When not in London, they spent winters in Hastings, summers in Whitby, and made frequent trips to Meanwoodside in Leeds to see relatives. He had been born in a house in Putney rented especially for the occasion, and two years later his parents were house-hunting in the same area – and beyond. As Caroline Oates wrote:

> Jan 11th, 1882. W & I go househunting in Putney – find nothing suitable.
> Jan 12th. To Swiss Cottage, Finchley Road and South Hampstead to househunt. No avail.
> Jan 13th. To see a house in Stafford Terrace, Kensington. Nothing at all.[3]

Despite the preoccupations of house-hunting, and the discomforts of repeated pregnancies, Mrs Oates took a keen interest in the welfare of her 'Baby Boy'. His sister Violet recalled that even as an infant he had 'an extraordinary firm mouth',[4] but he was also displaying a most worrying tendency to be delicate and, in an age when there was no cure for many childhood ailments and infant mortality was high, his mother's anxieties were understandable. There were many happy times, however. For a start, his second birthday, spent in Leeds, brought a firelit birthday tea, and some marvellous presents spread out for him: bricks from his practical mother, a tea-set (toy, surely, but china nonetheless) from his elegant father, a toy elephant from Lilian, a stable from nurse, and lots of painted wooden animals to live in the stable, a present from his aunt and uncle. His favourite toys, however, from the days when he could first discriminate amongst them, were the toy pistol and the wooden sword. On holiday at Ewe Cote, a hamlet near Whitby, there were all the joys of coast and countryside, and most exciting of all, real live donkeys upon which he took his first riding lessons.

In April 1885, his parents at last found a suitable house. It was not, perhaps, the home of their dreams, but it would do: a typically Victorian Putney mansion, large, detached and redbrick, in a quiet street. 263 Upper Richmond Road became their permanent home. The children must have explored it eagerly, and found a conservatory at the back leading to a large walled garden with a most intriguing shrubbery in which, no doubt, many campaigns were fought and many explorers met a grisly death. The Putney house brought them good neighbours, too: particularly a family called Parker who lived in nearby Colinette Road and had a son Patty who was exactly Laurie's age. They shared a love of wild games and rough-and-tumble.

Life, however, was not all fun and games. The Oates household may have seemed relaxed by Victorian standards, but the serious business of education was very much to the fore. A governess was employed, who gallantly attempted to interest Lilian and Laurie in the principles of reading and writing. To the boy, however, a row of silly little black marks on a page could never equal the attractions of the sword, the pistol and the shrubbery. Alas, for the ineffectual governess: the children occasionally arranged a strike, abandoning their chairs and taking refuge under the table. Despite the governess's embarrassed reassurances that Laurie was 'attentive and painstaking', Mr Oates soon perceived the true state of affairs, and Laurie was told that, after the summer holidays, he would be sharing Patty Parker's governess, Miss Payne, who, apart from being a more dynamic personality, actually knew some Latin – considered a vital accomplishment apparently, even for the pre-school Victorian child.

Illness intervened, however. Eagle-eyed, Mrs Oates watched her first-born son: no coughing-fit escaped her ears. She knew that his hands were often blue with cold in winter. He caught severe chills, which settled on his chest; he suffered an inflamed left lung. His skin grew pale and sallow, and shadows developed under his eyes. His mother hoped that the long summer holiday would restore him to health. First they went to Sidmouth in Devon, where mother and children gathered primroses in

9

the fields. Later, at Whitby, Laurie was given his very own donkey. His delight may be imagined: a donkey on the sands at Upgang or in the field around Ewe Cote became a fiery charger in the child's imagination. Yet even the delightful donkey could not work magic. On their return to London, Laurie was still far from well. While he had the first few Latin lessons with Miss Payne, his parents held urgent discussions about his health. They consulted the very best doctors – Dr Gunn of 74 Wimpole Street, for one – and received the same, reassuring but guarded diagnosis. There was no evidence of tuberculosis, but young Oates should go abroad for the winter, or the fogs, soot, frosts and damp might cause his health to break down altogether. A quick decision was made: he would go to South Africa to visit cousins who lived in Cape Town.

There was a harder decision for Mrs Oates. Should she wave goodbye to her son and entrust him to his father's sole care? Or should she leave her other three children (two of them still mere toddlers) and go south with her invalid? Quite apart from the claims of Lilian, Violet and Bryan, there were other considerations. She herself was a bad sailor and the sea-journey took almost three weeks. But she did not hesitate for long: of course, Laurie must come first. The other three children would have to be brave, and she would have to hand them over to the care of aunts, servants, and nannies. On 17 December 1885, when her children must all have been looking forward to Christmas, Caroline Oates set sail from England with her beloved Laurie, her trusty husband at her side. William Oates was to undertake his son's education during the winter, and to assist these studies, Caroline Oates gave her son a silver penholder as a New Year's present.

For her the voyage was dreadful. She was seasick and homesick, anxious about the little brood she had left behind, and to her alarm, four children on board developed chickenpox. Laurie, however, seemed blithe and carefree. He showed no signs of seasickness, played cricket on deck, made friends with some of the bearded old salts among the crew and proudly showed them his sailor suit. At New Year there were exciting celebrations and on 2 January, a parade of sailors on deck. Throughout the journey, Laurie accepted the tutelage of his father with a far better grace than he had shown towards Miss Payne or her unfortunate predecessor. In the depths of her seasickness and misery, Mrs Oates could not have failed to notice that Laurie was enjoying his voyage to the full.

On the evening of 14 January they dropped anchor in Table Bay. Here, miraculously, it was summer. The air did not bite his lungs as Laurie stood on deck staring at the serene mass of Table Mountain, which dwarfed anything he had seen before. For the first few days they stayed near Cape Town with an old family friend, Mrs Bushey. Laurie travelled into Cape Town with his mother, and they walked together down the fine straight avenues, and gazed at the street markets with their dazzling mounds of exotic flowers and strange fruit. Back at Mrs Bushey's they picked strawberries, chased butterflies, and played in the fields. The Victorian winter must have seemed a long way away as mother and son cavorted in the southern light.

No doubt Mrs Bushey told the little boy the legend of Table Mountain – how when it wore a dense cloud cap it was a certain sign that the Devil was about, smoking his pipe on a nearby peak. William Oates had tales to tell his son, too: tales of his own African travels twelve years earlier with his brother. William and Frank had ridden north from Durban in 1873 and followed in the footsteps of Livingstone and Stanley. Laurie's Uncle Frank had been a great naturalist, who collected birdskins, insects and reptiles, who knew how to talk to Bushmen, and who had been only the fifth white man to see the Victoria Falls on the Zambesi. Only a few weeks later, in 1875, he had died of malaria in Matabeleland, so sadly he was to remain an enigmatic figure to Laurie: a mystery, and probably an inspiration. An uncle who had died young (Frank Oates had been only thirty-four) hundreds of miles from home and alone in some of the darkest and most unexplored country in the world, was surely a hero.

After a few days the Oates family moved on to stay with their cousins the Burdetts who lived further away from Cape Town. They drove over the mountains to Hout Bay, where the sand was white as chalk and the sea a deep sapphire-blue. Laurie played with his cousin Jack, but they kept well clear of the booming surf. Mr Oates took the boys fishing, and back in the Burdett's garden there were more games. Mrs Oates watched hopefully as colour returned to her son's cheeks. Surely the air, the fresh fruit and the sunshine would work the desired miracle. But miracles are rare. By February Laurie was in bed again. He had sore legs and was very depressed. A mysterious rash came and went. So did a mysterious doctor called Smuts who prescribed a nasty medicine but seemed cheerful. And gradually Laurie did recover – at first sitting on the verandah and listening to the shrill birdcalls, later walking into the mountains with his father. The lesson, for his mother, had been learnt. Rome was not built in a day, and her delicate son still required much vigilance.

A brief trip to visit some more cousins in Caledon rounded off their South African winter. The weather was very hot, and it was threshing time in the fields. Laurie played among the stooks while his father sketched; his mother, lurking no doubt beneath huge white hat and parasol, watched, hoped, and noted it all down briefly in her large round childish hand. (She kept a diary all her life, though the entries were tantalizingly cryptic and commonplace.) On 10 March, she records that they set sail for England in the *Spartan*. Soon she had lapsed into her habitual seasickness, but Laurie made friends with a rumbustious family of three boys called Solomons from St Helena.

'Laurie was very happy playing with Mrs Solomons' three boys, but later we had a great fright as we thought he was lost. He was, for ¾ hour. He was found in the carpenter's cabin!'[5] He also enjoyed a swing which the quartermaster rigged up on deck, and on his birthday his mother gave him a most welcome present: another, smarter, toy pistol. They broke their journey briefly at Madeira, and on 2 April went 'on a little steamer to Santa Cruz, but Baby Boy and I were so sick that the expedition was a failure'.[6] In short, their voyage was losing its charm. They longed to be home, and in a few days were reunited with the rest of the Oates clan for a blissful holiday in Sidmouth.

The following autumn, a major adventure awaited: school. It was a big echoing house in Colinette Road called Willington School, established not long before by the Misses Hale whom Violet found 'daunting figures, wearing starched collars and with hair piled high'. After the wonderful freedom of South Africa, and lessons with his delightful papa, which were as likely to take place on a trek through the mountains as on deck in mid-ocean, Laurie must have found the Misses Hale dull. Reading, writing, arithmetic, Latin . . . how tedious they were. And he was already behind his fellows, having missed the much more rigorous schooling of an English winter. He may have enjoyed history, though, for history in those days was the study of kings and wars, campaigns and great men, and Napoleon was to remain a lifelong hero of his. It was typical of him to revere a great general irrespective of his outrageously foreign blood: for what was a Corsican, after all, but a mixture of Frog and Dago? But Oates, though xenophobic, could admire even generals who had trounced the British, if they were great enough.

Willington School was, however, a source of many new friends: future stockbrokers and clergymen and cannon-fodder. With Patty Parker or Rob Dick or the girls, but inevitably accompanied by a servant, he went on long walks and gradually the delights of Putney were revealed. If the Oates's servant girl had taken a fancy to one of the ostlers at the Fox and Hounds, a livery stables in the Upper Richmond Road, Laurie would have been allowed time to explore and sniff the delicious smells of hay and harness. The girls liked going up Putney Park Lane to pick flowers on the Common (for Putney wore in those days a distinctly semi-rural air, abounding in market-gardens, and cultivating the *rus in urbe* notion of haymaking parties at some of the great houses). If there were no riding-schools to be seen on the Common, Laurie might prevail upon the servant to escort them to the High Street. Many interesting establishments lined the route: a sweetshop kept by Mrs James, Henry Crocker's Saddler's and Harness Makers, and William Howell's smithy with its glowing forge and weeping white hot iron. And all the time, up and down the roads, horses moved, pulling all manner of carts and carriages. Biggest were the mountainous dray horses with their cartloads of barrels moving majestically through clouds of their own steam to the breweries in Wandsworth. Then there were the tired greys in pairs who pulled the buses. So many tempting places to explore – such as the dark alleys that skirted The Spotted Horse and The Rose and Crown, and especially Pepper Alley by the Bull and Star. But, as Laurie was no doubt reminded, he was a young gentleman, not a street Arab. Many a Victorian child must have seethed at his own gentlemanly destiny, and envied the street urchin his toughness and his freedom. Even freedom from shoes could seem romantic to the over-dressed, over-cossetted children of the middle classes. And as for a wild life, running amidst the flashing wheels of the street – picking a pocket here, pulling a face there – alas, it was probably as alluring as impossible to young Oates.

The Victorian Sunday cast its iron shadow across their young lives. Breakfast was early, and then the whole family would troop off to church at All Saints' on the Common. It was a fairly new church but no doubt still seemed draughty and dismal to the children, who had to endure an enormously long service which included the Litany and an interminable sermon. Laurie referred facetiously to the Litany as 'the long kneel down'. In the afternoons it was church again, this time at St Margaret's bordering on Putney Park Lane, where a special service for children was held by the ageing Reverend Henly. His wavering voice, butt of many secret impersonations and much mirth, rattled out simple questions. His verdict on the children's answers was invariably, 'Quite right, quite right!' On the way home Laurie would remark to Violet and Lilian, 'Old *Quite right* was in good form today.'

The next winter Laurie was again taken to South Africa, but this time Caroline Oates entrusted him to her husband. Once again the plan achieved its objective: serious illness was avoided. Mrs Oates sailed out to Madeira to meet her beloved menfolk on their return journey. They were reunited on 17 March 1887 – a red-letter day, Laurie's seventh birthday. His mother had come laden with presents from everybody at home: two pencil cases, one from Violet and one from Miss Payne;

chocolates and books; and from Patty, the inevitable revolver to add to his arsenal. To celebrate the occasion they went out in a rowing boat, looking back on the mountainous island and skirting round the long lava reefs. Every day they went out with a donkey and cart and two natives, Mr Oates carrying his camera. They saw a shipwrecked boat, walked on the beaches, and explored inland among the groves of laurel and chestnut.

The visit then began to turn sour. A man called Mackenzie staying in the same hotel shot himself. Laurie was taken out by his parents, far away on to the stretches of sandy beach, but he must have known something of what had happened, with that astute sixth sense of children which is so inconvenient. The next day the family saw a procession in the distance, with flowers and jangling music: a celebration of some sort. Grateful for the diversion, they approached more closely, Mr Oates preparing his camera. But it was no celebration. In the midst of everything they suddenly saw the body of a little girl lying pale as stone in her open coffin. The band played, the candles shivered, and the procession went on up the road. It was too late to shield Laurie's eyes. He had seen death, and floating in her sea of flowers, she had looked more like a bride. The return to England was hastened by a sudden surfeit of colds and coughs, and they left Madeira in the pouring rain – no doubt with mixed feelings.

At home things began to settle to a more cheerful temper. Young Oates appeared to be healthier. In 1890, he was sent to a preparatory school, Remenham Place at Henley-on-Thames. He grew tall and straight, and loved all sports, spending as much time as he possibly could on horseback. Living in Putney, the family looked forward eagerly to the annual Boat Race, which transformed an ordinary spring Saturday into a Gala occasion. The Parkers' grandmother had a garden which sloped down to the river and was ideally suited for seeing the beginning of the race. To this spot, rain or shine, the Oates family would repair. Leaning on the garden wall, Laurie would have seen the launches, the flotillas of boats, the crowds in boaters and late Victorian finery gathering on the newly built Putney bridge. The cries of vendors, the various blues sported by partisans, the laughter and the pranks would all have delighted him. Then, the sight of the two teams carrying their boat down to the river, and that electric second of suspense as both sets of oars stung the surface . . . a moment to be relished. Perhaps one day he would go to Oxford himself.

For the time being all grandiose notions of Oxford and great races between godlike young men had to give way to the harsh realities of growing up with sisters who could wield a savage cricket bat. Shortly after his eleventh birthday, Laurie was playing cricket with his siblings when Lilian felled him with such a violent crack on the head (whether through inexperience or exasperation is not recorded) that he had to retire hurt and go to bed. He was still in bed a couple of days later when his parents came into the room carrying bunches of spring flowers, violets and daffodils. They had, they informed him, been to somewhere called Gestingthorpe, where they had picked these flowers. And Gestingthorpe was to be their home.

Putney, though pleasant, was not the Oates's true element, and house-hunting of a fairly gentle kind had recently sprung up again, this time in the countryside surrounding London. After all, town life was exhausting, the London air was thick with soot and fog in winter, Laurie was still delicate, and Mr Oates had himself been ill early in 1891. In Gesting-thorpe Hall all their dreams were realized. A Georgian manor house buried deep in the Essex countryside (the county colonized by the Otes family so many centuries before): Mr Oates had found his parish, and the manor its lord. Preparations for the move were brisk. In June, Lilian, Violet and Bryan were sent away to Whitby but, significantly, Laurie stayed behind with his parents. Why? To help with the arrangements? He was eleven, so it was a possibility. But it is also quite likely that at such an exciting time Mrs Oates simply could not bear to be parted from him.

On 24 June 1891 Laurie went with his father and one George Oates to their new home. From London they took the train to Sudbury; thence by trap along high-hedged and wheeling lanes. The hamlet of Gestingthorpe was little more than a church and a few cottages. Opposite the church, their trap plunged up the drive to Gestingthorpe Hall. Dense trees fluttered overhead, then the drive swung round and the house appeared. Built of the same pink brick as the church, its blushes were veiled by ivy and Virginia Creeper, which skirted the long windows. Dark elms rose like a backcloth behind the house. The stage was set, and on to it stepped, possibly slightly dazed, the protagonists.

To an active boy who had been cooped up in a London suburb (how-ever pleasant) Gestingthorpe must have seemed a paradise. Behind the house were stables, before it, a vast park stretching lazily away into the distance. Fruit trees abounded and, near the road, a dark pool surrounded by bushes awaited his Naval Operations. There was a tennis court, and lawns as flat and smooth as carpets. But before he had leisure to explore everything, there was work to be done. Mrs Oates, having supervised the last of the packing in London, joined them, and every day vans arrived full of furniture. Their first Sunday visit to the little tumbledown church

15

must have been a delight after the vast impersonality of their London worship. And to be sure there was a throng of rural Essex faces taking a sly peek at the new Lord of the Manor and his family. What was their verdict on young Lawrence Oates? 'He looked as if a good meat pudden would've done him more good than going to the South Pole'[8] was the comment, many years later, of one Gestingthorpe worthy.

No doubt Lilian, Bryan and Violet were subjected to the same scrutiny when they joined their parents. No doubt the canny villagers did not miss a trick. They would have noticed Lilian's elegance, for she was very much the trainee *grande-dame* even at twelve; whereas Violet, shy and awkward, giggling and hectic, cherished a Romantic impulse towards mountains and watercolours (a very happy combination, as it turned out). As for Bryan, he was the archetypal younger brother: coltish, cheery and a bit of a ne'er-do-well. And the children must have explored their huge, romantic, creaking old house with rapture. Laurie and Bryan were convinced that there must be a secret panel in the dining-room, and they carried out experiments by tapping the walls and investigated with a rope in the chimney. If Gestingthorpe had any ghostly or ghastly secrets, it refused to yield them. As if the house itself were not enough of a pleasure, the surrounding Essex countryside was enchanting. Half an hour's walk from the house were dark woods where the family went for picnics and stayed until twilight to hear the nightingales sing. Another walk – Violet's favourite – was along the stream to Belchamp. On these banks, if they kept very still, they might see the blue flash of a kingfisher's wings.

Young Oates was approaching his fourteenth birthday, that rite of passage which would translate him from Henley to Eton. He had not distinguished himself academically during his three and a half years at Remenham Place, for his headmaster Mr Everard recalled, 'Oates showed a particular liking for sport. He was a quiet, plodding kind of scholar, and good at all games.'[9] Being good at games in 1894 however, was not regarded, as it sometimes is now, as faint compensation for intellectual mediocrity. Games were the cornerstone of the English public school education. During the nineteenth century the public schools had gradually been reformed by a band of enlightened and determined schoolmasters, of whom Dr Arnold at Rugby was the prime example. Dr Arnold brought Christianity back to what had become fairly heathen and hedonistic institutions. Other reformers saw that organized games could play a most important role, providing 'a civilized out-of-door life in the form of cricket, football, and wholesome sports, [which] took the place of poaching, rat-hunting and poultry stealing.'[10] The idea was that organized sports developed character by emphasizing co-operation and a sense of fair play. Character, the most important element in the education of a gentleman, involved the cultivation of manliness, godliness, courage and justice: that combination of unostentatious piety with athleticism which came to be known as muscular Christianity. The public schools asked no more of their charges. They certainly were not so interested in the dissemination of mere knowledge, especially (God forbid!) knowledge which might be applied to life. Lieutenant-Colonel Frederick FitzWagram declared that he left Eton 'without the slightest knowledge of any subject which has been the smallest use to me in after life'.[11]

It would certainly be wrong to suggest that Eton was an intellectual wasteland in the 1890s. H. E. Luxmoore, for example, was a master whose aesthetic enthusiasms extended to the Pre-Raphaelites. He persuaded G. F. Watts to let the school have a copy of his *Sir Galahad*, and Watts wrote, on presenting the painting to the school, that he thought 'it may be of use as a peg whereon to hang an occasional little discourse . . . upon the dignity and beauty of purity and chivalry, which things should be the characteristics of the gentleman.'[12] It is unlikely that young Oates fell under Luxmoore's influence: he was not an aesthete. He would probably think a 'little discourse' on purity and chivalry was 'the most fearful rot' but that did not stop him from being chivalrous to his fingertips, from his father's example. As for purity, probably the only thing he knew about girls was that they could wield a mean cricket bat. And that was probably the most important thing to know.

The headmaster of Eton in 1894 was Edmond Warre, a powerful man, an Oxford rowing blue who established the Eton Volunteer Corps and believed firmly in 'the British Empire, the military virtues and the cult of games . . . patriotism was virtually exalted into a religion and to die for one's country was the supreme sacrifice.'[13] This was the philosophy which enfolded Lawrence Oates as he arrived at Eton, an awkward fourteen year old in his starched collar and top hat. Violet used to joke that her brother looked just like the monkey which advertised Monkey Brand soap, but the photographs taken at about this time show an emerging adult face whose good looks are Roman rather than Simian. He was assigned to Mr Rawlings' House, Corner House by Barnes Pool Bridge. No doubt he struggled with Latin and Greek which formed the basis of an Eton education, but the school's emphasis on educating the 'whole man', the importance of sport and military values, must have suited him well.

He would have experienced the gamut of eccentricities which constituted Eton life in the 1890s: the fagging system (as a junior boy he would find himself acting as servant to an older one – cleaning his boots and making his tea), the reverence for 'Pop' – that Parnassian club which the most senior boys adorned, advertising the fact with their brocade waist-coats and lordly whiskers; the celebrations on 4 June – when the whole school was *en fête* and a throng of important and titled parents converged on the sleepy little town. Of course, Eton was the training-ground of the ruling class, and nothing was more certain than that some of Oates's contemporaries would go on to become Ministers of State, ambassadors, archbishops and generals. Trade and Industry, however, were still not quite the thing.

In his first year he played for his house in the finals of the Junior House Cricket Cup, but it was not a heroic performance: he was bowled by Pilkington for one. The following November he turned out as a foot-baller for the Lower Boys' House Cup, but Rawlings' House did not get to the finals. In the Lent Half he ran second in the 100 yards event of his House Sports. But all this exertion did not automatically mean health. Windsor is low-lying and very damp and cold, and Oates caught a chill which developed into near-fatal pneumonia. It was decided that he would not return to Eton, though he had made his mark there in a curious way. As a result of his illness the Lower Boys were permitted to wear sweaters – an innovation in their traditional dress which must have been most welcome. Instead of returning to Eton, he was sent to a crammer's at South Lynn, Eastbourne – a small establishment under the care of the Reverend H. E. Scott. This institution specialized in preparing boys for the army examinations, for 'from the more devotedly classical schools it long remained necessary for a boy . . . to go to the "crammer" if he seriously intended to go into the army'.[14]

It seemed as if Oates was making for an army career. Boys could obtain commissions by going to Sandhurst, Oxbridge, or through the Militia. For Oates, the Oxford route seemed the most appealing, as it would combine the benefits of a university education with an eventual commission. But both Sandhurst and Oxford had entrance exams, and a couple of years' hard study at South Lynn was required if he was to make up the ground lost during his much-interrupted education. By the time he arrived at Eastbourne, Oates was beginning to display a most distinctive character, as G. C. Coulton describes in *Fourscore Years*. 'He came to us quite young, perhaps at fifteen, an Etonian of rough offhand manners. Gradually he grew into a sort of honest, great Newfoundland puppy. Hence, again, he developed into a grown-up tame Newfoundland, boisterous but kindly. He was a fine middleweight boxer.

'One day, a major came to tea at South Lynn, bringing his son as a pupil. He sported rather conspicuous headgear, i.e. a brown bowler (alias "billycock"). Oates came in from golf and found this among other hats on the table in the entrance-hall. His reaction was: "What fellow has gone and been such a silly ass as to set up a brown billycock?" He kicked it round the hall, and finally thrust his fist through the exploded crown, plunging his arm through to the very brim. At that moment the major and his son emerged into the hall from their interview, shaking hands with Scott. After a few moments of hasty explanation and apology, Scott took the major back for another cut of tea, while Oates cycled off down St Anne's Hill at his usual breakneck speed into town, and reappeared with half a dozen brown billycocks at the major's choice.'[15] Soccer, boxing and kicking people's hats about remained a good deal more seductive to him than his studies.

At home, a new field of action was opening up. Around this time Oates must have experienced his first dance and his first hunt. The Oates family, though not lavish entertainers, did organize a dance and party at Christmas. The dance was held in the spacious drawing-room, its plasterwork ceiling and fine floor set off by the chandelier with its thirty-six candles glittering. Small Christmas trees, loaded with what Violet describes as 'ridiculous little presents' gave the room a festive air, and as the Broughams rolled up outside through the frost and fog, the small-time Sudbury band (led by the cadaverous Mr Sillitoe on piano) tuned up falteringly in a corner. The provincial band was more than made up for by the splendid buffet, and when young Oates had done his duty by the several local maidens to whom he owed a waltz, he would beat a retreat to a corner where an adoring manservant, Oscar, had saved him the most mouth-watering delicacies. Oscar, like a Jewish mother, watched jealously over Oates's appetite even at ordinary mealtimes, and if a third or fourth helping were refused, he took it as a personal slight and would stalk out with a martyred air.

Oates first hunted with the East Essex, and it rapidly became his most cherished activity. The danger, the open air, the escape from the drawing-room, the competition between fox and hounds and the combination of man, horse and dog all suited him admirably. The Reverend Bromwich, Rector of Gestingthorpe, recalled that 'we in Gestingthorpe remember [him] as a boy fond of every sport, who never knew the meaning of fear. Were he hunting and fell at a fence he was up and in the saddle and off again. The Belchamp Brook had no terrors for him. In hunting as in all his actions in life he went straight ahead. Always cheery, always good company, he was resolute to the greatest degree'.[16] After the kill, the talk might have been on the Irish question, the unemployed running amok in Pall Mall, Gordon's dramatic death at Khartoum, the impending Jubilee in 1897, or perhaps – in true sporting tradition – they only spoke of horses, hounds and the day's chase. Events in the wider world could still seem a long way away, in 1896. The world was not yet a village, travel across it was laborious, and some of its remotest corners remained as yet unexplored.

In March 1896 the Oates family decided to meet the summer by going out to Madeira for Easter. A half-competent soothsayer might have muttered warnings, given their mixed experiences there in the past. But all that was a long time ago and now it seemed a good idea: there would be sunshine, diversions, and much material for Mr Oates's camera and sketchbook. At first all was serene. Mr Oates found a most photogenic fountain to which the natives came with their water pots and stayed to chat in the bright sun. But picturesque water systems bring their dangers, and suddenly the family heard that there was an outbreak of typhoid on the island. Mr Oates was scrupulously careful, making his children drink boiled water, but soon fell ill himself. His wife immediately sent the children home, but stayed on herself to nurse him. It was a bad case. His condition deteriorated. Nearly frantic with worry, Mrs Oates sent cables home almost every day. Back in England, the children, paralyzed in a strange hushed world, waited for news. For once, 17 March passed without celebration. On that day Caroline Oates's diary records: 'a shocking morning of anxiety. I really believe my darling is sinking'.

Her diagnosis was correct. A fortnight later, her husband died. The island's regulations demanded an almost instant burial. Mrs Oates, supported by her brother-in-law who had arrived from England, attended to these last rites and then set sail for home. The holiday had turned to a lasting horror. To compound her grief, the boat docked at Plymouth, whereas Lilian and Laurie had been taken by their Uncle Charlie to meet her at Southampton. The family reunion finally took place in London, at the Great Eastern Hotel, and then they left for Gestingthorpe. As Laurie walked beside his mother into their silent home – both house and occupants muffled in the crêpe of deep mourning – he must have realized that he was now, at sixteen, the master of his house and the Lord of the Manor. Childhood was suddenly over and had given way to a world of sombre responsibilities.

Notes and references

1 Thomas Oates, born in 1554, lived in Thornhill Lees, and Lawrence, his brother, owned property in Woolley. The family tree leads to

Edward Oates, born in 1792 and grandfather of Captain Lawrence Oates, who lived at Meanwoodside. Edward had five children: Edward, Francis (Frank), William (Lawrence's father), Charles and Emily. Charles inherited Meanwoodside and when he died he left it jointly to Lawrence and his brother Bryan.

2 Also 'Hugh Le Fitz Oates, according to the Henry III Roll, was a Crusader in 1270, and accompanied Edward I to the Holy Land.' *The British Free Press*, 28 February 1913.
3 Caroline Oates, diary, January 1882.
4 Violet Oates, from conversations with Sue Limb between 1963 and 1965.
5 Caroline Oates, *op. cit.*, March 1882.
6 *Ibid* , April 1882.
7 Violet Oates, *op. cit.*
8 *The Halstead Gazette*, 18 March 1977.
9 *The Evening News*, 12 February 1913.
10 S. A. Cotton, *Memoir of Bishop Cotton*, p. 17.
11 Byron Farwell, *For Queen and Country*, p. 139.
12 Mark Girouard, *The Return to Camelot: Chivalry and the English Gentleman*, p.176.
13 *Ibid*.
14 Frank E. Huggett, *Victorian England as seen by 'Punch'*, p.158.
15 G.C. Coulton, *Fourscore Years*.
16 *The Essex Herald*, 19 February 1913.

2

Choice of Career

The Victorians gave death its due: deep mourning was in order for a year, and Caroline Oates, a woman of sober sensibility, was not one to make light of her loss. One imagines a certain grandeur in her grief: stoical and monumental. Throughout it, her eldest son supported her. Though Lilian and Violet were at home at this time it is 'Laurie' who is constantly mentioned in her diary. Mother and son talked deep into the evening, played billiards, and went for walks. He was never far from her side: he took his responsibilities seriously and it was his turn to watch over her with concern as, with great dignity, she embarked on her forty years of widowhood.

After a year, the air began to clear, and thoughts turned to the future and lives to be lived. Oates returned to Eastbourne to pick up the threads of his studies – a necessity no matter what course his life took. He seemed keen on Oxford as a route to the army, but the entrance exams were as yet beyond him, so back at South Lynn he dived into his books. At this time he also joined the 2nd Volunteer Battalion of the Suffolk Regiment – a kind of gentlemanly social obligation. It was natural to progress a year later to his father's old Militia Corps, the 3rd Battalion of the Prince of Wales's Own West Yorkshire Regiment, commanded by Colonel Sir George Hay. The Volunteers and the Militia were part-time regiments along the lines of the Territorial Army and the Home Guard. They were rather like social clubs, but held annual training sessions and at times of national emergency they could be called out or embodied. They could also be a back door into the Regular Army – a fact which was to be very useful to Oates. So while he struggled to master academic subjects at Eastbourne, he also experienced something of army routine at his annual Militia training at York.

In 1899 he paused for breath in the duel with the dragon Education. His mother had decided that a sixty-five day cruise to the West Indies in the R.M.S. *Solent* would be no bad thing. A tutor, one Blore, would accompany him so he could work on the trip, and it would be his first independent foray into adult society outside an institution. He gloried in it.

He looked on his fellow-passengers with a sardonic eye, especially the tutor. 'It is a fearful farce pretending that Blore is looking after me as I have to manage everything as with all due respects he is quite a child yet.' He was amused by two nuns 'who were babbling prayers all through the heavy weather and two or three ladies [who] got into hysterics'. He noticed how 'Lady Way wriggles about in her chair and talks very fast'. His chief friends and companions on the voyage were Sir Gibson Craig and his two daughters. 'They are very decent people indeed: quite the pick of all the passengers.' He seems to have seized his first social chances with alacrity, making the most of the nightly concerts and dances. Indeed he was sorry when they reached Barbados 'as we were having such a rattling good time.'

He must have rattled the hearts of some of the girls on board: a Miss Burstall, perhaps, who said she knew Lilian and Violet, or the two Misses Craig, with whom he went pony-trekking in the Islands. Indeed, he kept up a correspondence with one of the Misses Craig for many years after the cruise, so perhaps he was susceptible to the soft West Indian night air. It would be natural at his age and in his first celebration of independence, to fall in love a little.

He took the Misses Craig to a bullfight. 'It is the most brutal exhibition of Spanish cowardice you can possibly imagine. All the ladies in our party went out almost at once and I had to go out after they had killed the second bull as there is no sport in it only cruelty.' At Trinidad he delighted in a swimming pool. 'All the Government Houses out here have them,' he reported. 'I think we ought to build one at Gestingthorpe it would improve the place enormously.' Foresight indeed, for fifty years later, a swimming pool was built there.

He appreciated the natural beauty of the West Indies: 'St Thomas is the prettiest of the islands we have been to, the town is built on the side of a hill and all the houses are white with red roofs.' When they arrived in Venezuela, they found there was a revolution in progress. 'No one was allowed to talk about it so I did not hear many of the details. We did not see the President as he does not walk about the streets, but hides in his cellar.'

Despite such excitements and distractions, however, Oates was not unmindful of events at home. 'Mind you don't fade the carpet in the dining room by letting in too much light', he lectured his mother. Foremost in his mind were the dreaded exams which he had to face on his return.

'The work is a fearful nuisance and it does not progress very favourably but I must put it on coming home. I think you had better get me a tutor to be ready for when I arrive home as I must not lose a minute and I want someone to go up to Oxford with me, Algy or Mr Henly.' Other ways of easing his passage into Oxford occurred to him. 'I have some idea that Uncle Charlie [his father's brother, who lived at Meanwoodside] knows Pelham the President of Trinity so you might get him to write and tell Pelham he wants me to pass.'

On his return from the West Indies he went straight to Depot Barracks, York, for his annual Militia training. Here he took the Oxford exam. Whether or not Uncle Charlie delivered the subtle hint, Pelham proved a model of incorruptibility. In late May Oates received the stern verdict of the President of Trinity: 'Your papers are considerably below our standard, and I do not think it would be worth your while to stand again in September, as only very few vacancies are left.'

Oates was furious with himself. 'I don't think I was ever so annoyed about anything as I am about this exam as I really thought I had a chance of passing but I am afraid the Greek unseen and Latin prose did for me . . . I did 2 or 3 hours a day on the trip and thought it sufficient to pull me through, of course now it has turned out it was not . . . I feel almost as if I could chuck the whole thing up, army and all, so bored am I with exams.'

But he made it plain that he enjoyed his Militia training of five hours drill a day, and that the army still had great appeal. 'I do not mind getting up at six in the morning, in fact I rather like it. Could you send me a print of one of those photos which Father took in Madeira of some soldiers drilling? . . . If Trinity will not let me try again in October my best course I think would be to write to Merton and ask them if they would take me . . . as I am fearfully keen on the army at present so must go up in Oct somehow.' He continued to try and fit his revision into the routine of Militia training, usually managing '2 or 3 hours work but it is rather hard as after tramping about the parade from 6.20 all morning and part of the afternoon with your mind fixed on one thing all the time you do not feel much like work'.

Why did Oates have such problems with exams? It is clear that he possessed a good deal of native wit and shrewdness but his intellectual performance was poor. There had been no continuity in his education: it was a ragged succession of tutors, school and crammers, constantly interrupted by illness or family troubles. What education he had received, and so ill-digested, had been the public school model – that 'safe and elegant imbecility of classical learning'.[2] Science may have suited him better, but he never had the chance to find out. Though Germany was annually producing 3000 engineers alone, the universities of England and Wales turned out a meagre total of 350 graduates in all branches of maths, science and technology. He had, however, learnt some lessons. Life had taught him to be brave, in the face of illness and bereavement, and his public school had reinforced the idea of courage as the chief ornament of a gentleman. And in some eyes this stood for more than Homer – or even engineering.

For in some ways, the cultivation of vigorous and independent intellect was seen as downright dangerous, especially in the army. Intellectual curiosity might lead a man to question orders and the army could not function unless orders were unquestioningly obeyed. Bravery seems to have been more highly valued than strategy – and without qualms. 'Our present system, faulty as it is, has given us a corps of officers superior to any army in the world,' wrote W. E. Cairnes. 'In scientific military training they may be inferior to the highly-educated German officers; their professional attainments may be inferior to those of the French officers, but no one can surpass them in the high military qualities, in their courage, in their devotion, in their absolute forgetfulness of self.'[3]

Moral qualities, therefore, were most highly valued on the battlefield. Indeed officers were resistant even to the lessons of experience, if experience suggested that sophisticated strategy might outdo valour. For instance, the invention in the 1890s of the smokeless magazine rifle increased the tactical power of the defensive, allowing marksmen to remain invisible, safely entrenched, and firing long range shots every two seconds. But senior officers still insisted on the 'moral effect' of cavalry charges. 'The best protection from the enemy's fire is to overwhelm him with your own' thundered Major-General Marshall.[4] The quest for cover was pernicious, even cowardly; recklessly exposing your life to the enemy was what war was about; terrifying the blighters into submission by your incandescent bravery. 'Officers were expected to remain cool under fire and not to "bob" – that is, not to duck when bullets whistled close or shells exploded near them.'[5]

So a suspicion of meddling, innovating intellectuals threw the Victorian emphasis upon a moral education, especially for officers. Technology was alien, Germanic and un-British; sophisticated strategies undermined the army's death-and-glory traditions. But there was another reason to fear intellectual learning and academic success. If the army recruited officers by examination alone, heaven knows what social upstarts might arrive in the officers' mess, to disturb the gentlemanly rituals with their *arriviste* presumptions. Many recoiled at the idea of lowering the social status of the officer. 'It may sound snobbish to say so, but the fact remains that men will follow a "gentleman" much more readily than they will an officer whose social position is not assured.'[6] Such deference certainly did persist in some sections of the army, though Horace Wyndham may have spoken for many in the ranks when he argued that 'the average private would much rather follow an intelligent lance-corporal than somebody who is all blue blood but no brains.'[7] The officer corps, however, assumed that other ranks would resist promoted non-commissioned officers and prefer to defer, in uniform and out, to their social superiors.

There were many other urgent reasons to deplore the influx of the clever 'ranker'. The officers' mess enjoyed the protected atmosphere of a gentlemen's club. In peacetime, officers dined, drank, gambled, and hunted together. The regiment became their family, the mess, its hearth. An intrusion into this sanctum by lower orders who neither knew how to behave like gentlemen nor had the necessary private income to live like officers, was insufferable. Army pay was so abysmal that a cavalry officer would need a private income of £600 to £700 a year to fulfil his many obligations, and the officers' mess was openly hostile to any new-comer who fell short. Ensigns Bruce and Hodge, gazetted into the 4th Hussars in the 1890s, had private incomes of £500 and £300 respec-tively. 'They were informed by their brother officers that these incomes were quite inadequate. They were then bullied for over two months, subjected to a remorseless boycott, and forced to leave the regiment, with Hodge requiring medical treatment thereafter for a period of three months.'[8]

If the British Army emerges as hidebound and barbaric (albeit glori-ously brave) it must be noted that by 1899 it had already evolved away from its worst Regency excesses, when officers were reckless rakes and swaggering dandies, who wallowed in port and spirits and duelled upon the least provocation. Duelling had been outlawed (not without protests from the old guard who wished to cherish 'heroic, feudal and honorific' values). Flogging was no longer used as a punishment. Gradually the swagger, the sexuality, the hell-raising of Regency society shrank before Victoria's decorum, modesty and piety. By the end of the century the British officer had buried his licentiousness beneath 'manly attitudes of loyalty and courage, bravery and patriotism . . . Christian virtues became more pronounced – the unselfishness, the thoughtfulness and the sense of *noblesse oblige*, intrinsic aspects of Matthew Arnold's ideal of a Christian gentleman'.[9] This Christian refinement brought with it an increase in paternalistic concern for the welfare of the men.

However, the state of the army Oates was trying to join still left much to be desired. Gone were the days when a married soldier could only house his family in a corner of the barrack room, screened off with blankets. Yet in the new married quarters families were still often confined in one room each. Rations provided were bread and meat – everything extra had to be paid for out of a microscopic wage. As for a soldier's ability to shoot, that was left to chance more often than improved by practice. In 1902 army teams competing for a cup fired 1100 rounds, only five of which hit the target. Only in 1883 had the War Office been persuaded that it might be a good idea for officers to train with the men they commanded. Manoeuvres, something of an innovation, were so rigorously choreographed as to stifle all initiative and hardly resembled the unpredictable battlefield.

Many years of peace, broken only by the Crimean War and occasional colonial skirmish, had encouraged the British Army to slumber on its moth-eaten laurels. Meanwhile, the Industrial Revolution had changed society for ever – and with it, the nature of war. If the Boer War had not jolted the War Office out of its complacency, the First World War might have proved a much shorter, and for the British a much more ignominious affair. The nineteenth-century British Army has been compared to a dinosaur: when its tail was touched, it took two minutes to turn round. It was, however, a dinosaur that was lumbering gamely towards evolution and a higher form of life.

Many determined men prodded it on its way. Edward (later Lord) Cardwell, Secretary of War in Gladstone's government, had brought about many reforms in the 1870s, encouraged and supported by Lord Wolseley, one of the best generals of the late Victorian era. Experienced and shrewd, Wolseley was not blind to the army's faults, and campaigned for the abolition of the purchase of commissions; the introduction of short term service, the linked battalion system, and the Territorial Reserve; and the subordination of the Commander-in-Chief to the War Office. Wolseley had published a *Pocket Book* in 1869, which might be described as a Little Red Rule Book, calling as it did for officers to involve themselves more in their men's welfare, to take a lively interest in them, to treat them not as children but almost as equals. He attacked the very language of military life, suggesting that the socially divisive terms 'officer' and 'gentleman' should be replaced by 'soldier' – 'so that the private may really feel that there is no gulf between him and his commander, but that they are merely separated by a ladder, the rungs of which all can equally aspire to mount.'[10] Compulsory retirement for officers was also introduced and generals had to bow out at seventy. (At this, no doubt, General William Blakeney turned in his grave, for he had defended Fort St Philip in Minorca in 1756 at the age of eighty-four.)

Such dramatic reforms were resisted by many, including the Commander-in-Chief, the Duke of Cambridge. He clashed particularly strongly with Wolseley over the matter of promotion. He promoted by seniority alone, while Wolseley insisted that fitness should be considered and tested. Other abuses flourished, too. An officer's leave was absurdly generous, being three months' unbroken absence from his regiment. The rest of the time, hunting and racing constantly encroached on working hours. Officers too often had little or nothing to do with the training of their men: 'the Guards, as readers of Ouida's novels will be aware, had more leave than anyone else, seemingly dividing their time between hunting boxes in the Highlands and castles in Transylvania'.[11]

So while Oates struggled with his exams, the army he longed to join wrestled with itself, the radicals massing under Wolseley, the traditionalists clustering around the Commander-in-Chief and later Field Marshal Lord Frederick Roberts. Wolseley and Roberts, with one eye apiece, glared cyclopically at each other across the battle lines of reform. But then history burst in upon their confrontation, to bring them a massive challenge and a bitter education. On 9 October 1899 the Boers delivered an ultimatum to the British; three days later, war broke out.

Meanwhile, Oates had spent a dogged summer struggling with exam work at his Militia barracks in York, with occasional trips to his uncle's home at Meanwoodside in Yorkshire. Militia training was no substitute for a commission in the Regular Army. His irritation occasionally spilled over into adolescent indignation with his mother. 'I am rather insulted about your saying I am not good at accounts yet,' (he had previously asked, unsuccessfully, for his own bank account), 'I have had nearly £100 through my hands since the beginning of training besides my own and I can account for every farthing of it. I have to keep the canteen grocery account as well as pay my mess bills.' A week later, he was still smarting. 'My captain came back on Monday so I handed over my accounts money etc. they were right to a halfpenny. He said he thought I must be very good at accounts.' Several years later, however, Captain Scott was to endorse Mrs Oates's verdict on her son's mathematical ability. 'I had intended Oates to superintend the forage arrangements,' he wrote, 'but rows of figures, however simply expressed, are too much for him'.[12] And Oates himself admitted ruefully to his mother in 1904, 'if you were in the same way with your money as I am with mine we should soon be in the soup'.

In October he wrote a gloomy note from the Mitre Hotel, Oxford. 'I am afraid I have failed as there are 12 people up for Matric out of whom

10 have passed Responsions [13] and there are only 2 vacancies. I am perfectly sick of these exams.' Though he failed to get into Oxford, he was promoted lieutenant in the Militia, which somewhat revived his drooping spirits.

When the news of the Boer War broke, he was back at the crammer in South Lynn, working for one last try at the exams before 'chucking it'. Excitedly he wrote home asking his mother to tell Oscar to clean his uniform as it was possible the Militia would be called out. He waited impatiently throughout November, hopeful of getting a 'decent billet' as the Yorkshire Militia were forty officers short. At the beginning of December he began to write to senior officers to ask about getting a commission in the Regular Army through the Militia. He wrote to the commanding officer of his Militia Regiment and Colonel Hay 'wrote back and said it was very probable I should get one but before he could recommend me I must pass my "PS" . . . [the PS was a National Examination, roughly equivalent to O levels]. If I can get my "PS" in the beginning of Feb I ought if the war lasts till then, to get commissioned by March . . . It is of the most vital importance to get [it] before the end of the war as there may never be such a chance again'.

In January 1900 he moved to Wimbledon, sharing rooms with a friend called Druse who was also studying for the PS exam. Druse, however, was offered a commission almost at once 'so I think I shall go into London and stay at the Windsor as it is such rot being in rooms by oneself. I shall go and see Colonel Hay tomorrow and see if I can't do something in the way of applying for a commission as they seem to be knocking about cheap as dirt and to be had for the asking'. A fortnight later he reported that 'Colonel Hay says he will recommend me for a commission as soon as I am 20'. This would mean a two-month wait.

Oates fretted his way through February, dividing his time between London and Eastbourne, devouring any fragments of military gossip which came his way. 'There is every prospect I think of the 3rd [Prince of Wales' Own, his Militia Regiment] being called out as it will reassure the public, but I am afraid we shall not get out to South Africa.' A few domestic distractions arose: at Gestingthorpe, Jemima, one of the servants, landed in the usual sort of trouble. Oates told his mother he thought Jemima was more to be pitied than blamed. He ordered a tiger skin for a drum apron for Bryan. 'I don't think there can be much mistake about the swagger Bryan will put on when he is wearing it.' He went to see Othello. ('It was very good but I am afraid I did not appreciate it.') He asked for a dog, and ordered a watch 'with a clear face and as small as possible'. This last report hints at his less-than-perfect eyesight, another source of anxiety as entry to the army required strict eye tests. Whilst in London he consulted Surgeon-General Hamilton, an eye specialist, and a pair of glasses was prescribed for him. When he received them he complained, 'the glasses arrived all right but they are not a bit of good as they make everything misty'.

At last, a vital piece of news broke through the tedium and trivia of his life. 'Have you seen that they are going to give all qualified Militia officers commissions without any further exams, so I am pretty safe I think.' A month later, on 6 April 1900, the longed-for commission was his. He was not immediately assigned to a regiment, and strange as it may seem continued to work for the PS exam which he passed in early May. Shortly afterwards the 3rd were embodied and Oates was sent to Strensall Camp in Yorkshire as an embodied Militia officer despite his regular commission. 'It is no joke being an embodied Militiaman as they can kick you about as much as they like, and you are not allowed to resign.' But Oates undoubtedly recognized its value to him. The Militia, traditionally regarded as the back door to a commission in the Regular Army, was nonetheless a route followed by a good many distinguished officers and some of Oates's comrades. Militia officers varied greatly in their abilities and in their experience of training, their ranks being composed of crabbed aged and green youth with little in between. They had the reputation of being immature and ill-trained and when Militia regiments were called to the field of battle, they were regarded as 'second line troops of inferior quality', usually employed upon the lines of communication.

Oates was anxious to escape this ignominious identity as soon as possible. He wished to be gazetted into the Greys, and asked his mother to try to exert her influence on one Colonel Alexander. Women were frequently applied to in this way: Churchill was one who often called on his mother's influence to help him in his military career. On 27 May he wrote again: 'apparently Colonel Alexander has no say in the matter about me getting into the Greys, so I think you had better write at once to Mrs Simpson and ask her to write to her pal at the War Office and tell him how keen I am to get in the Greys and if he could use his influence to get me in, this must be done as soon as possible as I may be gazetted this week.' He was indeed: on 30 May he revealed to his mother that 'I am gazetted into the 6th [Inniskilling] Dragoons. I am very pleased about it as it is the best Heavy Cavalry Regiment in the British Army which is saying a good deal when it has to compete with the Greys and the Royals.'[14]

'I shall not try to thank you in writing for all you have done for me but what I say is this, that if it had not been for you I would still be rotting in the old 3rd [Prince of Wales' Own] and knowing how keen I was to get a commission you must if possible try to realise how grateful I am.'

Then, to London, to set about ordering his kit [15] and enjoying a few days' leave before travelling to join the rear party of his regiment in Ireland – only the young recruits and elements of the headquarters had not been sent to South Africa. Acquiring kit was a massive undertaking, and very exciting for the newly gazetted dragoon, as Colonel Sir Mike Ansell[16] remembers. 'The ordering of uniform was a thrilling and extremely expensive affair: scarlet mess kit, three drill tunics from Jones Chalk and Dawson; from Huntsman three pairs of uniform breeches, three white for polo, a cloak, two pairs of overalls from Tautz, three pairs of boots from Maxwells. A special room was put aside at home where polo helmets, boots and gold belt were all laid. When no-one was about, like any bride I used to examine my trousseau.'[17] The buying of his kit, however, was a mere fraction of the expense to which he as an officer would now be put. Officers had to pay subscriptions to the polo team, the regimental coach, the regimental hounds, the race fund, as well as providing servants' liveries, newspapers, china and glass for the mess.

In late June Oates sailed away to his regiment's headquarters at the Curragh. The garrison there was large, numbering several thousand, and including cavalry, artillery, engineers, infantry and departmental corps. 'Off parade the various units kept very much to themselves. Precedence was not only rigidly observed, but it was also carried to ridiculous lengths. Thus, the artillery and engineers affected to look down to the infantry, and the infantry looked down on the ordnance, medical and commissariat branches; while the cavalry from their superior heights looked down upon everybody.'[18] Oates slipped with alacrity into his place in this hierarchy: he had escaped from the Militia, he had his commission in the best cavalry regiment in the British Army, he might now look down on everybody.

He was eager to conform, as are all newcomers who arrive in institutions they have long dreamed of joining. 'Don't address my letters as Lieut but Esq', he warned his mother. 'Can you write to the stores and get me some cards printed Mr L. E. G. Oates, Inniskilling Dragoons . . . Could you let me have an account at Cox's as he is the military banker and everybody banks there; if you could let me have £100 in there I could use it for subs and mess bills etc. I should like it put in as soon as convenient to you as you have to pay these things as soon as you are ordered.'

This time he got his way – and his bank account. He bought ponies – one for polo and one for travelling to and from the stables where the regimental horses were kept. He was particularly keen on a colt which would cost £150. 'If you let me have the money . . . I shall be very careful and live as cheaply as possible to the end of the year. I have got my £100 at Cox's still which would keep me all right.' How could Mrs Oates have refused such melting pleas? 'Thank you very much for your letter and the cheque,' he wrote a week later, 'it gave me infinite joy as I hardly expected it. I shall buy the colt, he is a huge deep chestnut 16.3 with another inch to grow, it will be very interesting breaking and training him.'

Oates's relations with his mother were to be characterized by this constant fencing over the question of money. Though he was by the standards of the age a wealthy man, and left £29,000[19] in his will, his life was a continuing stream of requests for fairly small sums of money and attempts to convince his mother of his good husbandry. Caroline Oates seems to have understood very well the complicated relationship between money, power and love.

Despite the distractions of horseflesh, it was the progress of the war, and the possibility of being drafted to South Africa, which obsessed him. In September 1900 he tried unsuccessfully to get sent out with a draft. In October he was wistfully poring over the war reports. 'I suppose you saw the casualty lists – 1 officer killed and 3 wounded. The regiment has been in the thick of it all through; we are known out there as French's pets because he always puts us in front if there is going to be any fighting. We are very proud of our regiment and I only wish I was with them.'

He concluded ruefully, however, that he thought the war was 'all over bar the shouting'. So, at that time, did many British commentators. They were wrong. When Oates finally heard in November that he was indeed drafted out to the Boer War, he thought he had merely received an invitation to a glorious romp. In fact he was to witness the education of the British Army, and during his army career in the years following the war, he lived through a series of reforms which were to transform the weary old dinosaur into a dangerous modern animal.

Notes and references
1 L. E. G. Oates, letter to his mother, Caroline Oates, 22 February 1899. Some 340 of Oates's ill-spelt and scarcely punctuated letters home still exist. Most are owned by the Scott Polar Research Institute. Unless specified, all further quotes from Oates's writings are taken from this source.
2 Byron Farwell, *For Queen and Country*, p. 139.
3 W. E. Cairnes, *Social Life in the British Army*, p. xvi.

4 Edward M. Spiers, *The Army and Society, 1815-1914*, p. 210.

5 Byron Farwell, *op. cit.*, p. 108.

6 W. E. Cairnes, *op. cit.*, p. xvi.

7 Horace Wyndham, *Following the Drum*, p.63.

8 Edward M. Spiers, *op. cit.*, p. 25.

9 Edward M. Spiers, *op. cit.*, p. 26, quoting from W. L. Burn's *The Age of Equipoise*, p. 259.

10 E. S. Turner, *A Portrait of the British Officer*, p. 234, quoting from Garnet Wolseley's *A Pocket Book*.

11 *Ibid.*, p. 238.

12 R. F Scott, diary 22 October 1911, omitted from the published version.

13 The first of three examinations required for a BA degree at Oxford.

14 On 1 January 1690 the forces of Enniskillen were brought on to the Royal Establishment. The 6th (Inniskilling) Dragoons was officially formed. It was famous for its part in the charge of the Union Brigade at Waterloo (an Inniskilling soldier stands at one corner of Wellington's statue at Hyde Park Corner) and had a long distinguished history. Oates may well have been correct in what he said to his mother. However, the fact that in 1897 the regimental polo team won the Diamond Jubilee Inter-Regimental Cup, the premier sporting event for a cavalry regiment, may well have influenced Oates more than the regiment's history.

15 A scrap of paper exists at the Oates Memorial Library and Museum at Selborne which gives Oates's physical measurements at the age of 18. These include height 5 ft 11 ins, weight 12 stone 1 ½ lbs, neck 15 ins, chest (expanded) 38½ ins, waist 30¼ ins and biceps 13 ins.

16 Colonel Sir Mike Ansell joined the 5th/6th Dragoons in 1924. (This regiment was formed as the result of an amalgamation in 1922 of the 5th Dragoon Guards and the 6th (Inniskilling) Dragoons. It is now known as the 5th Royal Inniskilling Dragoon Guards.) He was seriously wounded and lost his sight while commanding the 1st Lothian and Border Yeomanry in 1940. He became Colonel of the 5th Royal Inniskilling Dragoon Guards in 1957. His father G. K. Ansell joined the 6th (Inniskilling) Dragoons in 1894 and was killed in 1914 while commanding the 5th Dragoon Guards, and his son N. P. G. Ansell commanded the 5th Royal Inniskilling Dragoon Guards from 1977 to 1980.

17 Colonel Sir Mike Ansell, *Soldier On*, p. 25.

18 Horace Wyndham, *op. cit.*, p. 77.

19 This sum is probably equivalent to £1,000,000 at 1995 price levels.

3

The Boer War

The Boer War had been brewing for years. For generations the southern-most tip of South Africa had gradually been colonized by scattered groups of British and Dutch settlers. By the late 1890s two landlocked Boer Republics (Transvaal and what later came to be known as the Orange Free State) had evolved, containing a large proportion of foreigners or *Uitlanders* (mostly British). These two Dutch Republics were surrounded to the south and east by Cape Colony and Natal (both British adminis-tered) and by Portuguese Mozambique, and to the north and west by territories controlled by the British South Africa Company, presided over by Cecil Rhodes (who was also Prime Minister of Cape Colony).

Paul Kruger, President of the Boer Republic of the Transvaal, was a Grand Old Man who typified the Dutch Boer at his most puritanical, devout and entrenched. And perhaps he could be forgiven for feeling entrenched, given his geographical position and the current of British Colonial thought. When gold was found in the Transvaal, his Republic was transformed. Foreign labour and capital (mostly British) poured in, turning Johannesburg into a booming city, and by 1895 the Uitlanders equalled the native Boers in number and contributed nearly all the coun-try's revenue in taxation. Still, Kruger refused to grant them political rights. Rhodes, who 'dreamt of a United South Africa and a Cape-to-Cairo railway running through British Territory all the way',[1] hatched a plot. It was to be a two-pronged attack on Kruger: a British uprising in Johannesburg and a simultaneous invasion of the Transvaal by a British South Africa Company force, led by Dr Leander Starr Jameson.

The plot misfired. The British in Johannesburg failed to rise, but in January 1896 Jameson led 500 men to an invasion into the Transvaal which ended in abject failure. This raid poisoned the already slightly nauseous Anglo-Boer relations: Rhodes had to resign; the Boers in Cape Colony, hitherto co-operative, began to resent their British over-lords. The Orange Free State fled to Kruger's side, his own support strengthened and he spent the next three years negotiating a settlement with Britain while secretly preparing for war. Kruger refused even more stubbornly to grant his Transvaal Uitlanders their civil rights. In April 1899 20,000 of these Uitlanders presented a petition to the British Government. The British then demanded a vote for every citizen after five years' residence in the Transvaal. Racial and nationalistic hatred was now rising to fever pitch, each side imagining that the other was intent on annexing for itself all the states of Southern Africa. The Boers how-ever delayed making a final move till after the rains came, bringing sweet new grass to feed up their horses, without which battle was impossible. This intelligent and sensitive use of their terrain was to characterize the Boers' strategy throughout the war.

By the autumn the Boers were ready: their army outnumbered the British by 2 to 1, and were all mounted on plump and fit horses; their arsenals and barns were bristling with German guns, and they were all expert shots. On 9 October 1899 they presented an ultimatum to the British: three days later they went to war. The British seem to have given less thought to strategy or preparations, preferring to bask in convictions of their own superiority. Joseph Chamberlain had said that the British 'were the greatest Imperial Race the world has ever seen'; Ruskin asserted that it was the task of England, 'still undegenerate in race . . . to found colonies as fast and far as she is able . . . seizing every piece of fruit-ful waste ground she can set her foot on'. As for Cecil Rhodes, he dreamt of a secret society with the aim of extending British rule throughout the world, 'especially the occupation by British settlers of the entire conti-nent of Africa, the Holy Land, the Valley of the Euphrates, the Isles of Cyprus and Candia, the whole of South America, the Islands of the Pacific not heretofore possessed by Great Britain, the whole of the Malay Archipelago, the seaboard of China and Japan, the ultimate recovery of the United States of America as an integral part of the British Empire'.[2]

Intoxicated by self-righteousness and exuberant chauvinism, crowds thronged pro-war rallies. Three brigades were despatched for South Africa under General Sir Redvers Buller, and the people cheered them off. Sir Arthur Sullivan set to music verses by Kipling which reviled Kruger and glorified Britannia. The words were on everybody's lips. British officials were complacent, believing that victory would be theirs by Christmas. 'The Army is more efficient than at any time since Waterloo', blustered George Wyndham, Parliamentary Under-Secretary for State at the War Office. British war correspondents reflected this com-placency, for though scores of them took off for South Africa, they relied heavily on the military for their lines of communication, were subject to

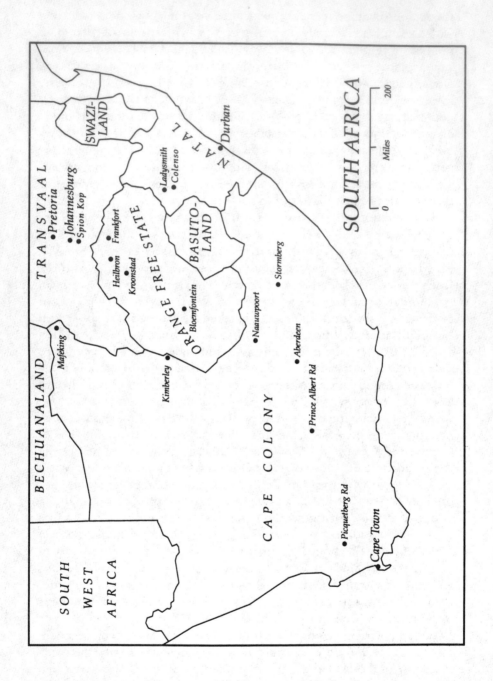

SOUTH AFRICA

0
Miles
200

SOUTH WEST AFRICA

BECHUANALAND

TRANSVAAL

SWAZI-LAND

NATAL

• Mafeking

• Pretoria
• Johannesburg
• Spion Kop

• Frankfort

• Heilbron
• Kroonstad

ORANGE FREE STATE

• Bloemfontein

BASUTO-LAND

• Ladysmith
• Colenso

• Durban

• Kimberley

• Naauwpoort

• Stormberg

• Aberdeen

CAPE COLONY

• Prince Albert Rd

• Picquetberg Rd

• Cape Town

strict censorship, and served up what their readers wanted to hear: they praised the 'dauntless bravery of English officers' and the daring deeds of the 'sweating, swearing, grimy, dirty, fearless and generous Tommy'.[3]

Within a few weeks, Buller's British force had been all but sewn up by the Boers. They were trounced at Stormberg, Colenso, Magersfontein and Spion Kop, and surrounded and paralysed at Ladysmith, Kimberley and Mafeking. Many of these defeats took place within a single week in December, 'Black Week' as it became known. The British had expected victory by Christmas; they were faced instead with disaster. There was deep shock and a great deal of recrimination, everywhere but at Court. 'Please understand there is no pessimism in *this* house,' Queen Victoria sternly informed Balfour. 'We are not interested in the possibilities of defeat. They do not exist.'

Lord Roberts took a more realistic view than his Queen, and he let fly a few salvoes at Buller, the Commander-in-Chief in South Africa. This must have been the more satisfying for Roberts since Buller was the protégé of Wolseley, Roberts's old enemy. 'Buller's reverse makes it clear that both our strategy and tactics are at fault,' blasted Roberts. 'We have had terrible losses without a single success, and unless some radical change is made at once, our army will be frittered away and we shall have to make an ignominious peace.'[4] Others took an even more desperate view. Viscount Curzon lamented that 'our disasters are so unbroken, our generals so uniformly incompetent, our inability to make any headway so consistent as to engender suspicion that our system must be rotten to the core'.[5] Argument raged as to whether the War Office or the Generals were to blame as, red faced and chastened, Britain set about repairing her losses. Roberts replaced Buller as Commander-in-Chief, Kitchener was appointed his Chief of Staff, the First Class Army Reserve was called out, and the Militia invited to come forward. There was an excellent response, but the fact remained that the Auxiliary Forces lacked the necessary training to support the Regular Army in a full-scale war.

The British had, however, reacted and acted, and soon the new brooms were sweeping their way through South Africa. The British relieved Kimberley, Ladysmith and Mafeking, were victorious at Paardeberg, and by June 1900 Bloemfontein, Johannesburg and Pretoria had fallen. In November, Roberts returned to England, having annexed the Transvaal, and received 'a hero's welcome, the Garter, an Earldom, and a grant of £100,000.[6] It was widely assumed that the war was all but over, and it was at this moment that Oates, with three other officers and some sixty Inniskillings, was drafted to join his regiment.

By early January 1901, they were nearing South Africa in the troopship *Idaho*. Oates had been put in the charge of Herbert Dixon, with whom he shared a cabin. 'Tomorrow we arrive at Cape Town. I wonder what the news will be. I am very much afraid I shall be stuck in Maitland Camp which will be a fearful nuisance.'

He was not, in the event, stuck in camp. The Inniskilling draft and one other were put into immediate action. Boers had apparently remained in the mountains of Cape Colony while the first great hunt passed by. Various British Columns had searched for them from Willowmore to Aberdeen but found nothing. Now fears existed that the enemy might infiltrate south behind the Columns and the drafts were used in blocking positions and mopping-up operations – trying again to flush Boer guerillas out of their hiding-places.

Though the British Army was beginning to learn from the mistakes it had made early in the war, it still had a lot to learn in, for example, the thorny problem of scouting. Much of the draft's operations were to revolve around this sort of reconnaissance work, and Oates is unlikely to have been adequately trained for it. Captain W. E. Cairns commented in 1901: 'cavalry scouting is made absurd and useless by the farcical unreality with which it is conducted on training and manoeuvres. A general sends his cavalry to ascertain the movements of the enemy: if possible without being seen themselves. As a matter of fact these patrols usually ride boldly up to within a few hundred yards of his columns, which they leisurely scrutinise, riding back to their own side . . . in a manner which would be absolutely impracticable in war. . . Successful scouting . . . takes time, and time is the last thing we can spare on a field day, when we are all anxious to get back to lunch'.[7]

However, it was a real war, not manoeuvres, which Oates's draft was to join, and negligence or foolishness on the part of senior officers would be highly dangerous, as Oates was well aware. 'The Captain who brought our draft out is not a popular man and I only hope I am not under him if I go to the front he is one of those fussy people who are I believe perfectly hopeless on service.' It was not the last time that he was to encounter what he considered to be incompetence in his superiors for a few weeks later he wrote: 'Old Parsons [a Column commander] is an awful old stick-in-the-mud, Colonel Greenhill said he would have nothing more to do with Parsons and cleared off so I suppose we must wait here for more troops.' However, despite the likely flimsiness of his training and the erratic qualities of his leaders, Oates had a job to do and was eager to do his best. At last action had come, in the form of war – not such an abhorred word then as it is now, with its overtones of Apocalypse. For in 1900 war was thought to be 'the supreme act in the life of a state', and a nation 'had to be kept up to a pitch of high efficiency by contest, chiefly by war with inferior races'.[8] The conviction of the Boers' inferiority had been the chief cause of early British disasters in the war, but young Oates was determined to do his bit to put this right, if the chance came his way.

At first, the Boers were frustratingly elusive – they always seemed to be about twenty miles away as the draft entrained and rode through Cape Colony, patrolling, scouting, and building 'three little forts so as to give the Boers a kindly welcome if they arrive'. The rigours of life on the march may have compensated somewhat for the absence of blood. 'We have been having fearful weather here the last 2 or 3 days: tropical downpours with a lot of wind. As we have no tents but are lying in the open we have had rather a wet time. I was out on patrol 7 miles from here the other night and it poured the whole night: if I had been in England I should have died of pneumonia by now.'

A few days later he apologized for the thumbprints which adorned his letter. 'Excuse this dirty paper but water is very scarce and I have not had a proper wash for 2 days. I have slept in a railway carriage the last two nights, tonight I sleep on the hillside if it does not rain.' Gradually he got acclimatized. 'I am getting accustomed to the weather out here, last night I slept soundly in the rain and am now sitting surrounded by my bedding which is drying nicely.' He loved roughing it, and the constant physical exercise was building him up to a pitch of rugged good health. 'I am enjoying myself immensely and I never felt so well in my life.'

In good spirits, he appreciated the Government horses he had hired. 'I have got two little fat country bred horses strong as elephants. One is called the Sausage.' One of his servants, Private McConnell, also earned high praise. 'That boy McConnell is a splendid fellow . . . he does the work of 6 men and is very good with the horses . . . he used to be a clerk with the Army and Navy Stores and then he was in Guinness's drawing £800 a year: he left it as he could not stand that kind of work.' His other servant, however, was not quite up to the mark: 'he is too fat and soft to do well here'. It is interesting that even campaigning in wild country this most junior of subalterns had two servants. Although England itself was 6000 miles away, its social hierarchy was ever-present.

The 6000 miles which separated the regiment from the mother-country made communications very difficult. Military censorship increased their sense of being cut off: 'it is very funny to think that you know a great deal more what is going on out here than I do, as it is very difficult to get news'. Letters to and from home were carried by the despatch rider, whose appearances could be sporadic: 'I have been out all day and only heard at supper that the despatch rider passes through tomorrow, so I am writing this on an empty whisky case by the light of a candle . . . just as I finished that last sentence my candle went out, fut, so I am finishing this morning as we cannot afford too many candles'. One day however the despatch rider brought news which must have brought the Column to a sudden stop. The Queen was dead.

Victoria had reigned for sixty-four years. No one in the draft could remember a time when she had not been Queen. It must have seemed as though things were falling apart and an old order disappearing for ever. The old century was gone, the old Queen dead, and a handful of Boer farmers had given a serious jolt to the military might of the greatest imperial power on earth. That night in camp, the home-thoughts must have been unusually poignant. 'We heard about the Queen's death while on the march, and were all very much cut up,' wrote Oates. 'It is awfully sad and the worst thing that could happen to England.' A psychological shock can make one more sensitive to physical discomforts, and now the southern summer was drawing to a close the nights could be bitterly cold. 'I had three blankets and my cloak over me last night but I could not sleep properly because of the cold.' Briefly, a mood of irritation creeps into his letters. 'There is half a gale of wind blowing and the sand is in everything . . . it is the sand which is making this pencil write so badly.' The Cape Town Highlanders arrived in the camp – a fact of which nobody could be unaware, for they were 'blowing their beastly bagpipes all day'.

Towards the end of February, however, the Inniskilling draft was ordered to join the column under Colonel Parsons. Oates perked up, for as Parsons was 'hunting a commando of Boers we may see some action at last'. On 24 February things were beginning to hum. 'I am now in Parson's Column about 20 miles east of Kaarkstoroom on the road to Willowmore. Yesterday morning the Boers attacked the camp. We turned out and fought with them for about 3 hours. I got a shot with a carbine at some of the blitters but I regret to say missed. If only I had a good long-range rifle with me I might have hit one. We are now sitting down waiting for another go at them, this time I hope with more success.' The second fracas was no more successful and afterwards the Column rested up for a few days at Willowmore as they had trekked 200 miles in six days. 'It is a great blessing to get into a town like this after being out on the trek, when we are trekking we march off when it is dark and you probably never get your clothes off the whole time.' At this point there was also a disagreement amongst the senior officers. Oates commented sourly: 'if all the Columns are run on the same lines as this one the war will go on for ever'.

He was experiencing at first hand many of the British Army's problems: bad leadership, inadequate fire-power (his carbine being sadly inferior to a long-range rifle) – and the discomforts of camp life when the enemy can hide out in his own barns and farms. Despite these trials, Colonel Parsons took the little wattle-and-daub town of Aberdeen on 5 March after a 'sharp scrap'. The Boers abandoned it and melted away into the hills. Next day, three reconnaissance patrols were sent out into the hills to locate the enemy. Each patrol consisted of a subaltern and fifteen men. At the head of the Inniskilling patrol was Oates. A patrol of fifteen men was an awkward size and had, as Major G. F. MacMunn later commented, 'many disadvantages. It was too small to put up a successful fight, and too large to escape observation'.[9] The fate of these three patrols amply justifies this verdict. One was pursued back to the town by the Boers, one was captured, and the third, Oates's patrol, was forced into a remarkable action. It was to be described as an act of 'conspicuous valour' at the news of which 'every Englishman's heart must have thrilled with emotion'.[10] Oates himself referred to it as 'the scrap on 6th March 1901'.

At 7.30 a.m. the patrol had already been out for two hours, and was advancing towards a hill. Two men, the scouts, had been sent up ahead and were within 100 yards of the crest. All seemed serene, and Oates noticed that a flock of sheep was grazing nearby. Suddenly an explosion of rifle fire broke out from the hilltop. His two scouts, two others with him, and two horses went down. Oates ordered the patrol back to a dry river bed while three men covered the retreat of the wounded. One of his scouts did not return – he had been captured.

The exchange of rifle fire continued for hours and as each man's ammunition was expended Oates sent him back to the town, staying himself with the rest of his party (some wounded) to cover their retreat. He refused to abandon his casualties, and soon found himself cut off in the riverbed, surrounded on all sides by Boers and vastly outnumbered. The Boers obviously decided that his defeat was inevitable, and despatched the man they had captured to Oates with a request that he surrender. 'I therefore decided to hold the place I was in,' reported Oates, 'being confirmed in my decision by Private Wild who repeatedly stated that there was no necessity to surrender.'[11] The Boer's invitation was declined, the messenger retained, and the fight continued.

At 10.30 a.m. a young Boer appeared with a white flag and a note signed by one Fouche demanding an immediate surrender and promising that he would release Oates at once and guarantee his private property.[12] 'While this flag was up,' commented Oates, 'several Boers who were lying in the grass within 100 yards . . . got up and strolled off.' They may have considered the surrender a foregone conclusion, but Oates did not. 'We came here to fight, not to surrender' was the message he sent back to Fouche. Firing broke out again and at about noon, some five hours after the skirmish began, the Boers suddenly dispersed. One of their parting shots, however, was all too successful: it shattered Oates's thigh. He ordered the last of his fit men back to town, and settled down with the remaining two soldiers to wait for the rescue party. They had to wait six hours before help came, a long time to be without water, under a hot sun, and losing blood from their wounds.

The reasons for the delay seem confused. As soon as the first men of Oates's party had reached the town, the beleaguered situation of his patrol had become known. Herbert Dixon had requested permission to go to his aid, but had been told that no men could be spared from the defence of the town. This outraged Oates's excellent servant McConnell, and another soldier, Private Malone,[13] so the two men stole out of camp without permission taking Oates's second charger, Mrs Butterwick, determined to rescue him. However, they were cut off from him by heavy fire and the horse was wounded, and much downhearted, they had to abandon their rescue bid. Meanwhile, Dixon was still agitating for a search party and eventually set off with Doctor Whyte towards the end of the afternoon. When they found Oates, Doctor Whyte decided to set the broken thighbone immediately, and they improvised splints from bits of old packing cases salvaged from a nearby farm. There was no anaesthetic. When the bone was set, Oates faced a six-mile journey back to camp.

'No words can describe what he must have suffered during that six mile drive across the veldt and the way he stuck it out,' wrote Dixon. 'It was here that he received his death blow, as he was never physically quite the same again.'[14] His bravery was also praised by the Senior Medical Officer, Lieutenant-Colonel O'Halloran. 'When I heard of his condition I had him conveyed by ambulance and comfortably placed in a doctor's house at Aberdeen with a brother officer who was wounded in several places, but not so severely. I expressed my regret to Oates for not being able to look after him earlier, but the poor fellow smiled and said it did not matter, as there were others in more urgent need of help . . . He never uttered a murmur, though he must have suffered considerable pain, as his thigh was shattered . . . I have never met a better soldier.'[15]

These reactions recall the last days of Sir Philip Sidney, after the battle of Zutphen in 1586. Sidney, also wounded in the thigh, had given up his last sip of water to a wounded fellow-soldier at his side. Sidney had also been lauded by his contemporaries, indeed, the example of his life and death became a golden pattern for his age. For Oates, however, there was still a future, and great things were predicted for him by no less a figure than Baden-Powell. He heard of Oates's refusal to surrender and recalled it a few years later. 'There's a young chap in the Inniskillings who did very well in the late war. He is a boy named Oates, and he is worth his oats – one of these youngsters that will go far; keen as mustard, and all that.'[16]

When Oates's draft eventually rejoined the rest of their regiment they were nicknamed by the Sergeants 'Lieutenant Oates's No Surrender draft'. 'We were all very proud of the achievement and the way in which this gallant young officer and his handful of recruits had valiantly upheld the traditions of our famous old corps.'[17] He was mentioned in despatches,[18] and recommended for a Victoria Cross. The medal however, eluded him.[19] Not that he would have welcomed such an honour, for his way was to refuse and endure rather than to bask in limelight. A few months later he remarked, 'Did you see that Kitchener has made surrendering a court-martial offence so people who hold out won't be thought little putty heroes as formerly.'

The immediate task was to reassure his mother. 'You will have heard about my wound and I shall be well again before you get this,' he wrote, with reckless optimism, on 7 March. It was to be nine months before he was properly recovered. 'This morning the Colonel commanding the Column came to see me and said I had done very well and my men had fought gallantly. I am now enclosed in splints in a private house. The lady who owns it is very good to me. I expect I shall be here 6 weeks and then I shall get home.' A week later, the most dismal aspects of his position were revealed.

'Col Parson's Column went on about 5 days ago and I was left here useless. I was very sick about it as the Boers are all around and plenty of chances of doing something. I am afraid this and my last letter are fearful scrawls, but I cannot move off my back and it is very difficult trying to write lying flat on one's back . . . it is awfully monotonous lying here with nothing to do.' But there he had to lie, in Dr Harvey's house, waited on by the good Mrs Harvey who looked after him 'all free gratis and for nothing'. She recalled years later, 'he was so good and grateful for anything done for him. I fancy I can still hear him say. "That's ripping!" when I took things in for them.'

Oates contrived a few entertainments for himself. He recollected the welcome his men had received 'as my lads came dribbling into camp the townspeople and soldiers all turned out to cheer them'. And he was amused by the distortions of the press. 'It is extraordinary how accounts of the fight got mixed. In one paper it said that as I was lying wounded the Boers came up and wanted to shoot me, but on my explaining to them that I was incapacitated from fighting any more, they refrained. Another said that I was the magistrate of Aberdeen!'

However, the constant pain (though his leg was healing, the bullet was still in place), the acute discomfort of lying on his back, the humiliation and disappointment of being left behind, all told on his spirits. 'My 21st birthday was not much of an affair, one person wished me Happy Birthday but the presents and rejoicings were conspicuous by their absence . . . I dreamt the other night that I was in England again drinking draught beer, and I woke up crying.' On 25 March he admitted 'I am getting into a wretched state as my back is becoming very sore and stiff, I do wish I could move from this position if only for a few minutes'. The next day at 4 a.m. he was moved twenty-five miles to a railway and thence to Naauwpoort and the hospital.

It was a wretched journey. 'The journey up here was terrible, three days in a red hot tin baggage van which nearly rattled your teeth out, the only things they had on the train were tinned milk tinned chicken and brandy; we fed ourselves the whole way.' At Naauwpoort Hospital plans were rapidly made to remove the bullet from his thigh 'they are going to do it without chloroform so it ought to be rather interesting'. However, his stoicism was not, in the event, to be tested. 'They gave me chloroform which rather upset me but now I am all right and shall be up in a week if it all goes well.

'The bullet hole in my leg is perfectly healed now, it was not a very big hole to start with . . . I am afraid I shall have rather a limp even after I am well again as my left leg is a good deal shorter than my right.[20] This is a rough sketch of the bullet which they took out . . . you can see how it is flattened and burst. It must have hit my bone sideways as it is bent in the middle and there is no mark on the end.'

The deterioration in his general fitness deeply depressed him and though he still longed for action, 'I would give anything to be out on the trek again', the realities of his condition were obvious. 'It seems it was months ago since I was wounded and before that the time went like fun . . . I never was so well in my life as the day I got hit and now I am as weak as a kitten. I must have lost nearly three stone.'

The nurses in Naauwpoort Hospital must have teased him a good deal. 'The sister in charge of this ward wishes me to tell you I am a fearful nuisance and she is about "fed up" with me, some of the other patients swore to her this morning they had seen me walking about the ward in my splint!' All the same, it was hard to keep his spirits up, though Captain Anstice, who had also been wounded, was there with him. Another blow was that his servant McConnell had fallen ill with enteric. 'I am writing to the doctor in charge to see if anything can be done for him', wrote Oates on 21 April. Alas for the master and the servant too: news travelled slowly, and as he wrote those words Oates did not know that McConnell had already been dead for a fortnight.

Only one thing could now cheer him up. On 8 May he reported that he had been given six months' leave, 'so boil the fatted rabbit. I will write from Madeira where I land so any sorrowing relatives can come on foot at pleasure'.

As he sailed home in the *Bavarian*, he certainly was not returning a sadder and wiser man, bloodied and bowed by the harsh realities of war. He regarded his wound as a kind of forfeit that had to be paid for the privilege for participating in a wonderful game. And the Boer War must in some ways have seemed like a game: a mixture of scouting, camping, orienteering, and playing hide-and-seek in some wild and beautiful country. It must have seemed to him a 'sporting' war, and was quite unlike the hellish horrors of trench warfare which were to engulf north-western Europe a few years later. To the Boers, of course, and to many Liberals in England, the latter stages of this war were far from sporting, with the use of concentration camps and the burning of farms. Campbell-Bannerman accused the British Army of 'methods of barbarism in South Africa'.[21] But there is no doubt that Oates had revelled in his first taste of action and was longing to be back in the firing line.

Experience of the army was beginning to develop his attitudes, which emerge as curiously unpredictable: neither a considered desire for reform nor an automatic Toryism which cherished the orthodox in the face of any challenge. Rather, his views seem to be the gut reactions of the sportsman. In October 1900 he had deplored the news of uniform reform. 'You will be sorry to hear that the whole of the British Army is going to wear khaki in the spring it is a great shame I think as they will never be able to recognise us from the Hussars or Dragoon Guards.' Now news of further army reforms preoccupied his convalescent world. 'I wonder what they are going to do in the Cavalry in these reforms, if they do too much they will drive a lot of people out, as it won't be much fun to spend £600 a year and be treated like the Germans are.' However, his first taste of military action had confirmed his hatred of people who fuss, and opened his eyes to the possible fallibility of his leaders.

Indeed, he himself could be seen as the victim of a tactical blunder. The fate of the three patrols amply supports this comment: one driven back to Aberdeen, one captured by the Boers, and Oates's patrol, whose achievement was moral rather than military. He had resisted, refused to yield, and had escaped capture. But he was himself badly wounded, as were four of his men and three horses. He had captured no Boers, gained no ground: seen in terms of strict military strategy he had merely been caught up in a silly débâcle. But his bravery and defiance transformed the event into something grand, something to be celebrated. For the British valued the heroic gesture, the spirit of self-sacrifice, most highly. It was a *gallant* act – and how that word resonates with implications of bravery in the face of failure or overwhelming odds. It is almost as if the British were driven into acts of extraordinary courage by the perils created by their incompetence.

His mother's first view of him must have been shocking. He was haggard, picking his way painfully along on crutches, his clothes hanging on him like the borrowed robes of a more substantial man. He found Violet and Lilian plump, rosy and well-fed, in the bloom of early womanhood, and Bryan was gangling and rather undecided as to what to do in life. The Essex countryside must have seemed very different from the veldt: full of grey-green spaces and crepuscular light. Kingfishers and croquet replaced rocks and rifles. England's fields and lanes were immaculate and serene. There were visits to be paid, tea on the lawn, stables to be organized. And there was one major celebration. He had spent his twenty-first birthday on his back and in pain, 6000 miles away from home, but now Mrs Oates was going to put that right. Saturday, 22 June 1901 was to be a gala day, with the whole village *en fête* to celebrate Oates's safe return from the war, and his coming of age. The village children were invited to tea at 3 p.m., all others to dinner at 4 p.m., and after early rain the sun broke through triumphantly to ensure a perfect day.

'Wherever you went in the village willing hands were busy putting up flags and banners as signs of welcome . . . long before three o'clock the children were joyfully wending their way towards the school, and within a few minutes of the appointed time were hard at work on cake, bread and butter and jam and steaming tea. A procession was then formed headed by Miss Oates and her sister, for the field where there was a steam roundabout, swings, cocoa nut shies etc. A steady stream of adults was seen going towards the barn and cart lodge, where 281 sat down to an excellent dinner consisting of beef, mutton, hot plum pudding and nut brown ale. Lieut Oates supported by Mrs Oates presided at the centre table, Mr Bryan Oates and the Vicar taking the other two. After dinner, all adjourned to the Hall grounds to present an address of welcome to Lieut Oates from the village. The Vicar in presenting the address said they wished Lieut Oates a long and honoured and useful life – a life which should be increasingly honoured and happy as the years tolled on . . . It was an honour as well as a pleasure to welcome Mr Oates – an honour because they honoured themselves when they did honour to the loyal and brave. Lieut Oates had shown himself a genuine soldier, a true Englishman to the backbone, loyal to King and country and with that sort of courage that did not know fear where duty was concerned.'[22]

The loyal address carried on in much the same vein, assuring Oates that 'every Englishman's heart must have thrilled with emotion when he read the account of your conspicuous valour . . . we say every Englishman rejoiced, but what shall we say for ourselves to whom you belong? We are indeed proud of you.' Oates's reply belongs to the same world of values. He thanked them for their address which would be kept as one of his greatest treasures, and then dismissed criticisms of the 'Continental papers' who had denied the bravery of the English soldiers, for 'if there were any Boers present here today they would be the first to extol the bravery of the English troops. We had some reverses at first, and there were blunders made, but these were probably due to the entirely new methods of fighting'.[23]

There was then a vote of thanks to Mrs Oates – for providing such a splendid day and also for her gifts to the church. Toast upon toast followed and the rest of the day was spent on the swings and roundabouts. The *East Essex and Halstead Times* devoted a column and a half to 'this important event in the life of the young squire', remarking that 'Lieut L. E. G. Oates . . . looks better than one might expect considering his experiences at the front, although a wound in the thigh still causes him to limp'. Its account summons up all the feudal satisfactions of the day, the 'gallant young officer' receiving three hearty cheers from the entire village assembled on the field in front of the elegant Hall, the 'hear hears', applause and cheers which punctuated the Vicar's paean of praise, the murmuring babes-in-arms, not forgotten by Mrs Oates, the distribution of tobacco to the men, the band playing in the field of roundabouts.

The picture is full of the contradictions of English social history, for though the scene is feudal, with a squire who presides over his social inferiors who know and keep their place, there is also a peculiarly democratic atmosphere to it all. These villagers were not peasants, worked into the ground by tyrannous landlords. They enjoyed the Oates family's protection and care and certainly cheered their returning hero as the villagers in *Adam Bede* cheered their young squire with 'a glorious shouting, a rapping, a jingling, a clattering and a shouting, with plentiful *da capo*, pleasanter than a strain of sublimest music in the ears that receive such a tribute for the first time'. The scene does not tell us the full story of their lives; their hardships, their poverty, their political subjugation. But it was a moment in which they felt a sense of meaning in a life with others. It is tempting to cherish such moments, and to lament the disappearance of meaning from our lives in a materialist, industrial age.

This sense of a coherent, rural squirarchical life was already threatened when George Eliot wrote *Adam Bede* in the 1850s, yet she celebrated its qualities and regretted its disappearance, and it is easy to see why. 'Old Leisure . . . lived chiefly in the country, among pleasant seats and homesteads, and was fond of sauntering by the fruit-tree wall, and scenting the apricots when they were warmed by the morning sunshine . . . he had an easy, jolly conscience, broad-backed like himself, and able to carry a great deal of beer or port-wine – not being made squeamish by doubts and qualms and lofty aspirations.' In other words, the squirarchy and its benign patterns of life resound with a thoroughly Georgian sense of peace and order. If Oates was a man of his anxious Victorian age in a restless desire for action, and in doing his duty and sacrificing himself, part of his heritage was something infinitely older and more gentle. It may be argued that the 'Old Leisure' described by George Eliot is an idealized fiction, that rural life was never so radiant and reassuring, except in people's imaginations. Yet what lives in people's imaginations is real too. It gives them their sense of what life is about – it is values and ideas which give an age its shape. Things invisible to mortal sight can be most powerful.

Although he was much recovered on 23 June Oates consulted Dr Herbert Waterhouse of Wimpole Street. Caroline Oates had insisted her 'Baby Boy' should visit the best specialist she could find. 'The injured limb is, and of course must remain permanently, nearly one inch shorter than the sound side. To counteract the limp that this would occasion a thicker sole must be worn on the boot of the shorter leg. I advise in addition massage with ordinary soap liniment, bathing with hot water and then, the cold douche. This will soon improve matters.' [24]

Oates then made his way to Leeds where he bought some horses. 'Tell Brujum [Bryan's nickname] I am suited with a quadruped.' Soon he was back at Gestingthorpe, returning early because 'I wanted to see my geegees put into condition for hunting. The men in the stables seem to have enjoyed our being away as they are looking fatter and sleepier than usual, however I am going to make things hum round a bit for them tomorrow – my gee-gees arrive tomorrow night.' The squire's chores also claimed his attention. 'They have started poaching in the Leys in an awful way, so I am going to put a man in there to pick up snares mend hedges etc.' However, these householder's tasks were not enough to absorb his increasing energies, and though the garden was very seductive with roses and oleanders blooming, and the new horses were a source of interest, his thoughts were elsewhere. 'I am desperately keen on getting out to the Cape again, and I think it would be a good thing for me to go as I am nearly quite fit for work and it would do me good at the W.O. if I gave up some of my leave.'

He had his way, of course, and was soon back in uniform, though he still limped a little. Maternal anxieties were quelled by his authoritative opinion that the war was nearly over, and he must have set off in high spirits, bound for action again at last. His first letter home, however, falters in its tone. He had arrived in Frankfort and found a countryside sadly devastated by war. 'I have changed my mind about this part of the country and I do not like it as much as the Cape Colony as all the farms are burnt and it looks so desolate.' He was also suffering from the usual uncertainties of the beginner. 'I feel rather out of my depth here at present as I have been away from work so long and know so few of the people here but I expect I shall find my legs in a week or two.'

He joined his regiment, with a draft of sixty men, on New Year's Eve 1901. The Inniskillings were now part of a column which Rimington, their Colonel,[25] was commanding 'with dynamic energy'. Rimington was 'inexhaustible physically and mentally, and his immense energy and drive, his unorthodox methods and his "schlimness" [as the army in South Africa referred to cunning] were intensely stimulating. Life in Rimington's column was never dull.'[26] It was, however, a series of small-scale operations, of individual escapades, of scouting and of light patrolling, that essential work which 'must of necessity be without a chronicler'.[27]

Rimington became famous for his *drives* – the only effective way of catching the elusive Boers. The British troops drove in a continuous line day and night till the Boers 'like fish in a net would dash about, endeavouring to find a way of escape, so wearying their horses . . . finally they would be compelled to surrender or fight'.[28] These drives continued throughout the spring, with a good deal of success. Rimington's command was unorthodox and challenging: when the column was troubled by men firing wildly at night, he issued the order that if any man insisted on firing at nothing, he would be sent out to attack singlehanded the thing which was annoying him, whether ant-heap or dead horse.

When not shooting in the dark at ant-heaps or dead horses, the British Army was occasionally known to fire at their own side. One such episode involved Oates. 'One particular night getting into camp very late, Captain Oates, who was Orderly Officer that day, had to post the piquets in the dark, so that he only had a very vague idea of the country. He had his black boy with him carrying his rifle, and with his usual thoroughness had posted us very carefully, spending a long time over the job.

'About an hour after he had left the post I was in charge of, we heard horses approaching from our front; instantly the whole picket was alert, and eight men with loaded rifles at the ready were peering into the darkness; presently two figures loomed through the night, and I rejoiced at the prospect of bagging two of the enemy. When I judged they were about twenty yards from us and impossible to miss, I gave the command "Fire". Eight rifles crashed out into the stillness of the night, and one of the figures dropped from his horse like a stone, the other did not move, but that dear familiar drawl came to us over the veldt. "Shut up, you blank fools, you will disturb the whole camp." We then found it was Captain Oates, who had mistaken his way, and had not the slightest idea he was in front of the outpost line. The black boy had simply fallen off his horse through fright. Captain, or rather Lieutenant Oates as he was then, said all the bullets had gone high, a good illustration of night firing, and convincing proof (although a lucky one as it happened) of the old musketry proverb, "Lights down, sights down." '[29]

On 2 February 1902 Oates was promoted Lieutenant (not, it must be said, as a result of avoiding assassination by his own men). For the next few weeks he played his part in the final moves in a war which was almost spent. At one point Oates captured a Boer waggon containing sewing machinery and babies' high chairs. Then, after a long absence of news, a letter arrived at Gestingthorpe from Heilbron Hospital, where Oates was recovering from enteric.[30] 'This is a horrid place – everybody gets ill here. They tell me I had a pretty bad go but personally I know nothing about it.' Military hospitals in South Africa were one of the scandals of the war (16, 168 men died from wounds or disease), their inadequacies of equipment matched only by the ham-fisted enthusiasm of the amateur nurses. One wounded officer in hospital at Pretoria was so irritated by their attentions that he pinned a note to his pillow which read 'too ill to be nursed'.

On 1 June 1902, news of the signature of peace was received by Heliograph at the Inniskilling Camp in a message worded 'Peace signed last night.' A telegram followed from Kitchener, communicating a message of congratulations from the King. Looking back on the Boer War, Lieutenant-Colonel Watkins Yardley wrote, 'it has shown us that, instead of the days of cavalry being past, this arm is just as essential to the success of an army as ever. A successful termination of a campaign is not brought about by the exertions of one arm alone: it is only by the skilful combination of the three that victory is to be attained. South Africa has shown

1. William Oates, father of
Lawrence. Gentleman, explorer,
and Victorian *paterfamilias*.

2. Caroline, Lawrence's mother.

3. Lilian (left) and Laurie in
petticoats. 'When he was small,
mother used to say, he was a very
pathetic little boy.' (Violet Oates)

4. 'Mother used to get angry, but
never with Laurie.' (Violet Oates)

5. The family on holiday at Sidmouth. 'Get a donkey for Laurie.'

(Mrs Oates's Diary, 22 April 1886)

6. 'We used to ride donkeys whenever we could on holiday near Whitby and at Sidmouth.'

(Violet Oates)

nothing to alter this principle of war; but it has proved that much of the former training of the cavalry in peacetime was useless.' He concluded, of the Boers, 'they have taught us much'.[31] Oates was to spend the next few years of his life in an army struggling to come to terms with those lessons.

Notes and references

1 Winston S. Churchill, *A History of the English Speaking Peoples*, Vol. IV, p. 294.
2 Michael Howard, 'Empire, Race and War in Pre 1914 Britain', *History Today*, Vol. 31, December 1981.
3 M. Prior, *Campaigns of a War Correspondent* p. 287.
4 Lord Roberts, letter to Lord Lansdowne, 15 February 1900.
5 Lord Curzon, letter to W. St J. Broderick, 8 January 1900.
6 Edward M. Spiers, *The Army and Society 1815-1914*, p. 241.
7 Captain W. E. Cairnes, *The Army from Within*.
8 Michael Howard, *op.cit.*
9 *The Cornhill Magazine*, April 1913, p. 473.
10 *Gestingthorpe Church Magazine*, July 1901.
11 L. E. G. Oates, account of action written for Major Jackson, 27 August 1907.
12 The note was a scrap of paper. It was later proudly displayed by Mrs C. A. Oates in the hall at Gestingthorpe.
13 L. E. G. Oates, *op. cit.* 'The man mentioned, Pte Malone, was a son of the old riding master Malone, V.C. He joined from desertion just before the regiment went on service and deserted again as soon as he was sent home. Nothing has been seen of him since.'
14 Herbert Dixon, letter to Mrs C. A. Oates, 5 July 1913.
15 *The Army and Navy Gazette*, 22 February 1913.
16 *The London Mail*, 22 February 1913. Lieutenant-Colonel (Later Lieutenant-General Lord) Baden-Powell commanded the 5th Dragoon Guards from 1897 to 1899.
17 *The Gloucestershire Chronicle*, 1 March 1913, quoting Sergeant-Major Denis Hartland.
18 Lord Kitchener's despatch to the Secretary of State for War, 23 June 1902.
19 Major-General J. M. D. Ward-Harrison, letter to Patrick Cordingley, recalling conversations with his father-in-law, C. A. Fleury Teulon, a contemporary of L. E. G. Oates in the 6th (Inniskilling) Dragoons. 'There was a strong feeling in the regiment at the time,

and for some years afterwards that Oates's gallantry was inadequately rewarded.'

20 *Ibid.* 'My father-in-law always believed that it was the war wound which finally let him down. It is not generally known that the leg always gave him trouble which he refused to admit.'

21 *The Times*, 15 June 1901.

22 *Gestingthorpe Church Magazine*, July 1901.

23 *Ibid.*

24 H. F. Waterhouse, FRCS, letter to Mrs C. A. Oates, 25 June 1901.

25 Lieutenant-Colonel (later Lieutenant-General Sir) Michael Rimington commanded the 6th (Inniskilling) Dragoons from 1901 to 1903. He was Colonel of this regiment from 1912 to 1922. On amalgamation with the 5th Dragoon Guards he became one of the two colonels of the Regiment, for a further six years.

26 Major-General R. Evans, *5th Royal Inniskilling Dragoon Guards*, p.106. General Evans commanded the regiment from 1929 to 1932 and was its Colonel from 1937 to 1947. His son, Major-General W. A. Evans, commanded the regiment from 1980 to 1982.

27 L. C. Bernacci, A *Very Gallant Gentleman*, p. 45.

28 Lieutenant-Colonel J. Watkins Yardley, *With the Inniskilling Dragoons*, p. 320.

29 *Journal of the 6th (Inniskilling) Dragoons*, August 1912, p. 263. Letter written by Sergeant-Major Williams.

30 Today the disease is called typhoid. The major epidemics during the South African War were caused by poor sanitation arrangements and polluted water. Recovery took some four or five weeks but the disease was sometimes fatal.

31 Lieutenant-Colonel J. Watkins Yardley, *op. cit.*, p. 345.

4

Ireland

Oates recovered rapidly from enteric and by the early autumn of 1902 was back at the Regimental Headquarters in Ireland: Ponsonby Barracks[1] at the Curragh, 'the Aldershot of Ireland'. His mother, delighted by his safe return, had the church bells at Gestingthorpe repaired as a gesture of thanksgiving.[2] The regiment returned to Ireland in November 1902 and after eighteen months moved to Marlborough Barracks, Dublin for a further two years. For Oates they were idle, slumbering years: little seemed to be happening nationally or internationally, and even in the army the reforms leaked slowly through the fabric rather than washing away all abuses in a flood tide of dramatic action. In vain Oates looked for excitement – and only found it sporadically in the practice of various gentlemanly sports.

Even Ireland, so often the scene of turbulent, tragic and thrilling events, seemed languorously becalmed. The period of 1890 to 1910, described as 'the doldrums of Irish political affairs,'[3] was a kind of Indian summer for the old Order. For much of this period the Tories were in power in England, pledged to 'kill Home Rule by kindness' – and apparently succeeding. Irish energies were being channelled in safe literary and *folkloriste* directions, such as the founding of the Gaelic League, the Gaelic Athletic Association, the National Literary Society and the Abbey Theatre. The years Oates spent in Ireland were a dead time, with nationalist spirits apparently dormant, and the shocking adultery and death of Parnell and the Rising of 1916 equally distant in past and future.

The army, however, was struggling to apply the lessons learnt in the Boer War, and the Inniskillings came once again under the influence of two most dynamic military personalities: Rimington and Baden-Powell. Rimington commanded the 3rd Cavalry Brigade, of which the Regiment formed a part, and Baden-Powell was now the new Inspector-General of Cavalry, and personally directed cavalry manoeuvres. 'We are in for some hard work this winter', reported Oates on 2 November 1902,

'Rimington does not let grass grow under his feet and he sees it does not grow under anybody else's'. However, the most striking of army reforms had to wait until 1905 and the arrival in office of R. B. Haldane.

Oates lost no time in amassing quite a stable of horses; for the next three years his life revolved utterly around them. It was customary for each young officer to provide himself with two chargers – one, a paragon 'free from blemish, noble in appearance, full of fire and equable in temper',⁴ and a second everyday horse of more modest endowments. However, there were a host of other activities for which special mounts were required: chiefly polo, hunting and racing. A polo pony had to be no more than 14.2 hands in height, very fast, and able to jump off at full speed at the shortest notice, like a rocket. Anything upward of fifty guineas would be thought a fair price for such a mount.

Hunting was not only an irresistible sport to most cavalry officers. It was considered excellent military training, for it was thought that 'sportsmen who had the Hunter's instinct' would require less military training than the officers of other European countries. 'By sportsmen,' explained General Parsons 'I mean men who can ride well to hounds . . . all officers can hunt if they have only strength of mind to give up other things for it . . . Time spent at these sports develops soldierly qualities . . . in hunting, riding hounds with judgement, studying ground, rapidly drawing deductions and forming decisions from them, committing country and ground to memory, screwing up one's courage to take risks, sympathizing with one's horse and learning his powers of jumping, pace and endurance. No practice is better than writing accounts of runs afterwards . . . . I did this when commanding a Battery in Ireland by having my reconnaissance instruction on hunting days, the enemy being the fox, the Army a certain pack of hounds. Next morning the operations against the enemy were described to me with 6 inch maps in the Battery Office.'⁵

Oates did not need to justify his hunting on educational grounds, however; he simply loved it. On 10 December he reported that 'while out hunting yesterday I hurt my hand and although it hurt me a good deal I did not give it much notice. This morning I find one of the bones is broken, the one leading down from the wrist to the knuckle of my little finger. I have got my left hand all done up in splints and can only use my right. I am most fearfully sick about it as hunting is the only thing that makes this life endurable'. The very next day, however, he was out again, splint and all. 'Just in from hunting had a good day rode Kate she's a topper.'

Even racing was seen as a good education for the cavalry officer, for 'on active service, in the moment of imminent danger, the self-reliance

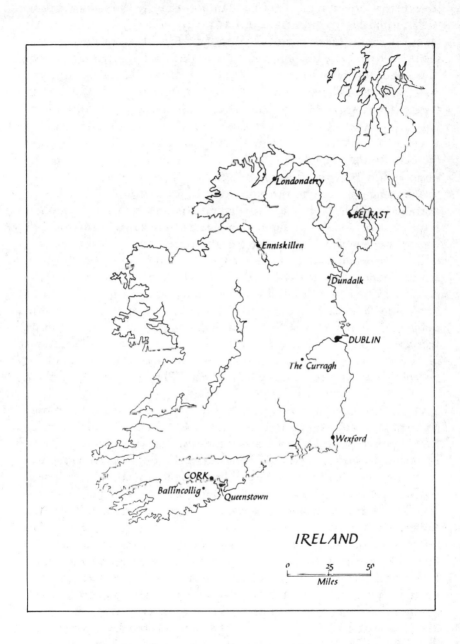

Londonderry

BELFAST

Enniskillen

Dundalk

DUBLIN

The Curragh

Wexford

CORK
Ballincollig
Queenstown

IRELAND

0   25   50
Miles

55

and quickness of resolution which are indispensable to the successful steeplechase rider cannot fail to be of utmost value to the soldier'.[6] With such formidable recommendations as to the educational value of his favourite sports, Oates could afford to indulge without qualms in what seems to have been his only vice. Two years running, riding his own horses, he won the Subalterns' Cup at the Regimental Meeting, firstly in 1904, and the following year when he finished in a dead heat with Lieutenant Holland. He also had considerable success at the Irish meetings, as an owner. With Gestingthorpe, in 1904 he won the Military Cup at Dundalk and again in 1905 he won the same race with a horse called the Cub. In 1904 Angel Gabriel won the St Stephen's Plate at Leopardstown and in 1905 the Irish Grand Military Cup at Punchestown. For Oates racing was an enterprise on some scale, for at one time he had seven horses in training with a civilian trainer. Before the 1905 triumph at Punchestown, Oates and his trainer Featherstonehaugh had words. 'I have quarrelled with F. and taken Angel Gabriel away.' Victory, when it came, was therefore all the sweeter. 'I was awfully pleased about Gabriel as I trained him myself and scored off F. and also everybody advised me not to let Wood ride.' Ireland was the perfect place for horse-lovers. 'A very funny thing happened yesterday,' Oates reported. 'I saw an old man dodging about my troop stables hiding behind the chaff cutter. He finally worked his way round to me and in a hoarse whisper said, "I know a great blood horse, Colonel, dam by Ascetic untried," and he would not say another word except that he would write. They are very funny, these people, on the subject of a horse.'

Oates obviously had a good eye for a horse. Rimington himself admired Daddy and told Oates he ought to sell him as he made the troop horses look so poor. One of Oates's horses which appeared, initially, to be below par however was Suffering Kate who on 3 January 1903 was 'suffering more than ever', but careful nursing improved her a great deal, for two months later he announced, 'Kate has long ceased to be suffering, she will make a beautiful mare with a summer's rest'. A little later, 'suffering Kate kicked my groom the other day which is a good sign'. His prognostications proved true, for in December 1904 he praised her to the skies. 'I knew she was a flyer but I did not know she was the best hunter I ever sat on.' Again and again his letters speak of horses seen, coveted ('could you let me have £100 as I have found a very useful horse which I want to buy'), bought ('my new horse is a ripper . . . goes in harness like a roaring tiger'), lost ('Judy died of pneumonia the day before yesterday. I think I shall sell all my horses and buy a bicycle') or sold ('I am going to sell Daddy if I can get a real nice price for him as I cannot afford to keep him in training all the year and he is a great tearing brute to go hunting on').

Now and again he felt a brief pang of guilt for spending so much money on horses, 'but it would be too dull without them'. Polo was not yet a passion with him, 'not half the fun a day's hunting or a horse race is . . . however, like croquet it is a nice summer's amusement and I believe improves your riding enormously'. Racing, however, seems to have transformed him from a rather laconic and reserved young man into a yelling and sobbing dervish. 'I was racing here today and ran Gabriel in the big Hurdle race . . . I was so excited I fairly screamed and rode an imaginary finish on top of the stand, much to everybody's amusement.' At the subaltern's cup, in 1904 – which he won – 'Murdoch and myself wept in each other's arms after the race'. And when Gabriel won at Punchestown, 'My eyes got so full of tears I could not see the horses and had to keep asking the man next to me how my horse was going.'

Horses were everything to him. He spent lavishly on them, was end-lessly fascinated by them: they were his business, his pleasure, and his passion. If this seems extreme, if it calls to mind the definition of the aristocracy as 'asses who care about horses', it must be remembered that horses were not then, as they are now, valued only for the pleasure they give. The economy depended on horses: transport and communications had until recently been totally dominated by them. The horse pulled the plough, the cab, the cart, the train, the barge. Though the railway had taken over for some long-distance journeys, and the motor car was still waiting in the wings, in the early 1900s the horse still triumphed, centre-stage. Everyday life was unthinkable without them. So to some extent a preoccupation with horses was not only natural but necessary. Nowadays, some men are fascinated by their cars: eighty years ago, the horse could fulfil a similar role. Quite apart from the fierce and often devoted fel-lowship of man with beast, horses could serve as status symbols and a focus for male energies. The continual buying, selling, care and careful tuning-up of fast machines, whether Triumphs or thoroughbreds, punc-tuated by thrilling bursts of speed, appears to be an unchanging ritual amongst young men – and one needing little explanation or excuse in 1900, in a society where marriage was often postponed until the mid or late thirties, and few outlets provided for male energies.

For though the nineties could be naughty for those of the Prince of Wales's set, for the bohemians of the theatrical or literary worlds, and though the Edwardian era which followed is often regarded as a time of licence if not licentiousness, in the army things were different. The Prince of Wales's first *amour* was at the Curragh (with a young actress called

Nellie Clifden, put up to it by his fellow officers) but some of his bachelor contemporaries led lives of blameless chastity. For a start, early marriage was not encouraged in the army. General Bellairs, writing in 1889, did not recommend young officers to fall in love. 'A subaltern,' he wrote, 'should not think of marrying until he is thirty-five years old.'[7] The rule of thumb was that subalterns may not marry, captains might marry, majors should marry and lieutenant-colonels must marry. Some senior officers believed that 'a soldier has no business to be married'[8] – *at all*. Frederick Stephenson wrote home to his mother, 'I have seen quite enough of married life in this campaign to prove to me that marriage and soldiering are totally incompatible'.[9] It was thought that once a man married, he became irrevocably softened and incapacitated as a soldier, because of the conflicting claims on his energies and sense of duty. As Kipling put it, 'he travels fastest who travels alone' a point he enlarged upon in a verse called 'The Married Man'.

> The bachelor 'e fights for one
> As joyful as can be;
> But the married man don't call it fun
> Because he fights for three
> For 'im an' 'er an' It
> (An' Two and One make Three)
> 'E wants to finish 'is bit
> An' 'e wants to go 'ome to 'is tea![10]

So matrimony wreaked havoc on the battlefield, but it was also frowned upon in the peacetime army. Married officers only paid half the usual mess subscriptions, seldom dined in the mess, and so the cost of maintaining the mess establishment fell more heavily on its bachelor members. In some corps, would be bridegrooms had to pay a fine of £100 to mess funds to compensate.

There were other problems, fertility for one. 'Married to a healthy young woman,' General Sir William Bellairs warned his young officer readers, 'you cannot reasonably expect to have fewer babies to provide for than one in every second year, six children after twelve years of married life, and very possibly more to follow later on'.[11] The most the army might be able to offer the married subaltern in terms of accommodation would be a couple of rooms in a barracks and, overseas, the matrimonial establishment might be reduced to a tent. Was it fair, asked Sir William, to invite a lady to share such a life? Given the sheltered background of most gentlewomen, the formality and restrictions of their lives, the deliberate state of idleness in which they were kept, and the suffocating routines of entertaining which the married state would involve, it is not surprising that Oates stayed well clear. He affected a playful horror of the very idea of marriage – referring to officers who got engaged as 'making fools of themselves' – and never giving the merest hint of his passions and affections being engaged by any Kates but the quadruped kind.

It is not simply that in his letters to his mother he presents himself as a caricature of a prematurely crusty old bachelor. Many a man might put up such a smokescreen to shield a mother's eyes from a world of indiscretions. But Oates seems to have been regarded by his brother officers as remarkable for his sobriety and indifference to women and society. Lieutenant-Colonel J. A. Brooke,[12] who served with him in Egypt, cannot remember Oates even once taking part in any of the forays to the wicked old city of Cairo. He certainly *affected* an indifference to women, but there is no doubt that he did not share Kitchener's and Gordon's preference for young men. During his late teenage years he struck up several friendships with girls which were sustained for many years by correspondence, for example the Misses Craig whom he met on his West Indies cruise.

Apart from the Misses Craig, there was a young lady in Leeds who had claimed his attention in the late 1890s: a Miss Florence Chambers who lived with her aunt and uncle. Oates asked her out, in a letter signed 'your ardent admirer', but her aunt was very strict and would not permit it. Oates then made a secret assignation to meet her in Commercial Street, and took a photograph of her there. Though she married in 1899, Oates clearly remained smitten for the rest of his life, as after his death she received a letter from Commander Evans saying she was a lucky woman to have had the admiration of such a man.

It was well within the chivalrous conventions of the age for a man in Oates's position 'to become her faithful servant, meet and correspond with her but never contemplate having an affair with her'.[13] It would also have been characteristic of Oates, and of his society, for him suddenly and quietly to marry, had he reached his late thirties and the rank of major. No doubt he would have had to present it most diplomatically to his mother, for her love of him was jealous, strong and ambitious. But it was the conventions of his profession and society, rather than the tyrannies of this doughty dame, which prolonged his bachelor days.

But were his bachelor days entirely innocent of dissipation? Even the most austere generals, Captain Cairnes tells us, have been subalterns in their time and 'must have sown, though no doubt soberly and discreetly . . . their little crop of wild oats'.[14] Some officers, torn between the irreconcilable demands of army discipline and sensual appetite, decided 'we'll whore it out to the end'. But not Oates. Though often reckless when taking risks in action or sport, he seems to have been remarkably restrained and judicious in his personal life. When he caught smallpox in India in 1908, the medical officer reassured his mother that his 'very healthy life and steady habits' would help him to recover quickly. Wine, women and song had evidently not undermined his constitution. Though in earlier times British officers in India had found that a native mistress could very conveniently teach them the language, by Oates's day a considerable influx of British women, and Queen Victoria's influence, had banished such liaisons and an atmosphere of purity prevailed.

Voluntary chastity, by present libertarian standards, may seem an aberration. For the Victorians, those champions of The Family, it was a necessity. Early Christianity had emphasized Christ's purity and St Augustine urged believers to turn away from the pleasure of the flesh and fix their eyes on heaven; in the nineteenth century the Christian prohibition was affirmed, and men were taught that they only possessed a finite amount of energy, and that energy was best saved for work or battle. Procreation, for the married man, was an occasional duty: that was all. This ascetic pattern is characteristic of many warrior societies.

Oates was a member of a warrior caste in a society which made early marriage almost impossible, sex outside marriage hazardous and degrading, and sex at all a reckless expenditure of vital energies. Respectable girls were virtually inaccessible and often reduced to near-imbecility by their lack of education and an obsession with the marriage market. Other girls were out of the question. Oates was a man who loved the outdoor life of violent exertion and gentlemanly sports; he hated the polite world of drawing-room conversation. He was watched over by a formidably powerful mother. To such a man, voluntary chastity must have been far from an aberration, but a style of life at once rational, elegant and natural.

Even without women, and with little wine, there was still a lot of enjoyment to be had in life – and some of it at the very top of the social scale. 'I do not think I have enjoyed 2 days better for a long time than I did at Punchestown. The King was there both days and the Queen the first. We got a tremendous reception. I got very much chaffed about riding myself but Titus is a terribly tiring horse to ride and I could not get anyone strong enough'.[15] 'We took the King down yesterday to lay a foundation stone and last night took him to the theatre and brought him back.' Oates also met the Duke of Connaught, but did not distinguish himself with great social *élan*, for 'he asked me if I knew his son at Eton and not knowing who he was, I answered that there were such a lot of people there you could not be expected to know *everybody*!'.

He was by nature fond of a solitary life, yet the Irish amused him exceedingly. 'They are extraordinary people, these Irish. There are about eight men outside who are supposed to be painting the huts. They do absolutely nothing except roar at each other and sing. There is one fat man, a most dreadful-looking being who is singing a song the first line of the chorus being "Oh the ladies the ladies the ladies." If I had my gun handy I would fire into them.' No doubt it was partly the splendours of the Irish race which led him to exclaim, 'I fairly love the Curragh' but also the easy availability of sport, especially racing, and 'Friday and Saturday I was away shooting and had a capital time'. At this time he also thought of offering his services as first whip to a hunt as a useful source of experience prior to taking on a pack of his own.

The local Irish were not his only sources of amusement. The army provided its share of sensations. 'Our mess caterer has just decamped and taken £500 with him, this has caused some excitement.' The characters of the men also gave rise to mirth. 'I have a very proper little sergeant here to instruct me, he was telling me with much hesitation a yarn about running after a Cretan and sticking his bayonet into him. "I struck him in the leg" he said, and then blushing continued, "only a little higher up."' Amongst his fellow officers there were of course the traditional army wagers, usually involving feats of strength or endurance. 'I have backed King to beat another Captain in the Corps, from here to the middle of the Curragh. I fancy our chances as King is really very strong and the other chap belongs to the fat non-sporting fraternity.' Some reg-imental wagers were simply, and satisfyingly, silly, such as one in the 15th Foot in which officers appropriately enough competed in the difficult art of standing on one leg. Domestic details claimed some of his attention – he wrote home to ask how to take some cuttings from geranium stumps in his window box. He also kept an unusual pet; a bloodhound puppy. 'It is leading me a dance – a foxhound puppy is not in it for mischief. We had snow here last night and as my hound had eaten nearly all the clothing in my quarters I was rather cold. It finished up with the Cavalry Drill Book but found it such thirsty work it stopped.'

A major pleasure, which he discovered at this time, was sailing, though his first steps were not auspicious. From Dublin he reported, 'I went out in a rigger the other day with the whole of Trinity looking on. I never made such a fool of myself in my life, they will not lend me one of their boats again which is rather miserable'. However, he evidently decided not to be dependent on the invitations of others, and in July 1905 bought a yacht. 'It is 48 ft long, 10 ft beam and has a small cabin; when I asked the Colonel for leave he wanted to know if I knew anything about it [sailing]. I said it was all right as my grandfather was an admiral.' Sailing in his yacht *The Saunterer*[21] became a favourite relaxation for him. Sometimes he managed to prevail upon Bryan to join him, and their sailing adventures together provoked some great memories and some shared jokes. 'I sent Bryan a picture p.c. the other day. It was one of those "Songs Illustrated" series entitled "The Return of the Swallows". When I saw it in the shop I laughed so [much] the proprietor came down and asked me to stop as a crowd was collecting outside.' He also enjoyed (or perhaps diplomatically pretended to) the occasional theatre trip with his mother. 'We will go to Veronique again next time I am over I do not remember ever having enjoyed a piece more.'

So there is no doubt that Oates's life was quite generously endowed with pleasures, as one would expect of an officer with his means. The point is one to labour because during these peacetime years in Ireland he developed a very strong sense of increasing boredom and frustration, amounting at times almost to despair. In a resourceful man who knew how to enjoy himself and had a range of pleasures, this growing bitterness and sense of purposelessness is interesting and significant. It is possible that he felt life offered him nothing but pleasure, when he hungered for work and a sense of meaning.

And there was little work for him to do. The late Victorian army was run by the warrant and non-commissioned officers. 'When the colonel, and half the captains and subalterns go on leave at the same time,' confided Horace Wyndham, 'the battalion somehow manages to get along without them. But it cannot do this if the sergeant-major and colour-sergeants are absent.'[16] It was assumed that officers would have little to do with the training of the men. On Sundays there was a Commanding Officer's full inspection of stables, horses, saddlery and barrack rooms, and the reason was felt to be that 'Sunday was the most convenient day for the officers, as it left them greater leisure to follow their social and sporting pursuits during the week'.[17] During the Boer War a storm of controversy had arisen about many aspects of the army, and the traditional role of the officer had attracted much sarcasm. 'We need an army which is an up to date fighting machine,' wrote Captain Cairnes, 'not a mere organisation for the purpose of providing an elegant employment for the leisure hours of the wealthy classes.'[18] A Select Committee investigating the attitudes of officers found that 'the majority of young officers will not work unless compelled: that "keenness is out of fashion"; that "it is not the correct form" and that the idea is . . . to do as little as they possibly can'.[19]

Was Oates one of these elegant, arrogant layabouts who was interested only in polo and hunting and anxious to avoid work as much as possible? The answer lies veiled in the most intriguing of riddles. For though he wrote, and certainly felt, 'the more work I do the better I feel', nevertheless Oates seems to resist the idea of reform, and even identified himself with the leisured old school of sporting officers: 'I am now thoroughly fed up with the army and would go tomorrow, the annoying thing about it is the War Office does not mind us going as they want to get rid of the people who are soldiering for amusement and are trying to get people who do not play polo etc'. He also seems to have found some of his commanding officers extraordinarily irritating. 'The new colonel is absolutely desperate, he picks quarrels with everybody and when he gets snuff he whines, for weakmindedness he really takes it, and he's always nag, nag, nag.' (Shortly afterwards this colonel was fired. 'I always said that man would come to a bad end', commented Oates.) But even the Commanding Officer who replaced him seems to have provoked in Oates some rebellious and arrogant moments. 'They offered to send me to the Cavalry School at Netheravon for 6 months but I refused as I told them it would interfer with my hunting. I thought for a moment the Colonel would burst but they calmed him down after a while . . . I have now to attend stables although I pointed out to the little man in charge of me that it is very hot and I have not quite settled with my lunch.' A few months later he was ordered to the Musketry School at Hythe. 'It is a great nuisance. When the Colonel told me about it he said in a very sarcastic voice, "I hope that falls in with your plans." I said it suited me admirably; it's no good being rude just because his manners are not quite what they should be.'

Indeed, it seems as if many people's manners, including Oates's, were not quite what they should have been. (His letters home sometimes provoked strong criticism from his mother, at which he thanked her for 'the two lectures, to the first I plead guilty to the second I also plead guilty'.) What is most striking here is the sense of men made uneasy, prickly and hostile by the uncertainty and redefinition of their roles. There is no doubt that the old army with its abuses and inefficiencies was crying out for reform. 'Pipeclay, antiquated and useless forms of drill, blind obedience to orders, ramrod-like rigidity on parade . . .'[20] nobody could defend such patently false values and practices. And when it came to battle, the muddles and disgraces of the Boer War had proved Roberts's analysis that the cavalry's old role, mounted, with sword and lance, would have to give way to defensive warfare, entrenched, with much use of firepower and cover. Bad leadership in the Boer War had provoked Roberts into sacking eleven of the seventeen cavalry commanders. Oates himself had experienced many of these inadequacies and railed against them. There is no doubt that he resented poor leadership (and obviously made his scorn very plain though he was capable of revising his opinion in the light of experience). That he was clearly not an apologist of the bad old ways is shown by his reaction to bad old army practices which persisted well into peacetime. 'It is very poor sort of work here,' he wrote in the autumn of 1902. 'Stables, riding-school, stables.' Endless parades jarred his nerves. 'I am really about sick of it, we were on parade for 5 hours the other morning.' Usually the Inniskillings turned out at 5 a.m. and went on parade for three hours. They then had nothing to do for the rest of the day. 'We are having an exciting time', Oates commented sardonically. When diversions arose in the form of manoeuvres or courses, they turned out to be even more frustrating and pointless than the endless tedium of daily routine.

The School of Musketry in Hythe, where he went in 1905, brought his discontent to boiling point. 'This place is absolutely desperate if I don't get away tomorrow I shall either murder someone or take to drink' – a sentiment shared, in his day, by Field-Marshal Robertson. The Cavalry School at Netheravon, Salisbury, where he had eventually to go, produced a similar response. 'In respect to my sojourn in this delightful spot, please never imagine me overworked the thing is an absolute impossibility what I complain of is having nothing to do . . . This is the worst place I ever dropped into there is absolutely nothing to do here and they won't let one go away. Why I go on soldiering is an absolute mystery to me I am beginning to think I am not quite all here.' Even taking up not one but two more sports, hockey and golf, could not dispel his irritation.

In this prevailing atmosphere of disillusionment and irritation, it is not surprising that the army reforms seemed to him merely to be an extra provocation. For a start, the reforms were not carried out in a smooth flowing, evidently rational and gradually unfolding series of changes which might have inspired confidence in some kind of overall plan. They were piecemeal, confused, sometimes ineffectual and often downright silly, as in the five changes of khaki jacket within one year. They were also hotly debated. The reasons for this were many. Broderick, Secretary of State for War during the Boer War tried to rush reforms through to placate public opinion, while the war was still going on. This was foolish. It did not take account of the needs of a peacetime army and the demands to be made on it (the manning of overseas garrisons, for example). What is more, Broderick tried to work out a system of reforms while his commanding officers, the best source of information and advice, were still

6000 miles away and deeply preoccupied with winning battles. It is no surprise that Broderick's reforms were soon discredited.

Even the arrival at the War Office of Roberts himself, fresh from the field and brimming with sound new ideas based on more than forty years' experience, did not work the desired magic. His excellent suggestions were often resisted, questioned and finally rejected, as in the issue of promotion by merit rather than seniority, and economies in uniform expenditure. Even the very substantial reforms which he did achieve met with scepticism or indifference – the Broderick reforms had aroused such a wave of hostility that some people felt that all reform must be ill-planned and misguided. The Liberals in Opposition did not help. Their fear of militarism led them to abandon all plans for army reform and their 'policy' was simply to plan for a huge cut in military expenditure. In the face of such overwhelming muddle it is astonishing to learn that the Balfour Government did somehow manage a considerable measure of improvement along the lines suggested by Roberts. No wonder Oates viewed it all with contempt. 'A circular came round from the Army Council saying the shortness of candidates for the cavalry was critical and ordering more discomforts to attract "the poor man with brains". The thing they have not yet grasped is that the man with brains knows too much to join the service.' As the weary months of tedium and confusion drew on, his thoughts turned more and more often to escape.

'King tells me he is leaving the Corps in June and they say Dixon will not come back,' he wrote from Hythe in 1905, 'so I think after this course I had better go too. I have given it very careful consideration since we discussed it and I don't see that things are any better. I do not want to leave solely because I do not like it. There are various reasons but the chief one is that I am doing neither myself nor anyone else any good, I am spending considerably too much money. You can look at the Army List and see for yourself what chance I have of promotion. They tell me you get such a good social position in the Army, damn the social position say I.' In early 1906 he reconciled himself to taking an equitation course, at the Cavalry School in Salisbury. 'We have our [veterinary] exam on Monday, I expect it will pass off alright but if bad teaching goes for anything we ought all to fail.'

In the event it proved fairly easy. 'I think I got through all right. They gave me a weed of a troop horse and asked me to pick out its faults. By the time I was halfway through the examiner burst into tears and was led away sobbing.' In his present mood of black humour, he obviously expected nothing from the army in the way of challenges or interest. Again and again he is tempted to thoughts of leaving, getting a little farm somewhere, or snatching in vain at every chance of going abroad. The prospect of escaping from the British Isles was always exciting. It was British society which irked him and the British Army which crabbed and confined him. There were no outlets for his particular energies. Only pleasure was allowed, and organized pleasure was sometimes the most excruciating of pains. 'Unfortunately I am now engaged to go to dinner and for a picnic on the canal, cold tea, hampers, bugs and backache all compleat.' No wonder he took refuge in energetic sports. It seems he was simply not allowed to do anything else, and they are a great safety valve for rage.

Then, soon after the equitation course, and perhaps in the nick of time, he received an interesting proposition. 'The Colonel, who I always said was cracked, came to me and asked me whether in the event of my being offered the Adjutancy I should accept . . . what should I do? It appears that my friends and relatives wish me to continue soldiering, this does not make me think any more highly of the intelligence of my friends and relatives. However, there is a slight increase of pay and it may lead to something better, thirdly if I soldier on atal I may as well do it properly.

'Against this it would be a great nuisance and take up a lot of my spare time also it would cost a good deal as I should have to buy a lot of new cloths and kit. I should also have to work with a crammer as I have not passed for promotion. What I propose is that I tell the Colonel I will take it and that you should increase my allowance by £100 in the event of my being made adjutant . . . If you think my allowance is already large enough please say so and I shan't be too upset.' Having decided to take the Adjutancy, he threw himself into the exams with characteristic scepticism. 'Certainly there are some awful fools passing so why not I?' In April 1906 the regiment was moved from Dublin to Ballincollig with a detachment of one squadron being sent to Belfast. Within fourteen days of this more orders were received of an immediate posting to Egypt. A good example of the eccentricities of army planning.

Notes and referenees

1 Named after Major-General Ponsonby, who commanded the 5th Dragoon Guards from 1803 to 1812 and was killed leading the brilliantly successful charge of the Union Brigade, which included the 6th (Inniskilling) Dragoons, at the Battle of Waterloo.
2 The 5th bell was inscribed in Latin: 'In gratitude to God for the safe return with honour of her beloved son Lawrence E. G. Oates from the dangers of the war in South Africa, C. A. Oates has caused this

and the sixth bell, for a long time cracked and useless, to be recast, 1901.'

3 Sir James O'Connor, *History of Ireland*, p.149.
4 W. E. Cairnes, *Social Life in the British Army*, p.15.
5 Major-General L. W. Parsons, *Training the Intelligence of Officers and Men*, p. 6.
6 W. E. Cairnes, *op. cit.*, p.53.
7 Sir William Bellairs, *The Military Career*, quoted in E. S. Turner's *Gallant Gentlemen – A Portrait of the British Officer*, p.239.
8 Byron Farwell, *For Queen and Country*, p. 231.
9 *Ibid.*
10 Rudyard Kipling, *The Barrack Room Ballads*.
11 Sir William Bellairs, *op. cit.*
12 Lieutenant-Colonel J. A. (Johnnie) Brooke joined the 6th (Inniskilling) Dragoons in 1907 from the Northumberland Fusiliers. He commanded the 5th Inniskilling Dragoon Guards from 1925 to 1929. He died in 1982.
13 Mark Girouard, *The Return to Camelot*, p.200.
14 W. E. Cairnes, *op.cit.* p.157.
15 Titus, ridden by Oates, was placed third in the Irish Grand Military Steeplechase at Punchestown, 1904.
16 Horace Wyndham, *Following the Drum*, p. 69.
17 Field-Marshal Sir William Robertson, *From Private to Field-Marshal*, p. 9.
18 W. E. Cairnes, *The Absent-Minded War*, p.146.
19 Edward M. Spiers, *The Army and Society 1815-1914*, p. 248, quoting from the 'Report of the Committee appointed to consider the Education and Training of Officers in the Army'.
20 Field-Marshal Sir William Robertson, *op. cit.*, p. 15.
21 *Saunterer* was Oates's second yacht. She was an Auxy Yawl, built at Cowes in March 1900 by C. Sibbick and Co. She was 47.5 feet over-all with a beam of 10.3 feet.

5

Egypt

'A well founded rumour prevails that the Inniskilling Dragoons . . . have
been ordered to Egypt where they will remain for two years,' announced
the Cork Examiner. It was indeed well founded. For decades, Britain had
been tangling and tussling with France and Turkey over Egypt. In 1875
Disraeli had bought the Egyptian Khedive Ismail's shares in the Suez
Canal (paying four million pounds for nearly half the total issue) and
so safeguarded the route to India. As a result, Britain's economic and
strategic interests were so irrevocably fixed on Suez that the question of
who governed Egypt, and how, was vital.

Though the Khedive ruled in name, Egypt had actually been admin-
istered for over twenty years by the British Consul-General, Evelyn
Baring, later Lord Cromer. Baring had witnessed a nationalist revolt
led by Colonel Arabi Pasha in 1881, and in 1884 the Sudan problem
in which the struggle with the Mahdi and his fanatical dervishes ended
with Gordon's death in Khartoum. Winston Churchill comments on
Gordon's end that the Government sent a 'hero of heroes' to
Khartoum with all the defects and virtues of his type and they paid the
penalty.[1]

Gordon's death and the outrage it provoked must still have been
vividly in the memory when in 1906 the Government decided to send
the Inniskilling Dragoons to Egypt to show the flag. This time it was the
Turks who had seized some Egyptian territory in Sinai, including Tabah,
a town at the northernmost tip of the Gulf of Akaba.

The British rattled a few sabres and sent an ultimatum to the Turks.
Some British cruisers, destroyers and torpedo boats mustered and hung
around menacingly in the eastern Mediterranean, and promptly enough
the Sultan gave way and promised to withdraw his garrison from Tabah.
He also beguilingly explained that the 2000 extra Turkish troops at Akaba
were not there for any sinister purpose, but to help build the Hejaz
Railway, which was scheduled to reach Medina the following year. In

the face of such wiliness, what could the British do but strengthen their presence in Egypt and show they meant business?

The French, sometimes equivocal in their behaviour over Egypt, for once did not grudge their support: 'Even if there were no Entente Cordiale, no civilised power could hesitate over which side to take in a conflict between England and Turkey'.[2] Apart from the note of cultural arrogance, what we see here is a sign of the old, old battle between the Crescent and the Cross, which had raged on and off in the Mediterranean since the Crusades. This time it was more of a Cold War than a bloody conflict, and the Inniskillings were to play their part in the threats and manoeuvres.

The telegram ordering the regiment to go had arrived at Ballincollig early on a Sunday morning, and was read to the Adjutant from outside his bathroom door as he took his morning bath. His reaction was perhaps not unexpected from a cavalry officer: 'But what about the polo ponies?'[3] *The Army and Navy Gazette* reported that the news had come unexpectedly, 'but it has given satisfaction nevertheless, for the gallant Inniskillings are never so happy as when they are up and doing'.[4]

Oates's own response to the posting was jubilant. 'The Egyptian move is quite first class. I'm awfully pleased about it. We are taking our horses with us, which is of course ludicrous as they will die like flies out there, however, if they sent me tied to a decomposing jackass I should be pleased.'

The detached squadron in Belfast, consisting of Lieutenants Oates and Bull and eighty-three noncommissioned officers and men, left Victoria Barracks, Belfast on 1 May to rejoin the regiment. The Enniskillen Reporter covered their departure. 'They marched to the Great Northern Railway terminus, headed by the band of 1st Battalion Royal Inniskilling Fusiliers. The troopers, with their beautiful horses, looked in the pink of condition and their march to the station was witnessed by large crowds. The special train with the squadron left for the south at ten o'clock.'[5]

Oates then enjoyed a few days leave at Gestingthorpe and during this time organized a trainer, one Mr Hallick, for his steeplechasers, which included the talented Angel Gabriel. 'Captain Oates was one of the best sportsmen I ever had any dealings with', reminisced Hallick in 1913, 'but I only saw a little of him, as he was always away on service. He was very fond of racing, but only military racing. His ambition was always to win soldiers' races, and especially races at the Grand Military Meeting at Sandown'.[6] Although Oates was not there to see it, Gabriel won the Grand Military Handicap Steeplechase in 1907 and finished second in the two following years.

OUT OF BOUNDS.

John Bull. "SHOO! SHOO!"

Punch, or the *London Charivari*, 9 May 1906

After his brief leave he returned to the regiment – on a motorbike. This was a new acquisition which he intended to take to Egypt with him.

The hired troopship S.S. *Cestrian* of the Leyland Steamship Company left Queenstown on a May evening for Alexandria via Southampton, having embarked 15 officers, 498 men, 76 women and children and 346 horses, all apparently in the best of condition and having no intention of fulfilling Oates's gloomy prophecy of dying like flies. The Inniskillings were given a rousing send-off by Generals Knox, Gore and Rimington. General Knox declared that 'he trusted – indeed, he felt confident – that the splendid reputation which the regiment had won would be more then maintained if they were called upon to do any fighting,'[7] sentiments echoed by General Rimington.

Colonel Herbert[8] replied that the regiment had never been in better form, and 'if occasion should arise, it would be found that the best traditions of the army would be fully upheld by the officers and men of the Inniskillings. The inspiring words which they had listened to from Generals Knox and Rimington would sink deep into the hearts of the men, who might be depended upon not to do anything to tarnish the glorious past which attached to the name of the Inniskilling Dragoons.'[9]

The troops cheered, the band assembled on the upper deck and played 'some appropriate airs'. This pleasing function having terminated and amongst these satisfying reflections the *Cestrian* steamed off from the quay.

Conditions aboard troopships varied a great deal. The wives and children were worst off: 'the discomfort, indeed, to which they were subjected was nothing less than disgraceful. Their quarters were dark and dismal, and below the water-line, and they were only permitted to leave them at certain hours.'[10] The troops were crowded into messes only six feet high, sleeping in hammocks slung from the beams.

'The atmosphere was horrible, and a stale smell of disinfectants, soap, and crowded humanity was everywhere . . . to be seasick in a comfortable, airy cabin is bad enough, but to be seasick in a crowded troopship is very much worse.'[11] Despite seasickness, military discipline prevailed. At four bells (6 a.m.) it was all hands on deck with hammocks and blankets, then half an hour for washing and shaving, breakfast at 7 a.m., after which there was a general fatigue, each mess clearing up its own quarters. A commanding officer's parade and inspection followed at 10 a.m. Dinner was at noon, followed by another fatigue and drill parade. It was tea at 4 p.m. and hammocks drawn half an hour later. By 8.15 every man was in his hammock.

Rations were rugged: ship's biscuit and tea (without milk) for breakfast, bully beef and preserved potatoes for dinner. The ship's canteen was open during part of the afternoon for the sale of 'microscopic sixpenny-worths of bread and cheese'.[12] Hungry, sick and hard worked, the men must have sought their hammocks with relief at the end of the day. It could hardly be described as a pleasure cruise.

The officers, however, observed one trooper in his memoirs, had very little of which to complain. 'Half the ship was given up to them, and they had well-appointed cabins, a big saloon, and the services of attentive stewards. Nevertheless, they grumbled from morning to night, and regarded themselves as martyrs.'[13] Thus was the British class system, enshrined in the British Army, perpetuated aboard a single heaving troopship. Divided, they ruled.

Luckily for Oates, however, the *Cestrian* did not heave. Nor did he grumble. 'We are due to arrive in Alexandria at 3 a.m. tomorrow. We have had a most excellent voyage, perfectly calm the whole way and a very nice ship. They say it will be very hot in Cairo when we land, but I suppose it will be alright as they don't appear to be going to work us too hard.'

The voyage had been spent by the officers in supervising stable hours, hearing lectures, map reading and work at sand tables. One officer recalled that only two horses had died en route[14] – apparently a good average – but the Regimental Historical Record disagrees. '24.5.06 . . . S.S. *Cestrian* arrived at Alexandria on the 24th, without a single casualty in either man or horses, and disembarkation commenced at once. The regiment proceeded by rail to Abassiyeh in three parties arriving at 11.30p.m., 12.14a.m. and 1 a.m. respectively.'

The train itself, if it was typical of Egyptian trains of the time, would have been 'little more than a glorified steam strain and the carriages set apart for the troops resembled cattle trucks more than anything else'.[15] Each truck had a canvas awning over the top and as there were no seats, the men had to sit on their kit bags. When they finally arrived at the dead of night, they found the Abassiyeh barracks antiquated and filthy, the woodwork infested with bugs. 'All ranks, and families, had to force open the doors, unroll piles of blankets, and for the first night, had to sleep on the floors. After a restless night, bitten by bugs, every face swollen, and eyes closed up, there were many pungent remarks about the country.'[16]

To some extent, of course, Oates and his fellow-officers would never get to know the country at all, for all their pungent remarks. The British Army of Occupation carried with it not only its women and children (albeit below decks and out of sight), its horses, its motorbikes, and (in the case of the Inniskillings) its Irish jaunting cars, but also its culture,

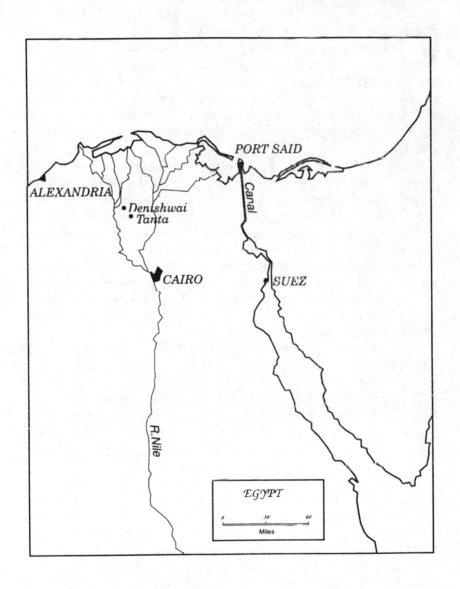

ALEXANDRIA

PORT SAID

Canal

•Denishwai
•Tanta

CAIRO

SUEZ

R.Nile

EGYPT

0   30   60
Miles

sports and habits of mind. Lord Cromer, British Consul General in Egypt when Oates arrived, had ample opportunities of observing the British Officers there. 'From the political point of view,' he concluded, 'the main characteristic of the British officer is his exclusiveness. In whatever clime he may serve, he carries his insular habits and national pastimes with him. In Egypt, he rarely mixes with any society which is not English . . . The British officers obey orders; they neither know, nor care to know anything about local politics: they rarely cause any trouble; they behave for the most part like English gentlemen.'[17] Whether an army of occupation could afford to exist in such Arcadian ignorance of local affairs is debatable. Cromer thinks 'these are ideal qualities' but in the light of some of the events which befell the Inniskillings in Egypt, one might venture to disagree.

Still, their first task, and indeed their *raison d'être* once arrived in Egypt was to be seen rather than to see. In those days the British could still muster a show of strength, and they were not going to let the Turk beguile them of Sinai, nor indeed of anywhere else. Parades and marches crossed and re-crossed Cairo, bands playing, sergeant-majors braying, and no doubt the Turks, watching at a distance, were duly impressed and deterred. As for the locals, who knows what went through their minds: was the British presence offensive or would the Turks have been worse? And weren't the British, despite all their puffing and blowing and marching up and down, nevertheless an inexhaustible source of income, not to say amusement?

For on all sides, the British in Egypt were importuned by teeming hordes of touts. In Port Said, for example, 'you could not move a yard without being pestered by men and boys to accompany them to a house of ill-fame where they boasted they could provide women such as the heart of man is supposed to hanker for. Moreover, all the charms of their women were extolled at the top of their voices, with a frankness that disgusted rather than enticed. The various shops and gambling hells were the only refuges from these pestiferous pimps.'[18]

In Cairo, British soldiers and officers alike would be pounced on by dozens of would-be guides. "You come with me, sah," one would shout, "Me quite high-class guide." "Him no good – him dam rascal!" would declare a second. "Me teetotal chap, sah. Got recommendation from Lord Kitchener," would add a third, pushing his way through the gang.'[19]

When it came to the hiring of donkeys (the best way of getting about in Cairo) the claims reached new heights of extravagance: 'Me spik English. My donkey spik English, too,' declared the first one. 'My donkey run like hell, sah – Him win beauty prize!'[20]

There was much in Cairo to astonish and indeed enthrall the innocent British soldier. And it was Oates's first taste of the Middle East. Another English Lawrence was to see it as 'a jangling place for its bells and bustle and running to and fro'.[21] There was the infamous Red Light Quarter of the Wishel-Birka and Clot Bey Street, once a respectable district of European hotels and consulates, which had degenerated into the brothel area. Here, hashish and gambling and plump prostitutes awaited the incautious British soldier. As for the local population, it is hard to imagine a more cosmopolitan mix. There were Bedouin, Copts, Turks, Circassians, Syrians, Sheikhs, Jews, Levantines, Greeks, Armenians, Tunisians, Algerians, Sudanese, Maltese, as well as native Egyptians and half-breeds numberless.

The city itself, with its mosques, minarets, bazaars, donkey boys and pilgrims, water-carriers and beggars, veiled women and strings of camels and mules, was an exotic, jabbering and hallucinatory place, a crucible of history, dirt and bad smells brought to boiling point by politics and the sun. The most remarkable old monument was the Citadel. Built by Saladin in 1166 on a spur of hills above the city, its domes and twin pencil sharp towers dominated the horizon. Inside, it was a kind of city within a city, containing a barracks (used at times by the British Army of Occupation) a hospital, prison, magazine, storehouses and several mosques.

From the ramparts of the Citadel there was a panoramic view of the whole of Cairo: mosques and palaces, and here and there the startling green of gardens, with the Nile glittering in the distance and beyond it the desert, with the shadowy outlines of the Pyramids of Ghizeh and the Sphinx clearly visible. Oates visited the Citadel, saw it all and wrote home: 'They showed me places which are quite ungetatable to the ordinary tourist . . . a stone box into which they used to put undesirables and then fill it with water.'

His initial impressions of Egypt had been disappointing – he grumbled at first about the cost of living and the bad state of the roads which did not suit his motorbike. But within five days his mood changed: 'This place improves on acquaintance . . . It is extraordinary what a rich country this is, everything seems to be going ahead,' and ten days later, 'That bike of mine is a great blessing. I use it nearly every day to go down to the racket and tennis courts. They have made me musketry instructor and assistant adjutant, whether this is a stepping stone or the offer of the other [i.e. the Adjutancy] was only a dodge to manoeuvre me into this I don't know.'

As assistant adjutant he would have several new duties to fulfil; he would understudy the adjutant who was in turn the principal staff officer to the commanding officer and responsible for welfare, drills and parades. Together they would also complete the Regimental Historical Record and from 13 June 1906 the entries in this book appear in Oates' spidery, casual script and eccentric spelling. Despite this increase in work, there was obviously still plenty of spare time for rackets, tennis, sight seeing, polo and cricket and a host of other emigré sports.

Still, the main purpose of the British presence was simply to be seen to be present, and with this in mind it was decided to send a body of mounted infantry on a march down from Cairo through the Nile Delta to Alexandria – a distance of about ninety miles. Some officers of the Inniskillings joined the march, including Captain S. C. Bull who, with Oates, had been with the squadron in Belfast just prior to the regiment's departure from Ireland. This march through the Delta, it was hoped, would ensure a quiet summer.

The town of Tanta, near the centre of the Nile Delta, was a notable hotbed of Moslem fanaticism and what was known as 'immorality among the lower native strata'.[22] Nor was this, for once, merely the Anglo-Saxon arrogance of the time. An example of this 'immorality' is a bizarre incident in which 'Derwish Zahran [of Denishwai] bearing a grudge against his neighbour Hassan Mahjonz, dug up the body of a young girl from the village cemetery and threw it into his neighbour's *sakha*, and, attended by numerous witnesses, discovered the crime and denounced his enemy.'[23] Rumours of native uprisings had often originated in the bazaars of Tanta; British and even Egyptian soldiers were rarely seen in its streets 'and the Tanta native is pleased to think that his city is *taboo* to the European invasion'.[24] There prevailed what seems to have been a simmering nationalistic fervour, with Europeans and Turks equally resented by the local Bedouin tribes and fellahin. It was not, however, exceptional for the mounted infantry to make a march through this terrain: they had done so the previous year with no trouble. They duly set out from Cairo on Monday, 11 June. Oates stayed behind.

On Wednesday, 13 June they arrived at the village of Tala and camped there. The officers were invited to lunch by the Sheikh. After lunch he offered them carriages to take them to a village called Denishwai, six miles away, where they wished to shoot pigeons, as they had done the previous year. There is little doubt that such a shooting trip was foolish in that area. 'It would be sufficient if instead of a pigeon or two a British officer's gun-shot damaged some village sheikh's young date crop for a disturbance to arise. A crowd would collect, and the knowledge that the offenders were "English soldiers" would speedily render the situation warm.'[25]

The pigeons began to come over, and the officers opened fire. 'There is no beast on earth', says the Koran, 'nor bird which flies with wings, but the same is a people like unto you: unto the Lord shall they return.'[26] There is no doubt that the native people did not regard the English officers as a *people like unto them*. At this moment a mysterious fire broke out on a threshing floor nearby. The officers, separated in order to occupy the best pigeon-shooting positions, were at a disadvantage as the local people began to shout at them, interfere with them, and throw mud.

As the officers tried to join forces, Lieutenant Porter was surrounded by villagers who attempted to take away his gun. There was no time to unload it and though he thought he had succeeded in putting it at 'safe', no sooner was it snatched from him than it went off, injuring four people, including a woman. This further inflamed the emotions of the crowd, and Major Pine-Coffin, who had served in the Boer War, and been mentioned in despatches, found himself strategically at a loss. He behaved exactly as a Perfect English Gentleman would have behaved: he gave up his own gun and urged his companions to do the same.

This gesture, however, belonged to a code of chivalry and honour which was entirely alien to the villagers. He had intended, by disarming himself, to disarm them, but all they saw was an absurd Englishman who had chosen for some mysterious reason to give up his gun. The crowd simply turned on the Europeans. As they tried to scramble away to their waiting carriages they were pursued by the angry villagers who hurled sticks and stones and clods of earth at them and struck them, when possible, with their nabouts.

Alas, the cabdrivers could not, or would not, drive away, and the furious villagers pulled the hapless officers out of their carriages and continued to beat them up in the road. There was no hope but to try and break away and run the six miles back to camp. Major Pine-Coffin, however, was thrown to the ground and given a severe beating, which broke his arm and caused other serious injuries. Lieutenants Smithwick and Porter came back in an effort to protect him. Captains Bull and Bostock, who were ahead, somehow managed to get away and ran on, bruised and bleeding, towards the camp. Bostock managed to stagger the full six miles, swimming a canal in the process, but Bull got left behind. When Bostock reached the camp at 3.30 p.m. he gave the alarm and instantly a patrol of mounted infantry set out to the rescue.

Meanwhile, back at Denishwai, the villagers took Major Pine-Coffin and the two other officers back to the place where the injured woman lay. They repeatedly drew their fingers across their throats (this seems to have been the only successful moment of communication) and the out-

77

look was obviously extremely black when help arrived in the form of some local sheikhs, gaffirs and other local dignitaries who formed a ring round the officers and succeeded in taking them away. This rescue party had been drummed up by the policeman who had acted as the officers' escort earlier in the day, and he now accompanied them back to their camp in the carriages.

Captain Bull was found by the patrol of mounted infantry, lying unconscious in a ditch about a mile and a half from the camp. He had bad head injuries and had been lying bareheaded in the blazing sun after running four miles and then collapsing. He died at seven o'clock that evening. Only an hour later the local notables arrived to open an enquiry: the Moudir of Menoufieh, Mohammed Shukri Pasha, Moberly Bey, Inspector of the Ministry of the Interior, and the Chief of the Menoufieh Parquet, Mohammed Bey Ibrahim.

Next morning these authorities went to Denishwai to continue the investigation. Some of the officers managed to identify a number of the villagers who had taken part in the affray. Seventy-five people were arrested and eventually fifty-two were charged. Captain Bull was buried in Cairo with full military honours, only to be exhumed later when the villagers set up a defence that he had died from the effects of sunstroke, and not from the injuries he had sustained. Dr Nolan, the pathologist, found that he had died of a form of apoplexy, 'caused or aggravated by concussion of the brain'.[27]

'We are indeed an unlucky regiment', Oates wrote home. 'It was a great shock to us, as he was the last man in the world to get into trouble with anyone: we are going down to the place where he was killed, to assist at the trial.' At first, Reuter reports suggested that the attack on the British officers might have been provoked because the villagers thought that the British had set fire to their threshing-floor, but gradually this interpretation gave way to a more punitive mood on the part of commentators.

'Everything indicates that the outrage was more serious than at first supposed, and that it was prearranged,' thundered the Alexandria correspondent of the *Daily Chronicle*. 'Fortunately this time Lord Cromer is convinced of the bad faith of the natives. They will be severely dealt with, and the sentence will be carried out with military severity. There will be no appeal.'

The court consisted of Sir Malcolm McIlwraith, Judical Adviser to the Khedive, one English judge of the Native Appeal Court, and the Egyptian President of the Native Court of the First Instance, with an officer of the Army of Occupation acting as Judge Advocate. The tribunal was established under a General Decree of 1895, which declared that 'All crimes and misdemeanours committed by natives against soldiers or officers of the British Army shall continue, in principle, to be tried by native tribunals.' However, in unusual cases a special tribunal could be summoned. There was no question of leniency on the part of the native authorities, nor indeed did their presence guarantee an overall balance and impartiality for as Oates wrote: 'The President is an Armenian and hates the fellahin like poison so I imagine they will get it pretty hot'. They did.

On 27 June, sentence was delivered: four sentenced to death, and twenty-one others to imprisonment and/or flogging. Of the four sentenced to death, two were Derwish Zahran (the grave robber and corpse-planter) and his hated neighbour Hassan Mahjonz. Loathing for the British had evidently united them in the end. 'The executions and floggings will take place at two o'clock tomorrow at the same time and in the same place in the fields where the assaults were committed', stated Reuter. 'The condemned men will be hanged in turn at one gallows in the presence of Officials, a detachment of British soldiers, the Press, and villagers.'[28] Oates was among the officers supervising the execution.

A cordon of soldiers and police was established with a radius of 300 yards, and the detachment of Inniskilling Dragoons was amongst them dismounted. Gallows and triangles (for the floggings) were erected twenty yards apart and two tents were pitched, one for those awaiting sentence, and one for those who had received their lashes. A third, more sinister tent was put up by the inscrutable hanutis who had brought the water and shrouds necessary to their trade. This tent was pitched near the gallows.

The official report records: 'At 1.30 p.m. the officer commanding the British Troops was requested to sound attention, and the Mudir of Menufiya . . . summoned Hassan Ali Mahfuz [the ringleader]. The Commandant of Police repeated the name and the prisoner was unfettered and brought forward to the Mudir between two Egyptian policemen with fixed bayonets. The escort was ordered to port arms and the Mudir read out the sentence of the court.

'The accused prayed loudly, and at a signal from the Mudir, the executioner and his assistants pinioned him. He was then led to the scaffold and guided up the steps. Hassan Ali Mahfuz, standing on the trapdoor before the cap was drawn over his head, paused in his prayers and in a loud voice invoked ruin upon the houses of those who had given evidence against him. The Mudir gave the signal, the bolt was drawn, and death was instantaneous . . .'[29] It was reported by Reuter that all the condemned men met their death calmly.

Although Oates never mentioned the incident again it provoked, in some quarters, a storm of protest. The Belgian newspaper Petit Bleu played upon the humanitarian heartstrings of its readers. 'The troops had assembled the prisoners in a tent. The first prisoner, an old man, was brought out and flogged mercilessly before the gallows on which he was to be hanged. Two other prisoners were then brought out, who in turn were flogged till the blood ran, a few yards' distance from the gibbet where the corpse of the first man was hanging. The latter being taken down, the rest were hanged in turn. Exactly the same scene was enacted with the other nine prisoners. Each one before death was flogged in a manner which drew forth terrible screams and in sight of the corpse dangling before him. Around the place of execution a crowd of natives cried and moaned on hearing the shrieks of those under torture.'[30]

Naturally enough the country buzzed. George Bernard Shaw in a letter to *The Times* suggested Sir Edward Grey, the Foreign Secretary, should be sacked and Mr Herbert Gladstone replace him.[31] But like all storms it passed, leaving the surviving protagonists to ponder the problems where a country with its own distinctive culture and body of law, is administrated by another, entirely alien, system. The Arab attitude to death is different from the European. The precariousness of the Arab's life was obvious. The desert consumes the careless man, and even the Nile, which brought fertility to the land, also brought bilharzia and malaria. Death was a familiar visitor. Moreover, fierce family loyalty combined with little responsibility towards the wider community had its inevitable results. A suspected slight on family honour, and a blood-feud or *thar* would be triggered off. Nor does the Moslem religion deter the violent man. A Christian is instructed, unequivocally, not to kill. The Koran is more accommodating: 'You shall not kill any man whom Allah has forbidden you to kill, except for a just cause. If any man is slain unjustly, his heir is entitled to satisfaction. But let him not carry his vengeance too far, for his victim will in turn be assisted and avenged.' A closeness to Allah the All-Powerful, it seems, will protect you from the threats of mortal authority as long as your cause is just.

Whether or not the villagers of Denishwai considered their cause just, it seemed to English eyes merely to be an inexcusable, brutal murder. The villagers may well have felt outrage at being encroached upon by the Turks in Sinai, let alone the occupying British, and today we would explain such incidents as evidence of understandable nationalistic feeling. Indeed, Lord Cromer, the Consul General, did show unfailing sensitivity to native feelings, and obviously understood and respected the Egyptian culture, or cultures, surrounding him.

However one of the most curious aspects of the Denishwai incident is the way in which Major Pine-Coffin gave up his gun. Surrounded by hostile villagers who had already shown signs of physical aggression, these British officers did not try to buy their way out of trouble, nor did they shoot over the heads of the crowd, let alone into it – all possible ways of attempting to ensure their own safety. Instead they resorted to this distinctively Christian, chivalrous gesture of giving up their weapons.

It seems that the Perfect English Gentleman (whose behaviour is wonderfully exemplified in this episode) is characterized by a striking mixture of arrogance and innocence. Arrogance, that he can occupy his imperial territories without the merest suspicion that his presence there might not be altogether a good thing. This arrogance is well illustrated and understood by Lieutenant-Colonel V. Prescott-Westcar: 'The Khedive was not popular and I believe he did not like us. I can quite understand his antipathy from the way the authorities of the army of occupation treated him. We used, for instance, to hold our King's Birthday Parade on the square outside the Abdin Palace, where he lived, march past and cheer our King without taking any notice of him, the nominal sovereign of the country.'[32] The same arrogance usually prevented the Englishman from learning the local language, so that when a hostile crowd surrounded him, communication was impossible.

His innocence, which borders on naïveté, convinces him that a chivalrous gesture will be universally understood and appreciated; that generosity will breed generosity, that a soft word will turn away wrath. A truly mediaeval idealism. Within the grips of this code, the English Gentleman was capable of reckless acts of courage. The society he lived in may have been sophisticated and industrialized, and have produced a materialistic and bourgeois culture and a hidebound and earthbound system of mores, but it still expected of him, and he provided, sudden flashes of extraordinarily primitive self-sacrifice.

In some senses the Denishwai incident, which happened so soon after the Inniskillings' arrival in Egypt, was to be the only major event of their stay. On his return to Abassiyeh barracks, Oates settled down to a peaceful daily routine. The time was filled up with training schemes and manoeuvres and the acquisition of horses (Arabs, Barbs and Syrian ponies) from the Mounted Infantry in Egypt, which was in course of disbandment. Under War Office instructions, a thorough series of tests was carried out to assess the capabilities of different sorts of horses with regard to feeding, water and marches.

'We did a horse trial to see how long horses could endure without getting a drink,' recollects Colonel Brooke, 'I was given the Arabs. When they did get a drink it was written down exactly how much they drank. One Arab drank six buckets of water – three gallons in each bucket – straight off.'[33] Scouting and treasure hunts were organized, and sometimes a big barrel of beer was substituted for the treasure buried in the sands of the desert.

The details of this somewhat soporific routine were noted in the Regimental Historical Record in Oates's ill-spelt scrawl: 'Sand was tried as bedding for the troop horses . . . puggares were issued and ordered to be worn on the karki helmet . . . Piebald drum horse died. He carried the drums since '96 . . . No cases of drunkenness occurred during the month of July . . .' On 16 July Oates records that he was appointed Acting Adjutant; two months later, Adjutant. A new draft of fifty-six men arrived with the S.S. *Sicilia*; instruction in the use of the lance was recommended (an interestingly archaic touch perhaps) and there were night operations in the desert south of Cairo.

Oates found the heat trying and suffered from headaches in the bright sun. He asked his mother to have some more glasses made and sent out from England – a rather pointless exercise as his prescription does not seem to have been known: 'the specs will not do atal they are made for different sight to mine'. There were occasional respites, however, from heat and discomfort. 'I went down to Alexandria last weekend, it was very pleasant down there, the hotel being on the beach and excellent bathing. I bought one pony down there.' (Not the first polo pony he had bought in Egypt.) 'We are sending some people to Damascus pony buying. I hope to be allowed to go with them, it should be rather a good trip.'

The horse trade, of course, flourished in the Middle East. Local Arab dealers would come regularly to the barracks to sell polo ponies: 'there is great excitement among the native dealers; two or three of them turning up every morning. They ask absurd prices, at the same time telling you that of course they take less.'

Oates's enthusiasm for polo was now considerable, but Colonel Brooke recalls that he was not an accomplished player: 'He was a good horseman but he couldn't really play polo. He hadn't got a good eye. He never played in a tournament.' He did, however, manage to make top score in a cricket match: officers versus sergeants. 'We persuaded the Col. to play for us and every time he played a ball such a roar went up from the men as could be heard a couple of miles away. . . We are going to Damascus on Friday via Port Said and Beirut. On the way back I hope to see Jerusalem and Jaffa.'

He was glad to leave Cairo, for its charms were beginning to pall. It

7. As a sickly child on his way to winter in South Africa, with his father.

8. The family home. Gestingthorpe Hall, Essex. There were rules in the visitors' book: 'Don't stay an awful time, ie., more than a week. . . Don't shiver. . . Don't ask what time the next meal is. . . Don't say "What fish?" when offered fish for breakfast.'

9. On his seventh birthday. 'Laurie: a pencil case, a book, chocolates and a revolver from Patty Parker.' (Mrs Oates's Diary)

10. 'I once saw Laurie with his shoes tied up with wire.' (Violet Oates)

11. 'He hated having his photo taken, and would either burst out laughing at the wrong moment or scowl.' (Violet Oates)

12. Whilst at Eton, 'We used to say he looked just like the monkey that was used to advertise Monkey Brand Soap.' (Violet Oates)

13. Oates during his period at the
Crammer. (His mother's favourite
photograph.) 'He came to us quite
young . . . an Etonian of rough offhand manners . . . a sort of honest,
great Newfoundland puppy.'

(G. C. Coulton).

14. When Frederick Ranalow
asked Mrs Oates for Lilian's hand
in marriage, and told her of his
income, she replied, 'Lilian spends
that on hats each year'.

(Sheila Blenkinsop, Lilian's daughter).

15. Violet Oates, who lived with her mother until the old lady's death
in the 1930s.

16. Officers inspecting the Subaltern's Ride at the Curragh Camp, Ireland, 1900.

17. Inniskilling officers' mess shelter, Boer War. Left to right: Johnson, Haig, Wyatt and Herbert.

had apparently been a 'bad season for Cairo. The hotels are only half-full and the place appears to be full of all the bad characters in Europe.' What is more, he had recently been moved to new barracks, where rats had visited him in the night and eaten all his candles and soap. So he must have been glad of the chance of the trip to Damascus with the Colonel to buy horses: it offered rest and refreshment. They sailed from Port Said.

Alas, the French boat which took them to Beirut was dirty and he fell ill with 'a touch of fever'. When they landed at Beirut they immediately left the jabbering city and travelled up through the mulberry groves to Aliih where they spent the night in the cool of the hills Next day they took a Turkish train on a tortuous route through the mountains of Lebanon eastwards to Damascus. The scorched mountain scenery was very fine, but 'this fearful Turkish train takes away all the pleasure' – and so, no doubt, did his illness.

The old city of Damascus, lying in the Syrian desert, has long been a centre for pilgrims and merchants. It was full of covered bazaars and curious narrow streets, including the Darb el Mustakim, once called the 'Street called Straight', overhung by gabled upper floors of houses which jutted out in the English sixteenth-century fashion, creating dark chasms below. Jostled by beggars, importuned by street vendors, his reaction was fairly disenchanted. 'This is the most extraordinary place, there are practically no streets, only sort of narrow passages, and shops full of all kinds of rubbish which I suppose they hope to sell to the visitors.' Nor did Jerusalem, on the return journey, arouse his enthusiasm: 'I was very disappointed with Jerusalem. They show you the exact spot where everything mentioned in the Gospels happened, my own opinion is that ⅞ of the things are humbug.

'The Roman Catholics and Greeks are there in great force and everywhere is incense, dirty ribbons and those glass balls you hang on Christmas trees. The Church of the Holy Sepulchre is a fine place but completely spoilt by dirty and tawdry decorations and noisy priests. The amusing thing is that they have to have Mohammedan soldiers in the churches to prevent the various sects bagging each other's relics. The finest and cleanest place in the city is the Mohammedan Mosque of Omar which stands on the site of the temple.' His reactions demonstrate a thoroughly English puritanism and scepticism, but he could give credit where due – even if that meant praising the infidel. Unlike many of his contemporaries, Oates was not bigoted.

On his return to Cairo, he finally succumbed to the sickness which had soured his entire trip. Four days in the military hospital put him on his feet again (if his letters to his mother are to be believed). It had been 'a mild touch of the ague'. The worst of the summer's heat was now over, though, which was a relief: 'The Guards arrived here yesterday . . . the officers are grousing about the heat and we are getting out our warmer clothing.' The pace of life, however, continued fairly leisurely. 'I must end as it is difficult to listen to what the Colonel is gassing about and write at the same time.'

Oates spent a lot of time worrying about, and working for, the army promotion exams. 'Certainly there are some awful fools passing now so why not I?' was his attitude. He got into the habit of asking his mother to send books out to him, not just for exam work but also for general reading. Some of the titles were *Pictures from the Balkans* by John Foster Fraser, *On the Spanish Main* by John Masefield, *Navigation for Yachtsmen*, *Operations of War* by Hamley, *Peninsular War* by Napier, *Wellington's Campaign* by General Robinson, *From Midshipman to Field Marshal* by Evelyn Wood, and *A Sailor's Garland*. ('I hear there are some good poems in it.') Though obviously far from scholarly, he read a considerable amount, deeply rather than widely. He was still poring over Napier's *Peninsular War* five years later in the Antarctic.

Apart from the intellectual ordeals of the army exam system, much of his spare time was taken up by sport. His motorbike met an early end when he was 'running and trying to jump on it and it got away from me and went tearing off down the road by itself. It finally flew over an embankment and came to a stop'. Obviously, the motorbike was capable of coltish behaviour. There were plenty of other diversions to console him for its demise.

The rifle ranges were quite near the barracks and shooting competitions were often held, and followed with keen interest. The regiment entered teams for National Rifle Association contests, and here the groundwork was done which enabled the regiment to win the Queen Victoria Cup in India in 1908. Oates, however, was not famous as a shot. Probably his eyesight was not sharp enough.

Undoubtedly though, the sport which most preoccupied him was polo. Polo, and occasionally camel racing, took place at the Turf Club, Ghezira, on the outskirts of Cairo. 'On most afternoons of the week there could be seen processions of ponies and Irish "jaunting cars" [brought from Dublin] which contained officers' servants with their masters' dress, for after 8 p.m., the officers of the "Army of Occupation" had to wear uniform.'[34] The Turf Club contained many a British eccentric besides Oates. 'Roly Barnard was one of the characters of the Turf Club; his ability to run backwards faster than most people can run forwards forming the basis of many a wager, the bet always being decided by a race down the wide empty street outside the club. Some of the subalterns had most exciting races in *arbuggis* – as the local cabs were named – their reckless cornering reminding one of the chariot race in *Ben Hur*, until a hint from above put an end to this diversion, fortunately before anyone broke his neck.'[35]

But it was polo itself which engrossed Oates and he was fascinated by the business of buying new ponies, so much so that at times it seems like his only reckless extravagance. It is interesting that he was still having to write home to his mother for money when he had reached the rank of Captain and the verge of his thirtieth birthday. Not so much a measure of his profligacy, one suspects, as a sign of the many subtle powers which Caroline Oates still exercised.

Certainly, Oates did not spend much money on his social life. According to Colonel Brooks, 'I don't think Oates took any interest in social life. He certainly didn't in Cairo when there was much gaiety in the winter. Numbers of people came out from England and there were dances in all the big hotels. But I can't ever remember Oates going to any of those sorts of things. He would appear in the mess I should say every night of the week. But I never heard of him doing anything in the social line . . . He was a very difficult man to get to know. He kept so much to himself . . . [His superior officers] had a feeling of affection for him but they couldn't get him to do the ordinary social round that was expected of officers.'

Oates's resistance to his social obligations was intense. Other British officers found Cairo 'a very cheerful spot' – so much so that they felt they must 'rub up' their dancing. Above all, what Oates seems to have feared and dreaded about social life was making a fool of himself, which some British officers achieved with distinction: 'I can well remember three of us – Pusscat Sladen, Croppy Moore Gwyn and myself going to take lessons from a little dago, in a greasy waistcoat and shirtsleeves turned up, who solemnly waltzed us round, while his bedraggled daughter strummed the tune on a wheezy piano. However, he taught us to reverse, a procedure that was banned when we'd learnt to dance as boys, and then a necessity unless one wanted to be left out in the cold.'[36] Oates, of course, wanted exactly that.

In the spring of 1907 he reported that 'there are rumours flying about that we go to India in October' and a little later, 'the regiment does not move to India until autumn twelvemonth. I am rather sorry as I am sick of this place and wanted to see something of India before I leave.' Leaving the army is a preoccupation which again recurs in his thoughts at this time. He seems to have felt an increasing irritation at the way the army was run: especially with the element of intrigue and influence which surrounded those who wielded power. 'If you happen to know one or 2 of the nibs at the War Office or better still their wives, soldiering is rather fun but if you don't it's better to stay at home and wash bottles.' So his increasing frustration in Cairo is no surprise. As usual, when depressed he tended to take a black view even of things he had not yet experienced: 'I do not think I shall soldier on much after the regiment goes to India, they tell me it is worse than this place . . . I loathe and detest this place in the season.'[37]

In the middle of the summer of 1907 he received a letter from Frank Chester, a boy who had been in the Regimental Band, and had been invalided home when he was injured on the voyage out. 'Dear Sir, I am writing to let you know that I am still suffering with my leg. It seems as if it will never get better. I am still on the list of the unemployed and will truthfully say that it is only by accident that a man gets into a situation now a days.

'I should also like to mention that I am badly in need of money (please keep this quiet to a certain extent) and having heard that Major Fryer has some for me I should very much like it sent on. Just now it would come as a God send from above . . . I should be very grateful to you as I am now for your tuition and testimonial and also for what you have done for me. Your kindness I shall never forget.'

Oates's reaction to this letter was immediate. He sat down and wrote to his mother. 'There is a boy who was in the band here and came out with the regiment; on the voyage out a beam fell on him while drawing forage and his leg never came right, consequently he was discharged from the army without any gratuity or pension of any sort. He is now in London without work and I believe practically starving. The boy is a teetotaller and while in the regiment bore a very good character. There are several charities which are trying to get him a job but having been brought up in a Military School he has no trade.

'Can you have the boy sent for and boarded out in the village, and we can discuss what is to be done with him when I come back. I believe the boy is in such a bad way that something should be done at once. If you will let me know what he costs I will pay his expenses and a small wage – he ought to be given a light job as soon as he arrives. I believe the case is urgent and the boy should be given something to do or he will starve.'

Frank Chester was a casualty of a society which demanded hard and dangerous work from its lower classes, without any guarantee of livelihood in case of accident. The Welfare State had not yet taken shape, so he and all similarly impoverished and helpless individuals were thrown upon the mercy of the ruling class and its paternalistic feelings. Oates's prompt response, his concern for Chester's dignity and the need to find him a useful job is a tribute to the sensitivity and magnanimity that could underlie the feudal patronage of the Tory squire.

The last few months of his time in Egypt rolled peacefully past, and he planned to spend his 1908 leave sailing in the *Saunterer* around the shores of Ireland, visiting Valentia Island and the Arrans. It was, however, threatened by army duties: 'unfortunately the Col. is going to Rome for the International Horse Show and wants me to go with him . . . it is really a great nuisance as I had arranged to sail in the *Saunterer* from Sursedon on the 6th . . . I shall try to get away from Rome a little before the show is over so I can hurry home for a day before joining the *Saunterer*. I wanted to have 2 or 3 days at Gestingthorpe before going yachting but King's leave is early and he has to get back.'

It was the visit to Gestingthorpe which was to be cut short, not the sailing trip. 'I am off to Rome tomorrow. We are going to spend a day in Naples which nowadays is considered long enough to see a place in. I am not so keen on the trip as I was as I have to take uniform and we are in communication with the Military Attaché so it looks as if I shall be let in for some social functions.' The Italian trip was indeed loaded with social duties: 'We were met with open arms and the Military Attaché is touting us round most assiduously as we are the only British Representatives.'

At last, he was free of his professional duties and sped north to his cruise. At first he was well pleased with the crew: 'we like the two men we have got very much, the new skipper is particularly nice, he appears to be a very careful man.' At Penzance, however, the new skipper insisted on turning back in some heavy weather and Oates was angry. 'I am seriously annoyed with Clark about this putting back and I suppose I ought to have been firm and held on but when you have a man on board who is supposed to be an expert and is drawing a princely salary you don't like to over rule what he advises.'

Things obviously improved, however, as by 1 June he was in Glengariff and in high spirits: 'I am very sorry you did not manage to get here as it really is a most beautiful place. We are having splendid weather and I am enjoying the trip thoroughly.' Then a shadow fell across the trip: he heard he had to go back to Egypt a week early, 'Really it is most sickening as it spoils my trip through France. It is bad enough having to soldier at all but when they start cutting bits off one's leave, it's about time to move or get another job elsewhere.'

Later in the Arran Islands, he was weatherbound and 'getting to dislike the place as I have been here 4 days now without money'. He speculated whether to cancel his projected motor trip through France with Fitzgerald or stay longer at Gestingthorpe. In the event, Gestingthorpe had to give way. The trip through France proved highly enjoyable. 'We had a first class trip down, tell Brujum we only burst 3 tyres, he said we should burst 6. I am not looking forward to going to Cairo atal as I hear things are not running quite smoothly.

'I think when I have time I shall do some motoring on the Continent on my own as it is a capital way of seeing a country. William King has left the regiment, it is a great mistake on his part and I believe his father is in a terrible state, however I can't say very much when I intend leaving myself.'

Their route through France had included visits to Beauvais, Fontainebleau, La Pallisse, Valence and Marseilles. 'The part of the road along the Rhone valley was most beautiful. It is most amusing and occasionally boring to be travelling with a motor enthusiast as he does nothing but talk about his machine. I suppose I am just as bad when I am yachting.'

As soon as he arrived in Cairo, it was time to pack and prepare for the regiment's next posting, India.

Notes and references

1 W. S. Churchill, *A History of the English-speaking Peoples*, Vol. IV, p.269.
2 *Le Figaro*, 12 May 1906.
3 Colonel W. Macpherson, *Unpublished Reminiscences 1906-1908* (Regimental Museum).
4 *Army and Navy Gazette*, 27 April 1906.
5 *The Enniskillen Reporter*, 2 May 1906.
6 *The Manchester Despatch*, 14 February 1913.
7 *The Irish Times*, 14 May 1906.
8 Lieutenant-Colonel E. A. Herbert commanded the 6th (Inniskilling) Dragoons from 1905 to 1908. '. . . he is the youngest and one of the ablest and smartest commanding officers which this distinguished regiment has ever had!' *The Enniskillen Reporter*, 4 May 1906.
9 *The Irish Times*, 14 May 1906.
10 Horace Wyndham, *Following the Drum*, p.213.
11 *Ibid.*, p.208.
12 *Ibid.*, p. 212.
13 *Ibid.*, p.213.

14 Colonel W. Macpherson, *op. cit.*

15 Horace Wyndham, *op. cit.*

16 Colonel W. Macpherson. op. cit.

17 Earl of Cromer, *Modern Egypt*, p.253.

18 Lieutenant-Colonel V. Prescott-Westcar DSO, *Big Game, Boers and Boches*, p.40.

19 Horace Wyndham, *op. cit.*, p.273.

20 *Ibid.*, p.273.

21 T. E. Lawrence, *Seven Pillars of Wisdom*.

22 From unidentifiable newspaper cutting in a scrap book made by Lieutenant-Colonel E. A. Herbert now in the possession of Colonel Sir Mike Ansell.

23 *The Times*, 14 July 1906.

24 *The Morning Post*, June 1906.

25 *Ibid.*

26 Bosworth Smith, *Mohammed and Mohammedanism*, p. 255.

27 *The Morning Post*, Reuter, 23 June 1906.

28 Reuter, 27 June 1906.

29 *The Egyptian Gazette*, 30 June 1906.

30 *Petit Bleu*, 4 July 1906.

31 Shaw also included an essay on 'The Denishwai Horror' in Preface for Politicians (*John Bull's Other Island*) in which he warned England that 'if her Empire means ruling the world as Denishwai has been ruled in 1906 – and that, I'm afraid, is what the Empire does mean to the main body of our aristocratic-military caste and to our Jingo plutocrats – then there can be no more sacred and urgent political duty on earth than the disruption, defeat and suppression of the Empire.'

32 Lieutenant-Colonel V. Prescott-Westcar, *op. cit.*, p.125.

33 Lieutenant-Colonel J. A. Brooke, during conversation with the authors.

34 Major-General R. Evans, *The 5th Royal Inniskilling Dragoon Guards*, p. 112.

35 Lieutenant-Colonel V. Prescott-Westcar, *op. cit.*, p. 119.

36 *Ibid.*

37 Though Oates disliked Cairo, he loved the desert. '11 May 1908. I have just come in from the desert where I have been for three days. I raised quite a good trotting camel and enjoyed myself. I had to report on some wells. It is extraordinary the fasination [*sic*] the desert has on one.'

6

India

A passage to India seems to have been an essential element in the British colonial experience. Kipling's barrack room Tommy, back home in the 'blasted Henglish drizzle' longed to return:

> Ship me somewhere east of Suez, where the best is like the worst
> Where there ain't no Ten Commandments and a man can raise a
> thirst . . .[1]

And east of Suez the Inniskillings were indeed shipped.

They were seen off from Cairo by practically the whole Army of Occupation, and the Egyptian Cavalry also sent their band as a gesture of good fellowship. The Regimental Historical Record boasted that 'in spite of the hospitality pressed on them the regiment left the station with only one drunkard'.[2] Oates was impressed with the send-off, '. . . the crowd around the train was about 40 deep' but the gilt was soon taken off his gingerbread: 'I was very annoyed on arrival on board *Dongola*, as instead of enjoying a rest I was looking forward to, I found I was ship's adjutant and was kept busy the whole voyage.'

Their one drunkard notwithstanding, the Inniskillings seem to have passed an exemplary journey, the Regimental Orders recording that 'work has been arduous and heavy . . . the weather hot and trying. In spite of these drawbacks, the Commanding Officer has never heard a single word of grumbling . . . and none has been brought to his notice'.[3] Oates evidently kept his mouth shut, as usual.

It was not the regiment's first trip to India, and they had been stationed at Mhow before, in the 1860s. The Regimental Orders of 12 October 1908 proudly record that 'when previously quartered in India the Regiment had an unbroken series of the most flattering reports from every General Officer Commanding who inspected them'. It went on to quote an extract from a Farewell Order published by Lieutenant-Colonel

C. C. Shute, dated 1 April 1861, to the effect that the Inniskillings were the only regiment which after three years in India was 'still on all points thoroughly English, and long may [they] continue to deserve this high compliment'.

What was the British Army doing in India? Major-General Evans explains: 'for many years military policy in India had been governed by the menace – real or imagined – of an invasion by Russia across the North-West Frontier, in 1907 the Anglo-Russian Agreement eased this situation, and the Government of India appreciated their military responsibilities to be the preservation of internal security and the control of the frontier tribes'.[4] In other (very different) words, as Kipling described the responsibilities of Victoria's army in 'The Widow at Windsor':

> Hands off o' the sons of the Widow
> Hands off o' the goods in 'er shop
> For the Kings must come down and the Emperors frown
> When the Widow at Windsor says 'Stop'.

Even if the Widow at Windsor's rule had given way to that of her pleasure-loving son Edward VII, he was still Emperor of India and the goodies in the Imperial shop still needed protecting. The British Army got the message across in periodic manoeuvres.

'At times we were sent to demonstrate to the tribesmen what they might expect if they gave trouble. I well remember one occasion: our composite force was detailed to "destroy a village". We moved off late one evening and bivouacked for the night in the open. Heads of local tribes were entertained to a tremendous breakfast by the Brigadier. A special village had been built up the valley and we had to destroy it . . . we attacked, dismounted under cover of gun and artillery fire, tracer bullets leaving little to spectators' imagination, after which Sappers moved in and blew up every house. Then another magnificent feast, and the tribesmen rode home – well, thoughtful, I think there's little doubt.'[5]

It is hardly surprising that in 1908 the Indian scene was peaceful and it was unlikely that the Inniskillings would have to perform more than a daily drill and the occasional manoeuvre. Such inactivity galled Oates, who, like Captain the Honourable Julian Grenfell, 1st Royal Dragoons, probably thought war was 'like a big picnic'.[6] 'We have come to India with an extraordinarily fine regiment,' he wrote, 'It is a thousand pities we could not have gone on service from Egypt during the last two months, we should have done very well.' Active service, however, was to elude him, and his energies and ambitions had to be channelled elsewhere.

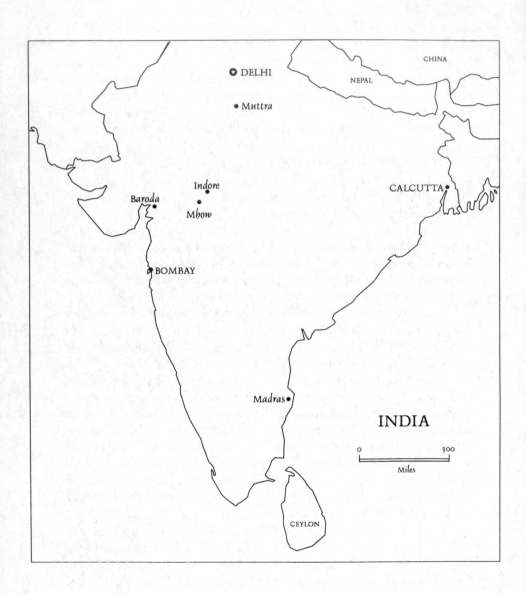

CHINA

NEPAL

✪ DELHI

● Muttra

Indore
●
Baroda
●
Mhow

CALCUTTA ●

● BOMBAY

Madras ●

INDIA

0   300

Miles

CEYLON

The quayside at Bombay, overlooked by the wooded slopes of Malabar Hill, swarmed with natives eagerly offering their services as personal servants. Somehow, in the mêlée, the Inniskillings managed to pack themselves into trains and leave for Mhow – a day's journey through the cotton fields of the black Deccan soil. Not without mishap, however, as Oates reported: 'Arrived at 1 am this morning and at present are in a state of some confusion owing to having lost half of our baggage between here and Bombay.' His first impressions of Mhow were favourable: 'I like this place very well and think it's healthier than Cairo.'

His intuitions were quite right, for as *The Illustrated London News* confided to its readers: 'It is impossible to conceive a more healthy looking station than Mhow . . . [it] is said to be one of the four healthiest military stations in Western India . . . It stands at an altitude of 2000 feet above the level of the sea. The Vindayan Hills, which gird it to the South, are a portion of an evolvement stretching from Champancer to Rajmahal. For 16 hours of the 24 the climate is delightful, but of course the Indian sun never ceases his unmerciful glare during 8 hours of the day.

'Mhow . . . has pretty much the appearance of a European town, having a church with a steeple, a spacious lecture room and library well furnished with books and a theatre . . . As I rode in from Indore in the morning, the first view I obtained was about 3 miles off. It lay embedded softly amongst luxurious foliage upon the lap of a range of low, irregular hills, and in all the glory of a chilly Indian morning atmosphere. As one approaches Mhow, letting one's horse pick its way between the grassy roadside and unmaccadamised boulders which had worked themselves up out of the mosaic bed, the station of Mhow . . . broadens out, and the church, surrounded by somewhat pretentious and very pretty bungalows, help to make the scene . . . one of the most attractive in India.'

Oates, along with other officers, was allotted one of these pretty and pretentious bungalows in which to live. He shared his with Fergus Nixon. The bungalows were large stone buildings, with a flight of steps up to a hall. There would be a long passage running down the middle of the building with rooms arranged on each side; large rooms with high ceilings, with a verandah on the outside wall. Furniture was hired from a contractor. The army provided none. Each officer had a sitting room and a bedroom of his own, and often a bathroom, too. (Regimental bathrooms were often pretty spartan, consisting of 'a tin bath and a cold tap, and the bearer used to boil up water in an old kerosene can'.)[7]

The bearer was the principal servant, the equivalent of an English butler, whose job was to oversee a vast entourage of lesser servants attached to each officer. Colonel Brooks, then a troop leader, remembers, 'we had lots of servants. I think I had 18 . . . one gardener (mali), one man who looked after the bullocks, a bearer, a *khitmutgar* who always went to meals with you and got what you wanted and stood behind your chair. One or two grass cutters who would bring in a load of grass for your ponies for the day, two punkah coolies . . . quite a number. Your bearer was a fairly good class man and he would provide what you wanted. I paid them all myself. It was quite small amounts. I just handed the money out myself once a month.'

Oates would soon have got used to a new vocabulary: *syces* were native grooms and were capable of amazing transformations in their personal appearance. When grooming the horses in the stables they were dressed in 'dirty old vests with twenty holes in them'.[8] But when it was time to turn out for an important polo match, they would appear wearing dazzling white long coats and white jodphurs, with a band around their turban and a matching cummerbund in their master's colours. All officers had their own colours, and if they had no racing colours would simply choose what they wanted for this eccentric livery.

The *khitmutgar* was the officer's personal waiter and escorted him to the mess at night, not just for ceremonial purposes but also to protect him from the wild life, especially snakes. 'Once a porcupine ran between my legs going to the mess', recalls Colonel Brooke. Safely arrived at the mess, Oates would have been waited on expertly by his white-gloved, barefooted *khitmutgar*. 'Some of the natives wore boots, which they were very proud of, but we never allowed them to enter tent or bungalow except with bare feet, the same as they had to remove their shoes before entering a mosque . . . They had to realize that they were our inferiors; and while they did so all was well with them, and with us, and with the whole land of India.'[9]

Keeping cool was the major occupation in the summer months, and it spawned a whole labour-intensive industry. From 29 March to 29 October every year the punkah-wallahs were busy operating an intricate system of primitive fans. Indoors were punkah-poles attached to large pieces of cloth measuring about 3 foot by 6 foot. 'In the centre of the room was the main punkah-pole to which the punkah-wallah attached the rope which set all the punkahs in motion when he pulled it from outside.'[10] The punkah-wallahs worked day and night in eight-hour shifts. Their efforts made life just about bearable for the cossetted English, though the temperature still regularly soared above 110°F.

Other seasonal servants were the tatty-wallahs and the bhisti-wallahs. All day long in summer, the doors of the bungalows were fastened back and a woven straw door fitted across the opening. This was called a tatty. The tatty-wallah crouched beside the tatty, dipping a small tin into a large earthenware bowl of water and throwing it over the tatty. This also cooled the room. The bhisti-wallah's job was to replenish the earthenware bowls from a goatskin of water which he would carry to and from, to and fro all day from the tatties to the washhouse and back. 'I'll never forget the smell of tatties', recalled Mrs Susan Ingall, who was a child at Mhow in 1908. 'It was a very sweet hay smell . . . a lovely smell, like Lucerne grass.'

So Oates found himself the master of a large establishment. He had ambitions for the garden around his bungalow. 'Our garden here is going along fairly well but I have a most frightful fool of a gardener – he sows all the seeds as thick as he can cram them and he has all the lobelias in a bed by themselves.' How did British officers – and men – treat these native Indian servants, on whom they were totally dependent for their survival and who in the population at large outnumbered them by 2000 to 1?

Frank Richards describes how as a newly arrived greenhorn in 1904 he was initiated by an old soldier into the mysteries of handling the natives, or rather, manhandling them. 'Since old Curzon has been Viceroy things are different, you see. An order has been issued, which every soldier in India believes comes from him, that Commanding Officers must severely punish men who are brought in front of them for ill treating the natives. We have to be very careful these days. If we punch them in the face they have marks to show, so we have to punch them in the body. Most of the natives on the Plains have enlarged spleens, and a good punch in the body hurts them more than what it would do us . . . Treat them kindly and they will show you no respect at all. What is won by the sword must be kept by the sword, and it's the only law that will ever apply to this country. Old Curzon is no damned good, this country wants a Viceroy who will keep the bleeding natives down.'[11] This may have been the way the men treated their servants (for in India the British servant-class had servants of its own and the novelty of the situation may have produced the brutality) but it is hard to imagine Oates punching Indians in the spleen. Though he did occasionally express a frustrated desire to kick people, he was not partial as to race or nationality.

The Inniskillings arrived in Mhow in October: the end of the summer, the beginning of serious army work, and the start of the social season. Almost immediately, Oates committed a considerable social gaffe, and deliberately so. Colonel Brooke recalls that 'it was the custom when a new regiment arrived for officers to drop visiting cards into little boxes at entrance gates leading up to bungalows. Most officers carried out this procedure but not Oates. But then, his unofficial motto was *Damn the social position, say I*. Manuals of etiquette insisted that 'leaving cards is the first step towards forming, or enlarging, a circle of acquaintances . . . cards should be delivered in person, and not sent by post . . .' And what is more, 'there is very strict etiquette in this matter of cards and calls . . . strict etiquette demands that a call should be returned by a call and a card by a card'.[12]

When a gentleman called, further rituals were observed, like the intricate dance or display of some exotic birds or animals when venturing on each other's territory or submitting in the social hierarchy: 'a gentleman, when calling, should take his hat and stick with him into the drawing-room, and hold them until he has seen the mistress of the house and shaken hands with her. He should then either place them on a chair or table near at hand or hold them . . . To leave his hat in the hall would be considered a liberty and in very bad taste . . .'[13] In vain the blooming daughters of the British inhabitants waited for Oates's card or call. His country house, yacht, racehorses, and private income must have impressed the mamas, and the daughters surely noticed his dark good looks, his glamorous limp, the curious look in his eye. It mattered not that it may have been astigmatism or myopia, for it was romantic . . . as was his war record. Oates, however, resisted. Ever the existentialist hero, he said no even to the ladies when necessary.

'It is very amusing here,' he reported to his mother on 30 October, 'there is the Chief Medical Officer's wife who has a marriageable daughter and she has all the unmarried members of the regiment there in turn to dinner, tennis, etc. I think a lot of that goes on in India, the daughters are touted round in the most barefaced way.'

Oates seems to have eluded the pack of baying mamas and gone safely to ground. One of his favourite sanctuaries was the home of his fellow-officer Captain C. R. Terrot. Mrs Terrot, a quiet, gentle woman, described by her daughter as rather retiring and self-conscious, was something of a favourite with Oates. He enjoyed being in a family atmosphere and was clearly happy to be with children and the pleasant and peaceable young matron who would demand no absurd gallantries of him. Here he could relax. At work, however, new challenges were in store – in January 1909 there was to be an Inspection by Major-General M. H. S. Glover, CB, Inspector General of Cavalry in India. As Adjutant, Oates felt a sense of responsibility. 'The Inspection commences on Monday. I hope it passes off without a hitch', he remarked anxiously.

The strength of the regiment at this Inspection was 511 men and 557 horses – of the men twenty-one were sick in hospital (four with venereal disease) and thirty-six attending hospital (twenty-three with venereal disease). The Inspections seems to have been a success, with the Inspector General complimenting the regiment on its air of 'business meant'. The drill was 'good and steady', the riding in the regiment 'of a high standard' and he appreciated the 'appearance and cheerfulness of the men'.[14] Especially, no doubt, those who had not got venereal disease.

'The Inspector General said he was very pleased, we went about doing everything in such a businesslike way and that we were a great acquisition to the army in India,' wrote Oates to his mother. 'This is first class for a regiment just out as they usually try to crab one. The CO is of course delighted. He walks about with a silly grin and chaffs all the subalterns.'

After the inspection came the Mhow polo week and a start to pigsticking. 'We have been very gay, dances, dinners, polo etc everyday', he told his mother. 'There is a gymkhana this afternoon and tonight we give a dance, the gymkhana I expect will be awful rot. Yesterday we started pigsticking and I went out for the first time. However there was no pig to be seen. I got a run after a hyena but lost him at once in the jungle.'

Then there were manoeuvres. But the next letter to arrive at Gestingthorpe from India was in Colonel Fryer's own handwriting. Oates had caught smallpox. 'He started to go on the manoeuvres with me on the 13th in spite of feeling unwell. On the way he got worse and was sent home in an *ekka*. At the time it was thought to be merely malarial fever which has been very prevalent here. I hear he is going on as well as can be expected. It is unfortunate that he had not been vaccinated. I did not know, till it was too late, that he had always got out of being done . . .'[15]

Here is another example of Oates's apparent disregard for his own safety. No doubt he felt that to be vaccinated would impugn his manly dignity: no doubt he felt a lordly contempt for germs and bugs; no doubt he assumed it would never happen to *him*. Dodging the smallpox vaccination is entirely characteristic of Oates's nature: reckless, socially an anarchist, bloody-minded. Fergus Nixon wrote to Mrs Oates to console her and promise her news by the next post. She also received a letter from Major F. W. Begbie, the medical officer.

'As you know, your son has been Master of Hounds here for some months, and as such is brought into very close contact with the native kennel men. I attribute his attack to this contact . . . I am taking all precautions to prevent his skin being marked by the disease . . . thanks to your son's very healthy life and steady habits I think he ought to pull round quickly.'[16]

Smallpox is a thoroughly unpleasant and often fatal disease. Although preventative inoculation had been practised since the eighteenth century, there was no known cure. Oates and a sergeant who had also contracted the disease were put into isolation tents. A nurse was sent from Bombay to attend the officer, but the sergeant was left to the tender mercies of native Indian servants. Oates heard about this and instantly refused to see the nurse again until the sergeant was brought into his tent so she could attend to them both.

Ten days later the medical officer was able to report to Mrs Oates that 'your son is now quite out of the wood and on the high road to recovery . . . and there is now no further cause of anxiety'. Oates himself reported fit to his mother on 11 March 1909: 'I have been discharged from hospital and am back at my job. I really had a very mild go of it and have made a good recovery. I am still a bit pulled down but shall hang on until I get my leave which commences of 1st May. I suppose I ought to be home about the 21st'.

It is possible, as Begbie conjectured, that Oates's smallpox was caught from his native kennel boys. What is certain is that he was absolutely obsessed by hunting while in India, and from his earliest days at Mhow he had set about organizing it. 'You may think it rash of me', he had written to his mother shortly after arriving in Mhow, 'but I have taken the hounds here. It used to be a station pack but owing to lack of funds and pretty bad management they got into a very bad way. We are supposed to start hunting in a fortnight and there are only 8 couple of hounds and we ought to have about 30 and hounds can't be got in this country so I don't know what we are to do.'

But he worked at the problem and was able to report two weeks later, 'I have got together a few more hounds, the sweepings from all the packs in India and I have had to pay through the neck for them, however its a start. I went out this morning and gave a jackal a rare trouncing. He got to ground in a fox earth just as I thought I had him.' By the middle of January 1909 his hard work had paid off and he told his mother, 'We had a capital day's sport yesterday. Killed twice; both times in the open after niceish gallops. The hound that pulled down the second jack had a regular rough and tumble with him and got knocked on his back. I almost burst a blood vessel screaming.'

Then he had an even more ambitious idea: to get a completely fresh pack of hounds for the next season, from hunts in England and Ireland. However, 'I can't do with them out here until the end of September and they leave the various kennels early in May; I have written to Bryan and asked him if they could possibly be kept at Gestingthorpe either at the

Pound Farm or the Brickfields. He would of course want a man and a boy to look after them but I would pay all expenses.' Once again we see Oates the Employer: many men's livelihoods depended on the pleasures and pastimes of the ruling class. But when it came to hounds, Oates was more than just an employer. He was obviously conscious of the squire's obligations and was keen to maintain the rituals that gave shape and meaning to English rural life. 'Unless the landowner makes a great effort now to look after the litters, there will be no foxhunting for the next generation and instead of being able to hear the sound of the horn and the cry of the hounds they will have to amuse themselves with motors etc and will blame us accordingly.' The hunting season ended in February, remarkable for 'a lady who was riding astride, the first I have ever seen'. Oates scrawled in the Historical Record, 'The Mhow hounds were hunted as a private pack by Captain Oates, 1st Whip 2Lt P. Symnate, 2nd Whip Major Haig.[17] 7 brace of jackal were killed. The pack consisted of 14 and hunted twice a week on Sundays and Thursdays' (Thursday was always a holiday in India. The meet was held at 6 a.m. to take advantage of the dew for scent and the cooler morning weather.)

Now he began preparations for his long leave: selling the rather indifferent hounds he had inherited to make room for the draft from England which would be sent out in the autumn. He also sold his bullocks and a pony 'So you see I am moderately well, but I don't think I shall do much good until I get away from here as the climate is against one picking up.' He did, however, pick up enough to find Mhow 'a dull little place, when we have finished discussing polo and shooting there is very little to talk about'. Some shooting trips helped to liven up the monotony of the hot season: it meant camping out in the jungle for three or four days at a time. The wild life of India was, in those days, extravagantly abundant.

'To hear a pack of jackals howling in unison is enough to curdle the blood of any man who is not well used to the noise. The hyenas and jackals scrounged around the camp at night, picking up what garbage they could find. Many a night I have been awakened by a pack of jackals scuttling through the camp. Another animal whose cry at night we soon learned to recognize was the cheetah, a sort of small spotted leopard. The cheetah, which is very fleet of foot, would hang around the camp in the hope of getting a dog for his supper. Many of the men owned dogs and they would never bark once they had smelled a cheetah, but used to shiver with fright and curl up as close to their masters as they possibly could.'[18]

Of course, the most awe-inspiring of India's wild life was the tiger. Indeed, an Inniskilling, Captain L. St P. Gavan, had been killed by a tiger whilst on an abortive shoot in 1863. Sixty years later officers were still fascinated by the creature – as Sir Mike Ansell reveals: 'Late one evening, Grant and I sat by the side of the path; I'd just unloaded the .500 rifle and was about to pour some tea, when he nudged me gently. Twenty feet away, a tiger. He stood, we gazed at each other, the slightest move of my unloaded rifle and I knew he'd be gone. Suddenly he caught our smell – and off. I was so transfixed by the silence and perfection of his movement, I hardly even regretted his departure.'[19]

Despite a sensitivity to the beauty of the beast, the British continued to blast away with guns rather than cameras. The eminent Court photographer Raja Lala Deen Dayal recorded a hunting party in the 1900s in which five Englishmen and one Englishwoman dressed in sacrificial white preside over a bag of three leopard skins and ten tigers. 'The British certainly did maraud the wild life of India', admits Mrs Ingall ruefully. 'I myself have sat up a tree waiting for a tiger, with a poor squawking goat tied up to the tree at the bottom. I prayed the tiger wouldn't come and he didn't and I never went again.'

Even if the hoped-for game did not appear, camping offered the chance to see the country. India was full of spectacular sights: some romantic, some gruesome. Mrs Ingall remembers travelling through Indian villages at night and seeing 'no electric light – only little fluttering candles. And smelling the smell of burning cowpats. They used them for fuel. The women would squat down and beat the cowpats, then stick them on the wall till they were dry and hard. Then they were burnt.' Sir Mike Ansell's experience of camping in India was at times delightful: 'close to a well, and under the inevitable banyan tree, we set up camp, so absorbed that when we looked up the entire village had surrounded us – and many offered the enchanting garlands of marigolds'.[20]

Not all was picturesque, however. Sir Mike Ansell's idyll was interrupted by the arrival of swarms of white ants. Frank Richards was also assailed by them: they ate holes 'in ground-sheets, blue rugs and everything else'. He also saw a more disgusting example of predation near 'an evil-smelling village . . . There we saw half a dozen pigs with their snouts buried in the bodies of three dead natives; by their grunts of satisfaction they were enjoying their meal. I never ate any more bacon or any pork sausages either so long as I was abroad.'[21] The Parsees, a religious sect, left their dead to be devoured by vultures, but they built special towers called *Dakshmas* (towers of silence) upon which the dead were laid. They worshipped fire and would not debase it for the purposes of cremation.

Oates, still weak after smallpox, found his camping trips arduous. 'The walking was very hard work as I am so unfit and I got very dead beat but

I was much better for the trip when I got back . . . It will be great fun to be home again. Tell Brujum I sail with *Saunterer* about the 1st June and there is a berth for him if he wants to come.' Thus with eager home thoughts from abroad, Oates approached his leave.

This leave was to be spent on an epic cruise around the English Channel, the Baltic and to include a trip to Amsterdam. Unfortunately for Oates it was a disaster owing to 'trouble with the men'. But it is not enough to dismiss the incident so simply. Oates's behaviour while yachting does call for a moment's scrutiny. In Penzance in 1908 he had been very impatient with his skipper for his caution, although he had earlier approved of this 'careful man'. On the occasion of this cruise, in June 1909, disagreements with the men caused the whole trip to fall through. Cecil Thresher, who accompanied Oates on both these sailing trips, recorded the incident.

'The trip was from Southampton to the Channel Islands and on to St Malo. Then back to Dover touching at Cherbourg and Le Havre. Oates had a great scheme of making our way from Dover to Amsterdam and then to the Baltic but the weather was bad and we nearly lost the yacht and our lives the second day out. It began to blow after we left Dover and got worse during the night and the skipper wanted to make for Flushing early the next morning. Oates said the yacht would stand a heavier sea and he meant going on to Amsterdam. Finally it got so bad and the skipper so insistent that Oates gave way and made for Flushing.

'About 3 miles out of West Kapelle we ran on a sand bank and it looked like being all up with the yacht and all, as the dinghy we had with us could not have lived in that heavy sea much less have taken four of us. As luck would have it a great gust of wind and a big wave caught us and flung us clear of the sandbank and we managed to put out to sea again where we picked up a Dutch pilot who got us safely into Flushing about 2 a.m. next morning. Next day when Oates wanted to continue our journey the 'crew' (the skipper and another hand) not only refused to go any further but wanted to return by the mail steamer. Oates then engaged two Dutchmen to come with us but finally we had to abandon our trip and return to England.'[22]

It is hard to disentangle the threads of this incident, but it seems as if the skipper, even if he was overcautious, was justified in the event. The fact that the crew virtually mutinied once in the safety of Flushing certainly suggests that they had been thoroughly frightened and regarded Oates as a reckless yachtsman. Both times he had trouble with the crew of the *Saunterer*, Oates seems to have been making light of dangerous conditions.

This incident is particularly interesting because of the almost universal affection and loyalty he seems to have inspired in his fellow men – especially men who worked for him. It was only aboard this yacht that things went so badly. Perhaps the clue to solving this mystery lies in the peculiar nature of a sailing boat. Oates was on board his own yacht, and thus in most senses the master. The skipper was a professional sailor, hired for his expertise, whose knowledge and experience should in theory have been deferred to, especially in moments of danger. All this Oates acknowledged.

However, the yacht also offered particular sensations. For a start, the escape from a shorebound society and the softening effects of the company of women, children and old men. Instead, there was a small group of men in the prime of their strength, in a position where to survive they might have to exert that strength to the full. And above all, there was the sea itself. Like the desert and the Antarctic, an implacable natural environment, empty of the detritus of civilization, and a pure element which could become a deadly enemy. Knowing the exhilaration which Oates felt in such circumstances, one is hardly surprised, after all, to find him driving each dangerous experience to the limits of sensation.

In the army, the sheer weight of institutional organization prevented his exercising too much his fascination with danger. When he was alone on horseback, no one else was involved. But on a yacht, other people's lives were at stake – and they obviously did not like the feeling, even if he did. Oates clearly relished sailing as the sensation of an escape from the refined and restricted society which so confined and frustrated him.

Having to abandon his yachting trip was a great blow. 'It is a long time since I have been so annoyed over anything as I have been over the falling through of this trip.' He sought consolation in a visit to his old friend William King, who had left the regiment some two years before. He 'was in great form and much to Mrs K's annoyance discussed shooting trips, rifles and game etc. He is I think like me, he gets restless and wants to be off after he has been about a week in a place.' And so his leave came to an end. The draft of hounds was despatched from England under the care of their new kennel man, Deighton, who had come from the Pytchley. By chance Oates's ship docked at Port Said at the same time as the ship carrying his pack. 'The hounds made a great disturbance when they saw me', he reported.

On his arrival at Mhow in October he was full of his new hounds and evidently very proud of them. 'The hounds are here looking extraordinarily well . . . everybody is much impressed with them. A vet in Bombay said they were the best lot he had seen arrive in India . . . The regiment is leaving here for Baroda on 23rd of this month but the Colonel has allowed me to stay behind to look after the hounds it is awfully good of him as I should have lost 2 months hunting if I had gone and now I can hunt 4 days a week all being well.' 'Deighton is most useful and the pack has improved enormously in the last week, we rode out with it tonight for the first time and the hounds went well.'

Oates had handed over the post of Adjutant on 1 August 1909 to Captain Terrot. He was now to command a squadron consisting of some eighty men and 100 horses, starting at the end of the year. This seems a fitting reward for three years' hard work as the Commanding Officer's personal staff officer. This is supported by his confidential report at the time. 'He is a man of few words. His action and energetic character speak for themselves. I have no hesitation in saying he is the most popular and generally respected and esteemed officer the regiment has in the present generation.' And so Oates was left in peace to train his hounds.

On 12 November he reported well of the opening meet and promised that the stuffed head of the kill would be sent to his mother 'from the hounds as a token of their esteem'. Deighton was still doing well, but Oates was looking forward to the return of the Colonel 'as it relieves me of the responsibility'.

There are signs that he worried about responsibility, and certainly he did not seek it. He was happiest when pitting his solitary strength against problems, most ill at ease when being forced to collaborate with people, whether senior or junior, in whom he had no confidence. Responsibility brought with it the possibility of making a fool of himself. And – perhaps its most unattractive constraint – responsibility encourages the grey virtues of caution, prudence and compromise at which his vigorous nature rebelled.

On 26 November he witnessed a moment of high drama in Indian colonial history. When the Viceroy, Lord Minto, moved about the country he travelled by train and was invariably met and escorted by a Guard of Honour or a Travelling Escort from the station. On this occasion no less than fourteen officers, 355 soldiers and 432 horses from the Inniskillings had been sent to Baroda to perform this duty. While part of the force was 'escorting Their Excellencies, Sergeant Spencer who was riding on one side of the carriage, cleverly intercepted a bomb, which was hurled at the carriage, with his sword. Lord Minto personally informed the Commanding Officer of Sergeant Spencer's behaviour.'[23] Oates, however, was not so impressed.

'The Viceroy had a miraculous escape . . . One of the bombs rolled underneath one of our subaltern's horse, if it had not happened to have been a sandy bit of road or if the horse had struck it with one of his feet the party would have been blown to bits . . . The Colonel is furious one of the escort did not ride down the man who threw it, but Minto seems to think they did very well in preventing the second bomb falling into the carriage.'

This was the only event which disturbed the calm routines of peacetime regimental life. The new pack flourished: 'we have had great sport with the hounds, 5 jack in 3 days and last Sunday we had 58 minutes as hard as we could split. All my old crocks are lame.' The Indian winter weather suited Oates very well: bright sunny days and cold nights, 'my only regret is that we have little or no rain and we hardly ever get that smell of damp earth which is so delightful at home'.

About this time, Oates's interest in animals was widening. As well as caring for the hounds (and he was planning to breed from them as well) he was assembling quite a menagerie in the compound around his bungalow. 'A native brought in 2 hyena cubs this morning he had got in the jungle and a man has lately given me a tame chinkara so my compound is getting more like a zoo than ever. The hyena cubs are extraordinary little brutes only about 4 weeks old but very savage and growl all the time you are handling them, they can never be got tame and when they get to big I shall have to turn them loose in the jungle again.'

So, though he hunted, his interest in animals was not primarily bloodthirsty. In fact he showed signs of becoming something of a naturalist, like his sister Violet. 'There is some beautiful birds out here. Yesterday I had a kingfisher in my compound, he was catching flies off my bone heap and did not appear a bit shy. . . Could you find out for me if there is a book on Indian birds with coloured photos if there is could you send it to me?'

The zoo was increased a few weeks later by the arrival of a deer. 'My deer has been playing the deuce while I have been away,' he admitted after a few days' absence, 'it is very fond of fresh roses and for 3 days it ravaged the gardens in the Mall and complaints came pouring in to the CO from the old ladies of both sexes who inhabit the fashionable road. However, it is home again now and sleeps contentedly in the coal hole.'

Oates may have been thought a little eccentric by the natives and by his fussy neighbours who objected to the noise of his hounds and the appetite of his deer, but the British officer's love of animals, which existed alongside his keenness for blood-sports, was legendary. Indeed, there are more bizarre examples than Oates. 'In the early Victorian era Captain Leonard Irby had a soldier servant whom he trained as a retriever, and no matter how deep the water where a duck fell, he quickly brought it to his master.'[24]

Mhow week, in January 1910, meant a busy time with a horse show, dances, dinners, polo and a 'swell meet' for fifty people – 'quite a crowd for us'. There was also an Infantry boxing competition at which Oates refereed, 'and have had headakes owing to the fug for my trouble. It is very hard to keep your attention fixed for 3 hours at a stretch in an atmosphere you can hardly see through especially if you have been up since 5 a.m.' He soon found more to grumble about, however, for in mid January he was sent to Muttra for two weeks of exercises. Muttra was a pretty place with thatched bungalows and beautiful gardens but he was in no mood to appreciate the scenery.

'There are seven cavalry regiments here and we have to make a three days march and then to fight a lot more. I am supposed to be an umpire, it is a job I simply loath and I shall be very glad indeed when I am safely back in Mhow. They sent me out here with no orders as to where I was to go and I arrived late in the afternoon having lost my tent and no horses and the place in a state bordering on insanity. However the Royals have been very kind and put me up but I am to be turned loose on the world again tomorrow.' To be bad tempered and bored when acting as umpire on manoeuvres is a *sine qua non* of military life. As the exercise unfolded, his gloom deepened.

'We have had a fairly strenuous time 62 miles I did the first day, it is quite impossible to take any real interest in them as everything they do is the same foolishness we did at home before the war . . . They have here 16 regiments and with the guns they make a fine show especially when they all charge in line . . . Rimington is up here as a spectator and if they make him Inspector General which is more than likely he will wake them up with a vengeance. The old Indian Generals commanding some of the brigades are extraordinary old blighters. I was galloping to one of them the other day he was a wonderful old fossil his gaiters had worked round back to front and all day he had a glittering drip on the end of his nose.'

Oates's amusement at this old fossil was matched in this letter by some affectionate remarks about Deighton, the kennel man. 'Bowen has been hunting the hounds while I was away. . . Deighton was I think disappointed he could not hunt them but his manners are not of the best and he would probably have insulted someone. He is nevertheless a most excellent man and I think he likes India.' In the depths of his bad temper at the manoeuvres he also found time to appreciate the spectacle of a major of a native cavalry regiment who as he went into dinner provoked 'a perfect roar from the subalterns. It appeared that the major had lost his temper during a night march and had seen fit to use a lot of very bad language.'

Shortly after this rowdy dinner Oates found himself in Base Hospital, Delhi, from which he wrote a letter to his mother which started characteristically and undramatically enough. 'Do not let the above address frighten you, I have merely drifted in here after eating a bad tin of fish on manoeuvres . . . This is a country in which you can't take liberties with what you eat and if you indulge in bad tuna fish and doubtful asparagus you are pretty certain to suffer.'

Having disarmed his mother in his usual dry way, however, he now dropped the bombshell of a lifetime. 'I have now a great confession to make. I offered my services to the Antarctic expedition which starts this summer from home under Scott. They wrote and told me to produce my references which I did and they appear to have been so flattering that I have been practically accepted. Now I don't know whether you will approve or not but I feel that I ought to have consulted you before I sent in my name. I did not do so as I thought there was very little chance of my being taken (as cavalry officers are not generally taken for these shows). . . Scott however appears to be a man who can make up his mind and having decided he told me so at once which was the first intimation I had I was likely to go.

'Points in favour of going. It will help me professionally as in the army if they want a man to wash labels off bottles they would sooner employ a man who had been to the North Pole than one who had only got as far as the Mile End Road. The job is most suitable to my tastes. Scott is almost certain to get to the Pole and it is something to say you were with the first party. The climate is very healthy although inclined to be cold. I shall get home twice within the next 3 years whereas if I stay here I shall only get once. And finally I am not so keen on India as I was with its smallpox and bad fish cans knocking about.

'Now the points against. I shall be out of touch for some considerable time. It will require a goodish outlay about £1500 as I have offered to subscribe to the funds. I shall have to give up the hounds. I shall annoy the Colonel very much . . . If it is decided that I go with Scott I shall have to come home almost at once probably in April. Let me know what you think about the affair but I think it had better be kept a secret until it is decided that I go . . . but consult anyone you like. It is a great nuisance being tied by the heels in this place the only blessing being I shall miss the COs first burst of fury at my wanting to go away. . . P.S. I am sorry this letter is so disgracefully written but I am in bed.'

A week later he was still fretting in the hospital and growing daily more furious as 'the miserable fool in charge here although he does not know what is wrong with me thinks it might have been something infectious and is keeping me here my full 14 days, it is fairly sickening but it has taught me a lesson and they won't catch me in their dirty hospitals again for some time . . . I have heard nothing more about the Antarctic Expedition, the question now being whether the War Office will second me'.

He was also concerned because 'the regiment is being inspected today. It is most annoying being away like this as one always feels things will go wrong if one is not there.' He need hardly have worried on that score as the Inspector General of Cavalry in India 'considered the regiment to be a magnificent one'. What might have concerned him however was that he had been recommended to attend a course at the Staff College which would certainly not have suited him, and which would have proved an obstacle to his Antarctic plans. After his fourteen days' quarantine he returned to Mhow and waited impatiently for more news.

Interesting developments were taking place at home. Lilian had been married in January 1909 to a singer, Frederick Ranalow, who had first visited Gestingthorpe as a performer, been engaged to give her music lessons, and finally succeeded in the Herculean task of persuading Mrs Oates that he was an acceptable suitor for the hand of her beloved elder daughter. The romantic atmosphere must have been infectious, for Bryan was next to succumb.

'I was wildly surprised to hear of Brujum's engagement . . . I feel quite out of it all the family getting married I suppose Violet will be fixing herself up next.' However, from now on his real preoccupation is evident: 'I have heard nothing more about Scott's expedition I am rather afraid the War Office may stop me going and it is useless my applying to the Colonel here as three Senior Officers have just gone away on staff jobs and he is not atal in favour of losing any more . . . I am getting very impatient to hear about the expedition . . . I am keener than ever on going as I am sure it will suit me better than soldiering on here.'

At last, on 12 March 1910, the long-awaited news came. 'I have had a wire from Scott saying the War Office have sanctioned my leave, it all depends on the Colonel now whether he blocks it or not. He is away at present so I can't see him but he has been written to. I am however taking it for granted I shall go and am making arrangements.' He occupied himself by getting his beloved hounds ready for sale. 'It is very sad having to give up the hounds especially now all the puppies are coming on so well and all the hounds are fit. I hope a decent chap takes them and they don't have to go to some native prince – they hate the sight of a black man'. The colonial English basked in a conviction of their own racial superiority which may sound absurd to us now. It is not surprising that Oates should have absorbed these arrogant assumptions. The very dogs seem to have done so.

By 18 March the Colonel had returned. 'I have had two interviews with him in the last 24 hours he says he will not allow me to go with Scott's Expedition if he can prevent it. I am equally determined to go, so it is a question of who is the most pig-headed. Personally I expect to leave here April 2nd . . . I have got someone in the regiment to take over the hounds[25] so that is fixed up and I can leave with a week's notice. We have now 30 puppies which are going extraordinarily well considering the heat.'

His last few days at Mhow were enlivened by a rather farcical trip to court. 'We had great fun here yesterday. I had a law suit which I eventually won we had six witnesses one was an old shihari who looks after the puppies we had to rig him out in some clothes for the occasion and he came into the witness box dressed in an old pyjama jacket of mine and a pair of polo breeches.' This episode would have appealed to the Lord of Misrule in Oates, especially in matters relating to formality and etiquette.

The Colonel was not the only Inniskilliner to resist Oates's plans for the Antarctic. Mrs Ingall's father, Captain Terrot, was also concerned. 'Father told me he sat up in the early hours trying to persuade him not to go on Scott's Expedition. He thought it wasn't properly organised, and besides they were short of staff officers and didn't want him to go.' In any case, the Colonel and his colleagues had in time to give way to the inexorable wheels of fate for 'Captain L. E. G. Oates is seconded for special extra regimental employment dated 26th March 1910 . . . Captain L. E. G. Oates is accompanying the expedition to the South Pole, under Captain Scott.'[26]

So off he went. Home via Bombay, where he met Lieutenant Brooke. 'The night before Captain Oates left Bombay I happened to be quartered in Bombay temporarily and he told me he was coming to Bombay and would like to see me before he left for Antarctica. I invited him to dinner at the Yacht Club and had a long talk afterwards on the terrace overlooking the bay. We spoke of what he hoped to achieve. On that occasion he opened up to me much more than I could have expected about his thoughts and desires as I was then only a junior officer.'

That last member of the regiment in India to see Oates as he set off, the extremely junior Brooke, survived Oates by over seventy years to recall: 'I don't think he was bored with India. He didn't think he was doing enough for his country enjoying life in India. He wanted something that would require a good deal of sacrifice on his part. I think he wanted adventure and he wanted something that would be a tough proposition.' For once he was to get what he wanted.

Notes and references

1 Rudyard Kipling, *Collected Works.*
2 *The Regimental Historical Record*, 30 September 1908.
3 *Regimental Orders*, 12 October 1908.
4 Major-General R. Evans, *5th Royal Inniskilling Dragoon Guards*, p. 122.
5 Colonel Sir Mike Ansell, *Soldier On*, p. 19.
6 Byron Farwell, *For Queen and Country*, p 116.
7 Colonel Sir Mike Ansell, *op. cit.*, p. 15.
8 Mrs Susan Ingall, conversations with the authors.
9 Frank Richards, *Old Soldier Sahib*, p.143.
10 *Ibid.*, p.190.
11 *Ibid.*, p. 75.
12 Leonore Davidoff, *The Best Circles*, p. 43.
13 *The Lady, A Magazine for Gentlewomen*, 9 February 1893.
14 *Regimental Orders*, 20 January 1909.
15 Lieutenant-Colonel F. A. B. Fryer, letter to Mrs C. A. Oates, 19 February 1909. He commanded the regiment from 1908 to 1912.
16 Major F. W. Begbie, RAMC, letter to Mrs C. A. Oates, 19 February 1909.
17 Lieutenant-Colonel N. W. Haig, the nephew of Field-Marshal Haig, took over command of the regiment in 1912. He was, according to Colonel Sir Mike Ansell, 'a remarkable character weighing seventeen stone. Every other afternoon he caught the local train to Brighton where he played real tennis: it was an exciting performance, for he didn't leave the house until he heard the train hoot, coming into the station; he then ran slowly down the village waving to the engine driver to wait.'
18 Frank Richards, *op. cit.*, p.98.
19 Colonel Sir Mike Ansell, *op. cit.*, p. 21.
20 *Ibid.*, p. 20.
21 Frank Richards, *op. cit.*, p. 94.

22 Cecil Thresher, letter to Lieutenant–Colonel Herbert, 15 March
    1913.
23 *Regimental Historical Record,* 23 November 1909.
24 Byron Farwell, *op. cit.*
25 This was C. A. Fleury Teulon.
26 *London Gazette,* 13 May 1910.

7

Antarctic: the Voyage out

Mankind knew nothing of Antarctica until the late eighteenth century. Some conjectured about a 'Terra Australis' — a supposed region of great riches at the ends of the Earth. But the men who first glimpsed Antarctica were not much impressed. Cook's response in 1775 was that to ' judge of the bulk by the sample it would not be worth the discovery'. However, once discovered, it continued to excite man's curiosity and, when seals were spied, his rapacity. Sealers and whalers were not merely ruthless profiteers, however. Some, such as Weddell, were eager to extend their knowledge, and during the nineteenth century a growing interest in the Earth's magnetic strength and direction led to a quest for the South Magnetic Pole. British, French, and American expeditions all tried to forge a way through the pack ice and fogs which shrouded the coastline in mystery. Sir James Ross, in 1840, was most successful in his two ships which were specially strengthened for working in ice. He had burst through the pack ice and at last beheld the distant peaks of snow-covered mountains which no man had seen before.

There were two volcanoes, which Ross named Erebus and Terror after his ships. He then sailed through what is now called the Ross Sea and tried to make his way towards the interior of the continent up the McMurdo Sound, but was stopped by 'a perpendicular cliff of ice, between one hundred and fifty and two hundred feet above the level of the sea . . . we might with equal chance of success try to sail through the cliffs of Dover, as penetrate such a mass.'[1] He had discovered the Great Icy Barrier (as he called it) or the Ross Ice Shelf. It is part of a vast ice-sheet which covers most of the continent and, like a huge glacier, inches downwards and outwards towards the sea. The Ross Ice Shelf covers an area larger than France, and as Ross sailed along the coast he reached a place from which he caught a glimpse of its surface. 'It appeared to be quite smooth,' he reported, 'and conveyed to the mind the idea of an immense plain of frosted silver.'

The forbidding face which Antarctica presented may account for the fact that by the dawn of the twentieth century the area was 'still largely *Terra Incognita* after 125 years of spasmodic and ill-coordinated expeditions.'[2] In the tropics, abundant animal and plant life and mineral wealth had lured European explorers, profiteers and settlers. But where the sultry tropics seduced, frigid Antarctica repelled. It was locked in icy inaccessibility, with temperatures on the 10,000 feet Polar Plateau averaging − 58°F, whipped by hurricane force winds of 100 m.p.h. or more, its only life-forms the most primitive algae, lichen and mosses. Amundsen called Antarctica the White Goddess yet some men seemed impelled to violate her immaculate snows. In the first years of the twentieth century she presented an irresistible challenge. In 1909, Peary reached the North Pole. This left Antarctica as the last unexplored corner of a rapidly shrinking world.

To conquer the South Pole became a 'patriotic duty', and the suffering it might entail brought a welcome dimension of heroism to the British effort. For Britain's Ship of State was beginning, albeit faintly, to shudder. The confident engines of colonialism, class and Christianity hesitated at the far-off, submarine murmurs of nationalism, revolution and scepticism. Marx and Darwin had dropped their depth-charges, Freud was about to complete the job. Heroes were needed − heroes who could prove that the British were still great. Physical endurance was highly valued for its own sake, because it proved manhood, and beyond that, there was a belief that stoicism ennobled the spirit, too: in the crucible of suffering the pure gold of honour would appear. Antarctica was the perfect setting for such exertions.

The continent obviously presented a most intriguing challenge to science, but the Pole was the real prize, with the international prestige it promised. On his *Discovery* expedition in 1902–3, Scott, accompanied by Wilson and Shackleton, had reached 82° 17' South. It was an unfortunate journey in many ways, for all three suffered from scurvy (Shackleton so badly that they feared for his life); Scott and Shackleton fell out, and Scott developed a prejudice against dogs for transport. He baulked at killing dogs at all, but especially killing them to feed their fellows, a necessary expedient on the vast Antarctic journeys. (The round trip from the *Discovery* winter quarters to the Pole would have been 1466 miles.)

On this first journey Scott's party did not discover the art of good dog-management − an inadequate diet at base camp meant that the animals started out sick and unfit and did not perform well. Scott came away from his first foray into the Antarctic convinced that dogs would not do, and was eventually to put his faith instead in an unwieldy amalgam of motor transport, ponies and, most unfortunate of all, the gruelling business of man-hauling, in which the explorers were themselves harnessed up to their sledges. They treated themselves like pack animals, and of course performed a good deal worse. Dogs were to play only a supporting role on the 1913 *Terra Nova* expedition, to which Oates had offered his services.

Most recently, in 1907, Shackleton had gone south in the *Nimrod* and got to within 97 miles of the Pole – 360 miles beyond Scott's previous record of furthest south. By now Scott and Shackleton were deadly rivals. Shackleton had very nearly pipped Scott to the Pole, but that all-important 97-mile gap was Scott's chance. He would go south again, across the Barrier, follow Shackleton's route up the Beardmore Glacier, and on to the Polar Plateau, and he would not turn back. Shackleton explained to his wife that at the critical moment he had found the willpower to turn back, leaving the Pole unconquered, because 'I thought you would rather have a live donkey than a dead lion'.[3]

This comment, with its disarming self-mockery, reveals a very different spirit from the one which radiates from Scott's pen – and from his recorded words. There is no doubt that despite the widely based scientific emphasis of his *Terra Nova* expedition, he longed to gain the Pole with a serious and elevated ardour. The more the breezy Shackleton basked in his success – and the live donkey was much lionized on his return – the more Scott fretted at 'the terrible vulgarity which [he] has introduced to the Southern field of enterprise, hitherto so clean and wholesome'.[4] It was clear that Scott's quest for the Pole was an almost Arthurian wish to retrieve a sense of nobility for his race. But also for himself there was the desire to exercise his frustrated energies. 'I seem to hold in reserve something that makes for success and yet see no worthy field for it.' And, perhaps, to exorcize a private sense of meaninglessness: 'I'm obsessed with the view of life as a struggle for existence,'[5] he wrote to his wife. Sir Winston Churchill once described depression as 'the Black Dog' and despite Scott's charisma and charm, the Black Dog was often with him.

Scott set about recruiting his team. Wilson, his old comrade, spiritual guide and peacemaker from *Discovery* days, was chief of Scientific Staff. Wilson ('Uncle Bill' as he was known) emerges as a saintly figure, who on rambles through the Cotswold spinneys would prostrate himself to kiss a tiny flower: a devoted Christian who venerated all living things as animated by a Divine Breath. His own life had been dogged by tuberculosis and doctors had advised against his going on the *Discovery*, but Scott instinctively took to him and insisted he should go. (In the event

Scott's instincts were right, for Wilson proved a marvellously healing and comforting influence and showed great physical stamina.) Apart from his Antarctic experience, Wilson had a medical degree, a keen interest in zoology, and considerable artistic gifts. Other scientists were Simpson, meteorologist, Priestley, Debenham and Griffith-Taylor, geologists, Wright, physicist and Lillie and Nelson, biologists. It was an impressive scientific team, and the shape of Antarctic exploration to come.

The other side of the expedition, the Polar journey, required several experts because of Scott's decision to use four forms of transport: dogs, men, motors and ponies. Bernard Day, who had been on Shackleton's *Nimrod* expedition, presided over the motors. Cecil Meares, an untidy, unshaven eccentric and a great traveller, was the dog man. Oates's job was to organize the ponies. Of these methods of transport, only dogs had been used by man for centuries in polar conditions, and proved their worth. The other two, motors and ponies, were the importations of a temperate civilization.

Why take ponies at all? The question might legitimately be asked, for there are many objections to their use in the Antarctic. Firstly, their food does not grow there. The Antarctic offers only flesh, in the form of seals and penguins. Herbivores are at a distinct disadvantage. Every scrap of their fodder would have to be shipped out. Secondly, ponies are vulnerable to low temperatures, and unsuited to travel over crusted ice and snow, or glaciers and crevasses, because of their small hooves and great body weight. But Shackleton had taken them, and got so near. (Shackleton had shared Scott's mistrust of dogs – a product of bitter *Discovery* experience.) Finally, horse-drawn power was the image of the old age. The new age was to be motorized. Scott was proud of his motors, for they proved how up-to-date his expedition was. But on the other hand, being still at the experimental stage, they could easily fail. The dogs were merely an insurance policy and not really to be trusted. It was upon the ponies that the main responsibility was to fall.

Oates's recruitment was straightforward. He had written offering his services and was prepared to subscribe £1000 to the Expedition funds if selected. He would require no pay and references were glowing – as Scott's Second-in-Command, Lieutenant E. R. G. ('Teddy') Evans put it, 'we learnt from several sources that Oates was a man of fine physique, full of pluck, energy and spirit'. Oates's arrival at the London office of the expedition was to cause some surprise. 'We had pictured a smartly-turned-out young cavalry officer, with hair nicely brushed and neat moustache. Our future companion turned up with a bowler characteristically on the back of his head and a very worn Aquascutum buttoned up

18. Convalescing at Naauwpoort Hospital, South Africa, following the injury to his thigh.

19. His yacht, *Saunterer*, purchased in 1905. When asked if he knew anything about sailing he said he would be all right, 'My grandfather was an admiral.'

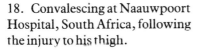

20. With Lilian at Gestingthorpe, during his convalescence.

21. The Inniskilling officers in Ireland, 1904. Oates (fifth from left, back row), Rimington (second left, middle row) and Baden-Powell (second from right, middle row).

22. With Bryan and the motorbike he took to Egypt, where 'it got away from me and went tearing off down the road by itself.'

23. Oates, sitting left of table, with a regimental team (probably boxing, as Oates often acted as referee), Cairo, 1907.

24. Example of postcards issued to commemorate the executions at Denishwai.

25.   Inniskilling officers in Cairo, 1907. 'The main characteristic of the British officer is his exclusiveness. . . . In Egypt he rarely mixes with any society which is not English.'   (Lord Cromer).

26.   With his hounds in India. 'The hounds are looking extraordinarily well . . . everybody is much impressed with them.'   (L. E. G. Oates).

closely round his neck, hiding his collar, and showing a strong, clean-shaven, weather-beaten face with kindly brown eyes indicative of his fine personality. "I'm Oates", he said.'[6]

Almost immediately Oates was taken to the West India Docks in London where the *Terra Nova* was being fitted out. Oates's appearance caused not a little stir among the seamen, for 'we could none of us make out who or what he was when he came on board – we never for a moment thought he was an officer for they were usually so smart! We made up our minds he was a farmer, he was always so nice and friendly, just like one of ourselves, but oh! he was a gentleman, quite a gentleman, and always a gentleman!'[7] It Oates looked a rough customer, the *Terra Nova* itself was rougher. She was an old Dundee whaler, built in 1884 and the shipwright exclaimed on seeing her that 'she looked an absolute wreck, fit only for the knacker's yard'.[8] But she was got into shape, and Oates made himself so useful about the place that Evans and the First Mate Campbell asked Scott if Oates could be enrolled as midshipman and be kept on the *Terra Nova* rather than go to Siberia to select the dogs and ponies with Cecil Meares.

Scott agreed. It was a mistake. Not his first nor his last, for Scott was thoroughly human in his capacity for error. But it was an important mistake. Meares knew his dogs but not much about horseflesh. He travelled overland by the Trans-Siberian Railway and then by horse and sleigh to Nikolievsk, where he chose his dogs by a very careful process, taking them on trial runs and rejecting the unsuitable ones. Then he turned to the problem of ponies. Since on Shackleton's expedition the dark ponies had died before the white ones, Scott had given orders that only white ponies should be bought, assuming them to be hardier. Meares, knowing nothing of ponies, asked a friend to buy them for him at a fair near Vladivostok. This friend took along Anton Omelchenko,[9] a jockey from the Vladivostok racecourse, to help him. Alas, there were few white ponies among those for sale and little choice. Anton recalled that the dealer pocketed their money and departed 'with a plenty big smile'.[10]

Meares persuaded little Anton to join him in taking the ponies and dogs on the epic journey from Vladivostok to New Zealand. He also enlisted the help of a Russian dog driver, Dmitri Gerov. More aid was sent from England in the person of Wilfred Bruce, Scott's brother-in-law, and between them they embarked their menagerie. Bruce recalled 'it was a dreadful experience, rain was falling in torrents, the streets and quays many inches deep in mud. The ponies were obstreperous, two of them breaking away twice.' Whilst Bruce was trying to fasten a rope on one of the ponies, the beast reared up (although Anton was seated on him) and planted a foreleg on each of Bruce's shoulders. 'We had been treating them very gently and carefully till then,' Bruce commented, 'but after this incident, we used brute force.'[11] These were not the only bruises the ponies were to bestow on Bruce: he arrived at Lyttelton with two black eyes and a swollen nose. That the beasts were well able to mis- behave and cause their handlers injury was to prove only one element in the full complement of their vices.

Meanwhile, back at the West India Docks, Oates was signed on as mid- shipman on 31 May, at a salary of one shilling per month. He worked hard on board and kept an eye on his future shipmates as they came and went. One of his regimental friends, William King, wrote that 'he some- times had a peculiar look in his eyes, as if he was sizing you up and seeing what you were good for'.[12] The sizing up process was slow, for Oates was not one to jump to conclusions. Bowers, one of the naval officers of the expedition, told Oates that his thought processes were like snails climb- ing up a cabbage stalk. Gradually, with his old dry humour ever to the fore, Oates reached his conclusions. He does not record his first impres- sions of Scott – but then, to Oates, first impressions never carried much weight. Occasionally he would take an initial dislike, and then revised his opinion in the light of subsequent events. He must have wondered that he was not sent to buy the horses, but he accepted Scott's decision. After all, Meares was already hundreds of miles away in Russia, and Oates had no reason to doubt Meares's abilities, nor, at this early stage, Scott's wisdom.

Scott must have been delighted when Evans and Campbell pleaded to keep Oates on board. Unlike Oates, Scott was emotional, responsive, and excitable, a man of spontaneous impulses, who celebrated exultantly when things went well, and pitched into gloom when plagued by uncer- tainties. He was a handsome man (his wife's description of him as 'ugly' is surely the perversity of the artistic woman) and Scott's morose good looks could crack into a dazzling grin. Though humourless he could sweep people off their feet with his charm. Cherry-Garrard, an observant young Oxford graduate who went on the expedition and chronicled it in The Worst Journey in the World, claimed that he had 'never known any- body, man or woman, who could be so attractive when he chose'.[13] To Scott, looks mattered. He would have warmed to Oates because of his impressive Roman profile and powerful physique, just as he initially recoiled from Bowers because of his squat, ungainly torso and huge hook nose. In fact, Scott soon revised his opinion in the light of Bowers's obvious competence, indeed his gluttony for hard work. For the time being Scott was delighted that he had recruited a handsome horseman who won friends everywhere and worked splendidly on the ship. For the time being Oates was content to enjoy the work, get to know his new comrades, and wait to see what sort of a leader Scott would turn out to be.

Amongst the ship's company were a number of naval officers – for Antarctic exploration had become a prerogative of the Navy. Lieutenant 'Teddy' Evans, the boyish and sparkling second-in-command, and Lieutenant 'Birdie' Bowers of the Indian Marine, the hook-nosed little Scot who stood 5 ft 2 in in his socks, were soon familiar figures, but the one who was to become Oates's special comrade on the voyage out was a naval surgeon, E. L. Atkinson. 'Atch' as he was known was a taciturn character who puffed at his pipe and preferred not to commit himself. 'He is an extraordinarily quiet man,' commented Oates, 'he hardly ever speaks but is a capital chap and a first rate boxer.' Atkinson must indeed have been silent if even Oates, that most legendary of quiet men, noticed it. 'Two more naturally silent men it would be hard to imagine,' remarked Teddy Evans, 'and one wonders how evident pleasure can be obtained from a speechless companion!'[14] It is not surprising that Teddy Evans could not understand the charms of silence. He was what the eighteenth century called a 'rattle' – an incessant talker.

Surrounded by new comrades, Oates nevertheless received visits from old ones. Geoffrey Herringham, an Inniskilling Dragoon, called on Oates while the *Terra Nova* was still in dock. Oates took his friends on a tour of inspection of the dirty little whaler. Herringham hesitated. 'I was horrified at the smallness of it, and especially the tiny place where he had to sleep, but he was as cheery as possible and looking forward to it tremendously.' Afterwards Oates stood Herringham breakfast at Lockhart's. 'I shall never forget sitting opposite Titus at a bare deal table munching huge slices of bread and jam and drinking coffee out of ¼ inch thick mugs, with the people round staring at us and wondering who in the world we were.'[15] People often seem to have wondered who in the world Oates was. It's clear that his appearance, in an age which set great store by outward show, was a deliberate snook cocked at authority and society, and a reaction to austere regimental dress.

The *Terra Nova*, duly fitted out and indeed weighed down with an already considerable cargo (to be augmented in New Zealand) set out for Cardiff via Portsmouth. At Portsmouth, visitors of all descriptions swarmed over the ship. Oates fumed silently at these invasions. 'The visitors and women are a great nuisance as we can't get really dirty.' At Cardiff, there was the same irritating tide of goggling well-wishers. 'The

Mayor and his crowd came on board and I never saw such a mob – they are Labour Socialists,' observed Oates. 'The only gentleman I have seen come aboard is the telephone operator.' He soothed his nerves with a brief visit to his old commanding officer Colonel Herbert, who now lived in Chepstow. Oates inspected various Welsh packs of hounds, and was himself inspected by Herbert's children. Like many people, they were at a loss to understand not only who but what he was. The small daughter decided that he must be a pirate. 'She was quite disappointed when she heard I was not,' smiled Oates.

No *Jolly Roger* snapped at the *Terra Nova*'s mast as she set sail from Cardiff on 15 June, 1910. Union Flags were the order of the day, and they flooded over the quayside in an endless red, white and blue sea. The crowds sang, ships' sirens sent up deep, whooping salutes, and, almost lost in the throng, a few special faces on the quay watched their menfolk depart. For Oates there were no such faces, for his mother had stayed away, and he approved. 'I am glad you are not going to see me off: I hate those awful goodbyes.' Once the cries and cheers had faded beyond their wake, Oates turned with relief to work and the shipboard routine. No more fuss now, no more absurd publicity and prying nosey-parkers, until they reached Cape Town. Oates shared a cabin with Atkinson. 'You won't find his photo anywhere,' he wrote to his mother, 'as he usually has a job elsewhere when a camera appears.'

Scott himself was not on board the *Terra Nova* so Teddy Evans was in command. The idea was that Scott should travel to New Zealand separately with his wife. Evans appreciated the way that Oates allowed himself to be hustled around and receive the same treatment as the youngest seaman on board. At the same time, Evans noticed that 'it was wonderful how Oates progressed in his seamanship'. 'He was very useful up aloft and would be one of the first on the yard in bad weather when a sail had to be furled.'[16] Oates wrote to Ansell to thank him for a book, although 'one does not get much time for reading as we are continually at work trying to keep the ship from falling to pieces'.[17] His affection for the *Terra Nova* emerges in a letter to his mother. 'This ship has only two speeds, one is slow and other is slower; however I can't abuse her as we had very strong weather last week and she behaved splendidly.' He celebrated the joys of being a midshipman. 'I do all kinds of jobs wire splicing, mending sails, stoking, trimming coal, painting etc: and one way and another I am picking up a lot of knowledge.'

Oates obviously delighted in his comrades. 'They are a capital lot of chaps with one or two exceptions, the exceptions will I think get rather a rough time as Scott and Evans are both men who say pretty quickly what they think.' Oates was himself appreciated by his new shipmates. Wilson wrote that 'Oates (or Titus, I need hardly add) is just beginning to come out now, and there is far more than meets the eye – or the ear either, for that matter – in his rather amused taciturnity. I began to suspect him of being the author of *Round the Horn before the Mast* when I saw him double up the ratlines and handle the sails as though he had been at it all his days. There's a delightful suppressed geniality in him which bubbles over now and again. When it comes to heavy work, he will be a great standby.'[18] Oates's geniality was not always suppressed, for it was the rowdiest mess he had ever been in, with Evans ('a splendid chap') leading the ragging. 'We shout and yell at meals just as we like and we have a game called Furl topgallant sails which consists in tearing off each others shirts. I wonder what some of the people at home would think if they saw the whole of the afterguard with the exception of the officer of the watch struggling, yelling and tearing off each others clothes the ship rolling and the whole place a regular pandemonium.'

They called briefly at Madeira, where Cherry-Garrard recalled they had a wonderful time, eating 'loquots galore' and Oates managed to slip away to visit his father's grave. 'It was quite tidy I thought but the lilies on it were of course a little faded and the roses had finished blooming. I had four dogs with me and they played about while I was in the cemetery. It was most quiet and nice.' He had also enjoyed a brief call at Trinidad Island. 'The birds on the island are so tame you can catch them in your hands; the booby birds (gannets) were most amusing they are great big birds and they sleep with their eyes shut, I stalked one and popped my hat over his head, his language was terrific and when the hat fell off he bit it savagely.

'On the very summit I found what I thought a very pretty flower so I stuck it in the band of my hat, on returning to the beach the surf was so heavy that the boat could not get in and we had to swim off and my hat was left on the beach; next day the hat was got off and I was wearing it with the flower still in it, the Botanist saw it and grabbed it. It turned out to be something not yet described and the best thing got in the vegetable line so I may yet make my reputation as a scientist.'

This uncharacteristically long letter to his mother positively radiates good humour and a sense of well being. Apart from the ragging and the joys of exploring, he revelled in the beauties of the open sea and of rumbustious weather. 'It was very fine to see those long seas coming up behind and looking as if they would smother us but the old bus riding like a duck and as dry as a biscuit.' He was enjoying himself immensely and was sorry the first leg of the journey was over, as once they arrived in South Africa it would mean 'collars and clean clothes and tea parties in the ward room at Cape Town'.

Sure enough, once in port, the invasions began. 'We get pressmen, hurrah parties, nibs nobs and snobs off to welcome us but they forgot to bring our mail or any bottled beer.' Oates and Atkinson escaped to the hills around Wynberg where they enjoyed a few quiet days and Atkinson was persuaded to change the habits of a lifetime, climb gingerly into the saddle, and join a hunt.

Oates and Atkinson also took the unusual step of dining with the men of their watches. 'They were very shy at first but soon warmed up,' reported Oates. 'I have never sat down with a finer looking lot of men and they are capital chaps. You can treat them as equals without their presuming on it.' Evans felt that Oates was 'more popular with the seamen than any other officer. He understood these men perfectly; he could get a wonderful amount of work out of them, and as he only had his Russian groom, he generally used volunteer labour after working hours to carry out his operations'.[19]

If Oates was getting to know his fellows, the ports of call also afforded a chance to see a little more of the expedition wives, chiefly Mesdames Scott, Wilson and Evans, who were travelling in a separate ship as far as New Zealand for the final farewells. Oates liked Mrs Evans and Mrs Wilson,[20] but he must have found Kathleen Scott too much of a formidable challenge, with her sculpture, her feminism and her assumptions of authority. In Simonstown, Oates, Atkinson and Cherry-Garrard were enjoying a lie-in after a hard day's riding and exploring, when they were awoken with the news that Captain Scott and his wife had arrived at their hotel and were awaiting them. Hurriedly they rose, dressed, and scrambled downstairs scruffy, unshaven and yawning. Mrs Scott must have raised an elegant eyebrow not only at their appearance but also at the fact that they had still been in bed at 8.30.

Mrs Scott had an artist's eye for Oates's eccentricities. At Sydney races a few weeks later, she espied him 'in the midst of a most brilliant and over-dressed crowd . . . the Soldier in Norfolk jacket, such boots, and marvellous trousers, and an indescribable hat, quite unconscious, I think, that he hadn't a top hat and morning jacket!'[21] Mrs Scott, accompanied by a gentleman of spotlessly immaculate attire, bore down on Oates and Atkinson (also a somewhat scarecrow figure). She introduced them as members of her husband's expedition, adding, 'They *are* officers,' in a satirical tone of voice.

If Mrs Scott looked askance at Oates, he certainly steered well clear of her if possible. His resistance to the fair sex had very soon become known on the *Terra Nova*. As Teddy Evans had sung on the voyage down, in a moment of inspiration:

> Who avoided female society?
> 'I' said Captain Oates
> 'Because I prefer goats.'

Squiring expedition wives was not his style. As a soldier and sometime boxing referee, though, he took pleasure in reporting the wives' campaigns. 'Mrs Scott and Mrs Evans have had a magnificent battle', he reported from New Zealand, 'they tell me it was a draw after 15 rounds. Mrs Wilson flung herself into the fight after the 10th round and there was more blood and hair flying about the hotel than you would see in a Chicago slaughter house in a month.'

There was another rousing send off, this time from Cape Town, and the *Terra Nova* steamed south. Perhaps to escape from the atmosphere of feminine fisticuffs, Scott had decided to join the ship at Cape Town instead of waiting until New Zealand. This caused a certain inevitable disappointment on board – a feeling of having to knuckle under and get down to business earlier than expected. Oates commented, 'this is not a very popular move but in a way I think it is a good thing as [Scott] gets to know the people better and we get to know him'. Oates enjoyed his last spell as a carefree midshipman. At New Zealand the ponies awaited him and his real responsibilities would begin. This initial period, though strenuous, was fun. 'Working at everything, chased round and never idle, strictly disciplined and subordinate and respectful to the ship's executive officers,' as Teddy Evans put it, Oates shared a watch with Bowers and acted as his 'snotty' (assistant). Their watch was from midnight to 4 a.m., their duties to watch the wind and its effects on the sails and ship, to maintain the course, and especially in rough seas, to supervise the pumping. Because of her extraordinary load, the *Terra Nova*'s seams had opened and she took in a great amount of water. Most days began with a working summons of 'all hands to the pumps!'

At New Zealand Oates hurried to inspect his ponies, waiting at their quarantine station, Quail Island, in Lyttelton Harbour. When Meares and Bruce had landed them there, they had been surprised at their skittishness, for 'although they were quite uncertain on their legs, they fought and kicked each other on every possible occasion'.[22] The ponies had been on their legs for fifty-two days on their journey from Vladivostok, so their unsteadiness was not surprizing. When Scott paid a visit to Quail Island, he was 'greatly pleased with animals . . . think dogs finest ever got together'.[23] Oates's reaction was quite different. He was simply appalled by what he found.

He made a melancholy catalogue in his diary of the ponies' defects. '*Victor* Narrow chest, knock knees, suffers with his eyes. Aged. Windsucker . . . *Snippets* Bad wind sucker. Doubtful back tendons off fore legs. Slightly lame off fore. Pigeon toes. Aged. *James Pigg* Sand crack near hind. Aged. *Chinaman* Has ringworm just above coronet on near fore. I think the oldest pony we have which is saying a good deal. Both nostrils slit up. *Christopher* Aged. Ringbone off fore. Slightly lame off fore. *Jehu* Aged, suffering from debility and worn out. *Nobby* Aged. Goes with stiff hocks. Spavin near hind. Best pony we have. *Michael* Lame near hind. Ringbone. Aged . . . In mentioning the ponies' blemishes I have only mentioned those which appear to actively interfere with their work or for identification.'[24] The ponies had cost £5 each. Oates was used to paying £100 or so for a horse. But simple economy was not the reason: the expedition's three motors had cost £1000 each.

The ponies' inadequacies were not the only shock, for in Melbourne Scott had received a cable: 'Beg leave to inform you, Fram proceeding Antarctic. Amundsen.' This was a bolt from the blue. Scott had thought that Amundsen was going north. Now he had a competitor and the Pole he had considered his by right was suddenly up for grabs. There was even news of a third expedition to the Ross Sea, by the Japanese. Scott believed that 'every explorer looks upon certain regions as his own.' He felt an almost capitalistic acquisitiveness about the territory he had explored, for a route pioneered by an explorer was to him 'as much a part of his capital as the gold and silver in the vault of a bank . . . no one else, without his consent, has any more right to take and use it, than a stranger has to enter the vaults of the bank and take its treasures'.[25] Scott's indignation on this point had been first aroused by Shackleton: now, against Amundsen, it was reinforced by patriotic chauvinism. The whole expedition buzzed with outrage, and Oates slunk ashore for a drink, and to write to his old friend William King.

'I am just ashore from Quail Island to get a skinful of beer. I took over the ponies the other day and am not impressed by them, they are very old for a job of this sort and four of them are unsound however we shall have to make the best of them. These b – y Norskies coming down south is a bit of a shock to us. I only hope they don't get there first, it will make us look pretty foolish after all the noise we have made.'[26] While most of his shipmates were grousing about Amundsen, calling him a blackguard and a cheat, Oates was taking a much more cautious and self-critical view – which he enlarged upon in a letter to his mother.

'What do you think about Amundsen's expedition? If he gets to the Pole first we shall come home with our tails between our legs and no mistake. I must say we have made far too much noise about ourselves all the photographing, cheering, steaming through the fleet etc etc is rot and if we fail it will only make us look more foolish. They say Amundsen has been underhand the way he has gone about it but I personally don't see it is underhand to keep your mouth shut. I myself think these Norskies are a very tough lot they have 200 dogs and Yohandsen [sic] is with them and he is not exactly a child, also they are very good ski-runners while we can only walk, if Scott does anything silly such as underfeeding his ponies he will be beaten sure as death.'

This last remark brings into focus a problem which was to cause him constant anxiety for the next year. Although Scott had appointed Oates for his experience as a horseman, he seems quite often to have resisted Oates's opinions about the ponies. In Lyttelton this process began. He could not believe that Oates's account of the ponies' condition was accurate. Fascinated by men's personalities, Scott decided that Oates was a 'cheery old pessimist' and attributed his criticism of the beasts to a gloomy outlook. Furthermore, Oates reckoned that Scott's estimates of the fodder to be taken fell far short of what they would actually need.

Scott said there would be room only for thirty tons, as much of the stowage space simply had to be used for coal. Oates insisted he needed forty-five tons 'When I tackled him,' wrote Oates, 'he said not one over 30 so it's no good arguing, however we argued for one hour and he has given way which shows that he is open to reason but they will have to leave some coal behind to get the extra forage in. He told me I was a something nuisance.' Oates also smuggled in an extra five tons at his own expense.[27]

He was quite clearly anxious about the prospects for his 'wretched load of crocks'. Responsibility had not always appealed to him, and he had occasionally tangled with his superiors when he thought they were not up to the mark. Now he was in sole charge of the most important of Scott's methods of transport; the ponies were wrecks, and Scott had showed himself capable at times of dismissing Oates's advice or simply refusing to believe him. Amundsen's arrival on the scene threatened to turn Scott's expedition into a foolish also-ran, and looking a fool was something Oates did not enjoy. A tense, truculent air began to creep into his comments about Scott. The journey that had begun in the sunshiny atmosphere of schoolboy frolics was gradually darkening.

However, whilst the *Terra Nova* was in Lyttelton docks, many of the local notables strolled down to look her over, and Oates's unkempt appearance caused some amusement. One day Debenham observed that Oates 'was passing along the deck in an old dirty shirt with his hair cropped close and somebody on the wharf asked Petty Officer Evans who it was. When he said, 'Captain Oates,' the man roared out laughing, whereat Evans proceeded to show him he should give more respect to members of the *Terra Nova* staff'.[28] Two days later, Oates himself reported another bizarre episode. 'I had a job helping the ship's carpenter to refit the cross trees on the foremast. It was rather amusing as a parson came up belonging to the Missions to Seamen. He heard I was a soldier and came up to me. He said he had been a private soldier and had raised himself to a parson and it was sad that I who had been a Captain of a Cavalry Regiment should have come down to be a carpenter's mate. I think somebody had been pulling his leg.'

The final goodbyes were said on the afternoon of 29 November 1910. A flotilla of little boats followed the *Terra Nova* out of the harbour, and a tug took the wives off and returned to Port Chalmers. 'I decided not to say good-bye to my man,' wrote Mrs Scott, 'because I didn't want anyone to see him look sad. On the bridge of the tug, Mrs Evans looked ghastly white and said she wanted to have hysterics. Mrs Wilson was plucky and good'.[29] Later, on the shore, Mrs Wilson 'sat sphinx-like on the wharf', oblivious to Mrs Scott's attempts to organize a tea. By then, the *Terra Nova* had disappeared over the horizon.

The ship had steamed away from New Zealand so heavily laden that Gran, the Norwegian ski expert, felt she was 'ready to sink'. Three heavy motor-sledges were lashed to the decks, nineteen ponies and thirty-three dogs had been taken on board. The space between decks under the forecastle was converted into fifteen stalls, 3 ft wide and 19 ft long (although the length varied owing to the curve of the ship). Four more stalls were built on the upper deck between the galley and the ice-house.[30] 'One takes a look through the hole in the bulkhead,' wrote Scott, 'and sees a row of heads with sad, patient eyes come swinging up together from the starboard side, whilst those on the port swing back: then up come the port heads, whilst the starboard recede. It seems a terrible ordeal for these poor beasts to stand this day after day for weeks together . . .'[31]

The *Terra Nova* carried 455 tons of coal, 2½ tons of petrol in drums, 2 tons of oats, 30 tons of compressed fodder, 5 tons of bran, 6 tons of oil-cake and 2 tons of hay. And even its human cargo had increased, for several of the scientists had joined the ship in the Antipodes: Debenham and Griffith-Taylor, the Australian geologists; Meares and Bruce, and Ponting, the expedition photographer, who not only took a series of beautiful still photographs but made a cine film. Debenham's first

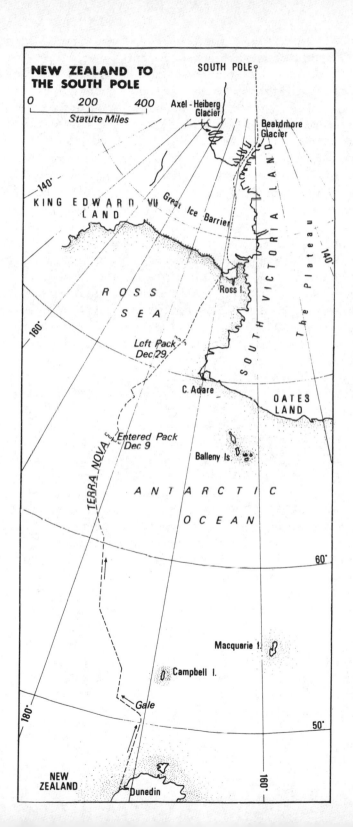

NEW ZEALAND TO
THE SOUTH POLE

0   200   400

Statute Miles

SOUTH POLE

Axel - Heiberg
Glacier

Beardmore
Glacier

140°

KING EDWARD VII
LAND

Great Ice Barrier

SOUTH VICTORIA LAND

The Plateau

140°

ROSS
SEA

Ross I.

Left Pack
Dec 29

C. Adare

OATES
LAND

160°

Entered Pack
Dec 9

Balleny Is.

TERRA NOVA

ANTARCTIC

OCEAN

60°

Macquarie I.

Campbell I.

180°

Gale

50°

NEW
ZEALAND

Dunedin

160°

impressions of Oates were that 'Soldier is a fine big chap with a most genial face and is eminently teasable. He and Bowers are always at each other.' On the mess deck, the seamen must have been feeling squeezed, for much of their space had been encroached upon by the ponies, and they had to share hammocks, one watch turning out as the other turned in. No wonder the *Terra Nova* looked ready to sink. As for the Plimsoll line, it had been painted out.

Oates's last letter from New Zealand shows a mixture of relief and uneasiness. 'The ponies fitted in splendidly and were very good, not giving the slightest trouble, even Hackenschmidt behaved like the little gentleman he is! Scott was kind enough to say he was pleased with the way they went in. Fancy, we had fifteen ponies and five tons of forage in that upper fo'castle. I have to climb in and out of the sky-light to get at them and it is a long job feeding them. I only pray we don't have any heavy weather going south, or there is bound to be trouble.'

Alas, this was a vain hope. The *Terra Nova* was running into the 'Filthy Fifties', an area of ocean notorious for its storms and through which every Antarctic expedition had to pass. On 1 December Cherry-Garrard, looking green with foreboding, invited Oates to inspect the barometer. 'It makes me feel sick just to look at it', groaned the young assistant zoologist, perhaps wishing he was back among the serene staircases of Christchurch College. A great storm was brewing, and soon the weather was so bad that the ship was lurching with what seemed like sickening finality at every minute. Despite a liberal use of oil to keep heavy seas from breaking over the ship, the decks were swept by the waves, the ponies falling about and the dogs being hanged by their chains.

For Oates the vital work was to try and keep the ponies on their feet, but this was no small task as the ship hurled them alternately one way and then the other. Helped by Atkinson, he spent sixty hours on his feet and soaked to the skin in a desperate attempt to keep his charges alive. 'I can't remember having a worse time', he confessed to his mother. 'The motion up in the bows was very violent and unless one had been through it one would not believe any pony could keep its feet for five minutes. I was drenched all night, the water continually forcing the skylight up and pouring over the fo'castle in a regular torrent. During the night one pony was down as many as eight times and I was unfortunate to have two killed. One fell and broke its leg and the other got cast so badly that without proper tackle it could not be got up and I had no one who could do anything to help me as everybody was busy with the ship.' (Appropriately enough, these two unfortunate beasts were called Davy and Jones.)

'About 4 in the morning the fo'castle got half full of water and on looking out I found the whole forrard part of the ship deserted and one solitary dog washing about loose. I began then to think things were getting a bit serious as I knew they would not let dogs about loose unless things were bad. It appears what happened was she was making so much water they could not keep the furnaces going and the water rising above the fires, made the water hot and the pumps would not suck. Finally they got it under control by means of a chain of buckets. Noon next day the gale ceased and it was about time as we were all nearly beat. The reason the ship made so much water was the great load she had in her which opened the seams in the deck. When I turned in for a couple of hours in the afternoon I could hear the water running down the bulkhead into my bunk.'

Oates was not the only one to suffer thus. For some of the seamen things were even worse. After the gale the deck under the ponies started to leak badly and the ponies' urine seeped through onto hammocks and bedding beneath. 'The men living in that part have done their best to fend off the nuisance with oilskins and canvas, but without sign of complaint', Scott marvelled. The two ponies who had died were got out through the fo'castle skylight. 'It was a curious proceeding,' remarked Scott, 'as the space looked quite inadequate for their passage.' [32]

After the storm had abated, a dazed and sobered company counted their blessings – and their losses: two ponies, a dog, 10 tons of coal, 65 gallons of petrol, and a case of the biologists' spirit. There had been certain gains, though of an intangible kind. Bowers, who was rapidly developing a deep devotion to Scott, declared that at the height of the storm 'he was simply splendid, he might have been at Cowes'. And Evans had noticed and appreciated Oates's efforts, declaring that he would 'never forget his strong, brown face illuminated by a swinging lamp as he stood amongst those suffering little beasts. He was a fine powerful man, and on occasions he seemed to be actually lifting the poor little ponies to their feet as the ship lurched heavily to leeward and a great sea would wash the legs of his suffering charges from under him . . . He himself appeared quite unconscious of any personal suffering, although his hands and feet must have been absolutely numbed with the cold and wet'.[33] Bowers put the whole thing in proportion when he remarked, with Christian piety, that 'God had shown us the weakness of man's hand and it was enough for the best of us – the people who had been made such a lot of recently'.[34] But even the loyal Bowers seems to have faltered at the thought of what might have been: 'the terrible ocean is our best friend, except when you tamper with him by running heavy risks'.[35]

A week later the *Terra Nova* entered the pack ice. Gran, the Norwegian ski expert, rhapsodized at the sight. 'It was as if we sailed over a lake where thousands of white lilies lay and swayed in the evening breeze.' Albatrosses wheeled slowing around the ship, and on 7 December the first fulmars and a McCormick skua were seen, and shortly afterwards, an Antarctic petrel. At first the ship thrust her way easily enough through the bobbing floes then gradually she was slowed down as the ice thickened. Then the day came when she could no longer butt herself a passage through the brashy sea-ice: she was stuck fast, and remained so for three weeks.

Gran took advantage of the moment, and of the surrounding ice, to give some ski lessons. Almost the whole party were absolute beginners and most of the seamen, with characteristic British stubbornness, refused even to try. Petty Officer Evans, a big beery seaman and veteran of the *Discovery* expedition, dismissed the skis as 'planks'. The officer and scientists were at it with a will, but compared to Amundsen's team, who had been expert skiers all their lives, Scott's men were pathetically inept. Oates and Atkinson stripped to the waist and skied around in snow goggles, for the sun was dazzling in the new world of ice and penguins. 'They are really most amusing, they come running up to you on a flow exactly like a stout and aged lady running after a bus'.

Christmas Eve in the pack ice brought frustrated energies to a head in a display of high spirits, recounted by Cherry-Garrard. 'Jane [Atkinson] and Soldier entered the mate's cabin and said that they did not want to use force, but they wanted the return of twenty matches which he had taken from the Eastern Party. There was such a fight that afterwards Campbell was hanging over the side feeling very sick! Titus dragged all Bill's clothes off and Bill burst naked into ward room dragging Titus along on his back.'[37]

For Christmas dinner, the mess was festooned with decorations, and an excellent meal was served: tomato soup, penguin breast stewed as an entree, roast beef, plum pudding, mince pies, asparagus, champagne, port and liqueurs. The whole company stayed at the table for five hours afterwards, singing. Oates, who had always sneered at 'the infernal pianola', now astonished everyone by bursting into song. He gave then the 'The Fly on the Turnip', an old favourite which had rocked them in the aisles back in the mess, and now appealed enormously to his *Terra Nova* comrades in view of one of his nicknames: 'Farmer Hayseed'. 'We actually got Oates to sing for the first time', noted an amazed Bernard Day in his diary.

Despite the festivities, Oates was deeply worried about the ponies, which had lost condition badly since the gale. One of them collapsed, and was taken out onto deck as a last resort in an attempt to revive it. 'I'm anxious, anxious about these animals of ours',[38] brooded Scott. Communications seem to have failed between him and Oates, for on Wednesday 28 December Scott wrote in his diary, 'Oates is unremitting in his attention and care of the animals, but I don't think he quite realises that whilst in the pack the ship must remain steady and that, therefore, a certain limited scope for movement and exercise is afforded by the open deck on which the sick animal now stands.' Why did not Scott simply suggest this to Oates?

It seems extraordinary that such elementary, such simple consultations could not, somehow, take place. Instead, no doubt, Oates would have been conscious of Scott's brooding, dark-blue eyes fixed on him, and the sense of buried anxieties and resentments. Scott watched his men closely, fascinated by human beings in any case, but usually quick to criticize and make suggestions. There seems to have been something about Oates which made him hesitate. Perhaps Oates was a man whose respect he would have valued, but could not feel.

Certainly Oates would have found Scott's watchful, pained look extremely galling. Cherry-Garrard remarked that 'few who knew [Scott] realised how shy and reserved the man was, and it was partly for this reason that he laid himself open to misunderstanding . . . Add to this that he was sensitive, femininely sensitive . . . and it will be clear that leadership to such a man may be almost a martyrdom.'[39] Delayed in the pack ice for day after day, with the expedition devouring valuable resources and wasting precious time, Scott was working himself up into a frenzy of impatience. 'To Scott any delay was intolerable', says Cherry-Garrard, and waiting for the Southern summer conditions to break up the ice required more patience than many men could muster. Oates may well have felt that Scott's bad temper was directed towards, or provoked by, himself. He had never got on well with men with fussy, fretful natures, and now he was trapped with one as his leader, in a situation where he could feel no faith in his ability to produce the results. He retreated further into his shell whenever Scott was around.

On 30 December the *Terra Nova* escaped from the pack ice and two days later land was visible. Wilson recorded the moment in his diary. 'It was a very beautiful sight as we saw first a brilliant white line appear on the horizon to the left of Mount Terror and then, as we came nearer, this white line developed into a long irregular line of white ice cliff standing out of the dark inky water. The water here at a distance has an inky blue look, but when one looks into it over the ship's side it is a dark sage green . . . As we came closer in the number of Adélie penguins in the water became extraordinary. They were leaping in and out like little dolphins all round us in small schools . . . the water was as though hundreds of rifle bullets were dropping in around us everywhere.

'As we came close into the Barrier we had a grand view over its surface which was much curved. In the cliff just before us we had the usual wonderful green colour in the caves – a wonderful holly green – also cobalt blues and a line of emerald green along the water line . . . The peace of God which passes all understanding reigns here. . . One only wishes one could bring a glimpse of it away with one with all its unimaginable beauty.'[40] The final selection of a landing site had to wait until the last moment, because local conditions might greatly have changed, with the movement of the ice, since Scott's previous voyage. In the event, ice blocked the way to the desired sites, so he decided to land on a small promontory at the foot of Mount Erebus, about six miles south of Cape Royds, fifteen miles from the *Discovery* hut. It was named Cape Evans in honour of Scott's deputy, and here the expedition disembarked, built its prefabricated hut, and set up in business.

The transport was instantly landed, so it could be used to haul the rest of the cargo across the ice to the land. Two of the motors came first, followed by the ponies. Scott recorded the scene. 'There was a good deal of difficulty in getting some of them into the horse box, but Oates rose to the occasion and got most in by persuasion, whilst others were simply lifted in by the sailors. Though all are thin and some few look pulled down I was agreeably surprised at the evident vitality which they still possessed – some were even skittish. I cannot express the relief when all seventeen were safely picketed on the floe. From the moment of getting on the snow they seemed to take on a new lease of life, and I haven't a doubt they will pick up very rapidly. It really is a triumph to have got them through safely and as well as they are . . . Poor brutes, how they must have enjoyed their first roll, and how glad they must be to have freedom to scratch themselves! It is evident they have all suffered from skin irritation – one can imagine the horror of suffering from such an ill for weeks without being able to get at the part that itched. I note that now they are picketed together they administer kindly offices to each other: one sees them gnawing away at each other's flanks in the most obliging manner.'[41]

It was typical of Scott to anthropomorphize these ponies and see their compulsive, exploratory gnawing as a deeply social act, a 'kindly office'. Next the dogs were landed – and goaded beyond endurance by the penguins, who waddled up to inspect them like so many tipsy operagoers in evening dress. Gradually the stores were brought ashore and the framework of the hut began to take shape. The dogs were very unfit after their long journey, and the motors were giving trouble, so Scott was impressed with the ponies. 'I was astonished at the strength of the beasts I handled', he wrote, 'three out of the four pulled hard the whole time and gave me much exercise'.[42] On 8 January the third motor-sledge was unloaded, but before it could reach the shore it plunged through the ice and sank many fathoms deep, beyond all hope of salvage. The ponies' importance was becoming daily more obvious.

They did not all, however, take easily to the novelty of drawing sledges. There were many incidents of bolting and Scott noticed the animals' nerves and experienced the difficulty of handling them. 'Oates is splendid with them – I don't know what we would do without him',[43] he mused. But also, the ponies' friskiness convinced him that they were stronger and better beasts than first appeared. 'Their condition can't be half as bad as we imagined', he thought. Other ideas occurred to him at this time. 'I am wondering how we shall stable the ponies in the winter', he wrote on 7 January. It seems extraordinary that this was the first time he had given the matter any thought.

At first the ponies were made fast by their halters to a stout hempen rope secured between two rocks. They were spaced far enough apart so as not to be within reach of each other, to avoid any kindly – or unkindly – offices. Eventually, 'on the leeward side of the hut . . . a rough stable was built running the length of the northern side of the hut. This contained stalls and chut-board and was roofed with scantling and covered with rubberoid. A stove was installed at the end farthest from the entrance, and with this, burning a combination of blubber and coal or wood, sufficient ice was thawed out daily for the ponies' water. The outer back wall of the stable was composed largely of the bales of compressed fodder which made an excellent firm wall for protection. When a bale was needed for use it was removed from the inside and replaced by boarding.'[44]

On Sunday, 22 January Oates took up his pen to write to his mother and survey his situation. In three days' time he was to start out on the two-month depot-laying journey under Scott. Scott's orders for the preparation of this journey had been rather abrupt. Evans and Bowers had a bare week to organize it and make out the rations while Scott busied himself with sledge details, though, he complained in his diary, sounding rather like Alice's White Queen, 'my mind doesn't seem half as clear on the subject as it ought to be'.[45] The purpose of the depot-laying journey was to deposit stores of food and fuel along the route to the Pole, to be used the next season on the Polar journey itself. The ponies were to play a most important part, as Oates was well aware.

'The transport is of course the great question', he wrote to his mother, 'and between you and me things are not as rosy as they might be. To start with we had three sledges the best of which fell through the ice and sank in 100 fathoms to arise no more the other two have developed serious defects which prevent them being used on this depot journey, secondly I went a journey yesterday to Glacier Tongue with Meares and 9 dogs only 14 miles there and back and we returned both walking, one dog being dragged on the sledge two more not able to pull atal and the rest dead beat: now for the journey eleven is the team and they are expected to pull 450 lbs personally I am glad I have not much to do with them.

'The ponies are alright but as I say nobody understands severe marching with ponies except Meares and myself and Meares goes with the dogs and I can't run the lot especially as there are three people over me to give orders. Scott and Evans boss the show pretty well and their ignorance about marching with animals is colossal, on several points Scott is going on lines contrary to what I have suggested, however, if I can only persuade him to take a pony himself he will learn a lot this autumn. That is all the growl I have got.' It wasn't quite though, for after some remarks about the beautiful weather (the Englishman's traditional resort when assailed by strong emotion) he is drawn irresistibly back to exercise his anxieties.

'The ponies have improved out of all recognition since coming ashore they are fat but of course soft as after we had finished hauling stores ashore they have had no exercise no one being available for the job, this is a point Scott cannot see the force of but if he wishes to march with soft animals I am content. We shall I am sure be handicapped by the lack of experience in trekking which the party possess, Scott having spent too much of his time in an office, he would fifty times sooner stay in the hut seeing how a pair of Foxs spiral puttees suited him than come out and look at the ponies legs or a dogs feet – however I suppose I think too much of this having come strate [sic] from a regiment where horses were the first and only real consideration.'

After another brief digression about the beauties of the landscape (another device by which the Englishman seeks to cool his temper), Oates returns to the most interesting topic of Scott and his chances. 'I wonder what has happened to Amundsen. Scott thinks he has gone to the Weddell Sea to try for the Pole from there, if it comes to a race he will have a great chance of getting there as he is a man who has been at this kind of game all his life and he has a hard crowd behind him while we are very young. Don't think from what I say that Scott is likely to endanger anyone, it is quite the reverse and I may be maligning the man altogether as I admit I am annoyed at him not having taken my advice more freely about the marches.' He then speculates about what would happen if Scott failed in his first attempt to get to the Pole and tried to enlist Oates's services for a second season. 'I don't know yet whether I shall stay or not as it is early yet and I shan't decide until I see the mail . . . I am afraid you will think my letter is full of growls,' he concludes guiltily, 'but as a matter of fact I am having a first class time am very fit and looking forward to the sledge journey.'

At about the same time Oates wrote to Colonel Haig telling him that Scott wanted mules for 1912 (the ship would return with fresh supplies for the last season's work) and Oates had advised him to get them from the Indian transport. He asked Haig to put in a word for the expedition with his uncle, Douglas Haig, the Commander-in-Chief in India, as they would only be able to get government mules as a favour 'and if Scott goes elsewhere he will get stuck as he did with this lot'. He seemed doubtful about staying on a further season himself, and seemed disposed to 'come back to the regiment as soon as you have room for me. I have had a top hole time so far but should like to have a morning in Mhow after the jack'.[46] After having made arrangements to ship the mules out to the Antarctic, Oates had a momentary qualm. 'I shall look pretty foolish if they all die of cold on landing but they should be better than the crocks we have here.' At 9 a.m. on Tuesday, 24 January 1911, the depot-laying journey began and Oates could set aside his growls, resentments, anxieties and fears of looking foolish and get to grips with the business of leading his ponies on the march.

Notes and references

1 Sir James Ross, diary, August 1840.
2 H. G. R. King, *The Antarctic*, p.215.
3 Quoted by Roland Huntford, *Scott and Amundsen*, p. 245.
4 R. F. Scott, letter to Kathleen Bruce, 1908.
5 R. F. Scott, letter to Kathleen Scott, 17 January 1909.
6 Commander Evans, *My Recollections of a Gallant Comrade*, a booklet reprinted from *Strand Magazine*, December 1913.
7 Tom Crean, quote from Violet Oates's collection.
8 Lieutenant-Commander F. E. C. Davies, *With Scott before the Mast*, p.11.
9 Anton became Oates's stable boy. After fighting in the First World

War he joined the Red Army and was later involved in helping to set up a Kolkhoz, or collective farm, at Bat'ki. He was killed by lightning in 1932.

10 Quoted in diary of Frank Debenham, 18 June 1911.

11 W. M. Bruce, *Blue Peter*, June 1932.

12 William King, from Violet Oates's collection.

13 Quoted by Reginald Pound, *Scott of the Antarctic*, p. 243.

14 Commander Evans, *op. cit.*

15 G. Herringham, from Violet Oates's collection.

16 Commander Evans, *op. cit.*

17 L. E. G. Oates, letter to Major G. K. Ansell, 14 August 1910.

18 Dr E. A. Wilson, letter to Scott, 25 June 1910.

19 Commander Evans, *op. cit.*

20 'I am being most honoured by the wives of the expedition. Mrs Scott marked all my clothes, and Mrs Evans is going to send you some papers. I like Mrs Evans very much.' L. E. G. Oates, 28 November 1910.

'Wilson is a first-rate chap, perhaps you remember him, he has a very nice wife.' L. E. G. Oates, diary entry-notes for letter home.

21 Kathleen Scott, diary, 13 October 1910.

22 W. M. Bruce, *op. cit.*

23 Quoted by Roland Huntford, *op. cit.* p. 326.

24 L. E. G. Oates, copied by Violet Oates from his diary.

25 R. F. Scott, letter to Scott Keltie, 20 February 1907.

26 L. E. G. Oates, letter to William King, 15 November 1910. In this letter Oates also discusses a possible trip to Nova Zembla. He had first mentioned this on 14 August 1913. 'Bowers's great ambition is to go exploring on the upper reaches of the Amazon. Mind you, I think if we could afford it that would be a very nice trip for us. That chap you met [Campbell] is already talking about a trip to Nova Zembla when we get back and wants me to go – let me have a letter in New Zealand.'

27 Oates reports the first exchange with Scott on the forage subject on 17 November. On 23 November he adds 'Scott has been kicking up another fuss about the forage but I succeeded in defeating him, also we smuggled in an extra two tons.' On 28 November he reports 'I have dodged in a little more forage, I have now ordered just a little more which I shall try to get in on the quiet this afternoon, and my ambitions will be attained, ie to go south with 50 good tons.' But later he says 'I have succeeded in getting in the extra forage except three bales of hay which were mildewed, it is a bit thick a man sending down rotten stuff for a show like this.'

28 Frank Debenham, conversation with Sue Limb.

29 Quoted by Reginald Pound, *Scott of the Antarctic*, p. 209.

30 On 17 November 1910 Oates had written of these arrangements, 'I have had 15 stalls built in the fo'castle for the ponies and 4 are to be built outside. When I look at the stalls sometimes I think they are too small and the ponies won't go in, and sometimes I think they are too big, next minute I think we shall never get them out again if we do get them in, until I feel positively sick with anxiety.'

31 R. F. Scott, diary, 1 December 1910.

32 *Ibid.*, 3 December 1910.

33 Commander Evans, *op. cit.*

34 Birdie Bowers, quoted by Apsley Cherry-Garrard, *The Worst Journey in the World*, p. 55.

35 Quoted by Roland Huntford, *op. cit.*, p. 332.

36 L. E. G. Oates. 'They keep up a fearful fug in this wardroom. There are 24 of us sleeping down here and practically no ventilation. I hook back the door everytime I go on deck but Scott keeps sending up and having it closed; in the morning you could make iron clads of it.'

37 A. Cherry-Garrard, diary, 24 December 1910.

38 R. F. Scott, diary, December 1910.

39 A. Cherry-Garrard, *op. cit.*

40 E. A. Wilson, diary, 2 January 1911.

41 R. F. Scott, diary, 4 January 1911.

42 *Ibid.*, 6 January 1911.

43 *Ibid.*, 7 January 1911.

44 *Terra Nova*, Miscellaneous Data.

45 R. F. Scott, diary, January 1911.

46 L. E. G. Oates, letter to Major N. Haig, 20 January 1911.

8

The Depot-Laying Journey

Twelve men set out from Cape Evans. The aim was to travel along the Polar route for the first hundred miles or so, on the Barrier, leaving depots for the next season. Wilson and Meares went with the two dog teams, and Oates, Scott, Bowers, Cherry-Garrard, Gran, Atkinson, Crean, Petty Officers Evans, Ford and Keohane led the eight ponies, or marched alongside them. The load was an estimated 5385 lbs, including fourteen weeks' food and fuel. Each sledge weighed 52 lbs and the drivers' skis and sleeping bags, and pony furniture, weighed 65 lbs. Other gear was distributed amongst the sledges: examples being cooker and primus (40 lbs), oil (100 lbs) tank containing biscuits (172 lbs), box with tools (35 lbs), sack of oats (160 lbs), tent and poles (28 lbs). Each man had spare gear, mostly extra clothing, amounting to 12 lbs. The two dog sledges averaged 490 lbs each – the pony-drawn sledges around 570 lbs.

Scott initially took a hand in driving a dog team and decided to withhold his opinion, unsure whether they would be a real success, 'but the ponies are going to be real good. They work with such extraordinary steadiness, stepping out briskly and cheerfully, following in each other's tracks. The great drawback is the ease with which they sink in soft snow; they go through in lots of places where men scarcely make an impression – they struggle pluckily when they sink, but it is trying to watch them.'[1] Scott's language here betrays a tender-heartedness towards the animals which had already clouded his judgement of dogs. He attributes moral qualities to the ponies: pluck, cheerfulness, and so on, and when they suffer, he suffers with them. His sentimental attachment to animals is quintessentially English, part of his emotional nature and indeed his charm, but still, not necessarily a help to him in organizing Antarctic travel.

At Camp 1, Scott reported that 'the ponies are doing excellently,'[2] at Camp 2, Keohane's pony had gone lame, with a possible strained tendon. 'The Soldier takes a gloomy view of the situation, but he is not an optimist.'³ By Camp 3, Scott's own optimism was beginning to be eroded. 'A great shock came when we passed the depoted fodder and made for this camp. The ponies sank very deep and only brought on their loads with difficulty, getting pretty hot. The distance was but miles, but it took more out of them than the rest of the march.'⁴ Scott panicked slightly at this, and the idea of snow-shoes for the ponies became a most attractive one. They only had one pair with them, and they were tried on Weary Willie.

'The effect was magical,' enthused Scott. 'He strolled around as though walking on hard ground in places where he floundered woefully without them. Oates hasn't any faith in these shoes at all, and I thought that even the quietest pony would need to be practised in their use.'⁵ Scott sent Meares and Wilson with a dog team back to Cape Evans to look for more snow shoes. Meanwhile, Oates and Scott disagreed about other matters, too: chiefly the overall plan of the depot-laying journey. Oates wanted to march some of the ponies as far south as they could go, then kill them and depot their carcasses for meat for men and dogs for the following season. Scott, again showing signs of squeamishness, preferred the idea of getting all the ponies safely back to Cape Evans for the winter.

Oates was sharing a tent with Gran, the young Norwegian, and Petty Officer Keohane. Sitting on his sleeping-bag before turning in, probably puffing away at his pipe, Oates recorded a few thoughts for his mother. 'The surface of the barrier is very bad for travelling as the summer sun has melted the crust on the snow to a certain extent and the ponies break through almost to their knees . . . These poor ponies are having a perfectly wretched time they have their summer coats on and this wind which is blowing now is bitterly cold for them I don't know how they will get on atal, the dogs have bucked up a lot but don't drag much of a load. These reindeer sleeping bags are beastly smelly things but wonderfully warm in fact you could not get any sleep without one. I am very fit indeed it is marvellous how little one feels the cold I suppose it is owing to always being out in it. I have had no snow blindness yet as most people have and I hardly wear goggles atal the reason of this is I think that my eyes are sunk fairly well into my head and so don't get affected so quickly. This is a wonderful country and a great delight to travel in it but one can hardly call it travelling for pleasure with 8 ponies to look after and if you take off your mitts you lose the use of your hands almost at once.'⁶

The next day the dog team returned from the attempt to get the snow shoes, unable to get back to Cape Evans because of the break up of the sea ice. In fact the whole party would have to wait for the sea ice to freeze over again at the end of the season before they would be able to rejoin

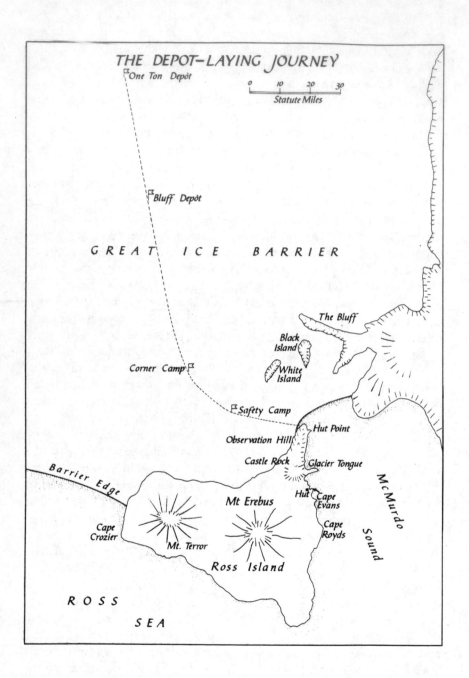

THE DEPOT–LAYING JOURNEY

One Ton Depôt

0   10   20   30
Statute Miles

Bluff Depôt

GREAT   ICE   BARRIER

The Bluff

Black
Island

Corner Camp

White
Island

Safety Camp

Hut Point

Observation Hill

Castle Rock

Glacier Tongue

Barrier Edge

McMurdo

Mt Erebus

Hut   Cape
Evans

Cape
Crozier

Mt. Terror

Cape
Royds

Sound

Ross Island

ROSS

SEA

their comrades. No extra pony snow shoes were therefore available.

Next day they turned out at 7 a.m., but progress was slow as the surface was too soft for the ponies. It was decided to travel by night instead, when the temperatures would be lower and the surfaces firmer. Moreover, this plan had another advantage: the ponies would rest in the comparatively higher daytime temperatures. Midnight marching did not involve darkness, of course – most of the time the sun was low on the horizon. Once again the pony shoes were tried on Bowers's pony – and once again Scott saw them as the answer to their prayers, concluding, 'It is trying to feel that so great a help to our work has been left at the station'.[7] One wonders who was responsible for this omission: Oates presumably, since he seems to have had a rooted objection to the pony snow-shoes (probably because they would have been so difficult to put on to temperamental ponies).

Scott painted a very heart-rending picture of the shoeless ponies' plight. 'Now and again they have to stop, and it is horrid to see them half engulfed in snow, panting and heaving from the strain. Now and again one falls and lies trembling and temporarily exhausted.'[8] Scott clearly thought the snow-shoes would have made a great difference to the ponies' performance. Yet he acquiesced in the face of Oates's opposition to the idea. Perhaps this is a sign of Oates's power in matters relating to things equine – or evidence that Scott could accept advice even if it contradicted his own opinion?

On 4 February Oates experienced his first Antarctic blizzard. There was a sudden rise in temperature (in this case from zero° F to about + 24°F) and a driving wind. Cherry-Garrard described it as 'raging chaos. It is blowing a full gale: the air is full of falling snow, and the wind drives this along and adds to it the loose snow which is lying on the surface of the Barrier. Fight your way a few steps from the tent, and it will be gone. Lose your sense of direction and there is nothing to guide you back.'[9] In such circumstances, the party could only lie up in camp. Most slept, dreamed or read, rousing themselves for meals, but Oates was kept busy tending the ponies. The dogs enjoyed blizzards as a rest, curling up in the snow and sleeping: for the ponies the suffering was intense. 'During this first blizzard', Cherry-Garrard recalled, 'all our ponies were weakened and two of them became practically useless.'[10]

Three days later, they dug out the sledges and the march resumed. The average march was ten to twelve miles a day, but the weakened ponies were finding it desperately hard going. Scott had the idea of building low walls to the south of the ponies when they were at rest, and these proved a good protection against wind and drift. The surface hardened, the going was better, and Oates pressed his argument for going on with some ponies as far south as possible, and killing them there. Scott disagreed, and on 13 February he sent Evans, Keohane and Forde back with the weakest ponies: Blossom, Blucher and Jimmy Pigg. The outward party now consisted of the dog teams still driven by Wilson and Meares, and five ponies: Scott with Nobby, Oates with Punch, Bowers with Uncle Bill, Gran with Weary Willie and Cherry-Garrard with Guts. Oates found himself sharing a tent with Bowers and Gran. It is to be hoped that Bowers's efficiency compensated for Gran's adolescent casualness, for Oates had found Gran both 'dirty and lazy' as a tent-mate and had one or two rows with him. Gran had some difficulties on the expedition as the youngest, and as a Norwegian his position was bound to be awkward. At one point Scott gave him a public wigging for his alleged laziness. Bowers felt sorry for him, believing that 'he always meant well' and 'a year at an English public school would have worked wonders for him as he is in every respect a nice fellow'.[11]

On this sledging journey, Gran believed that Oates's dislike of him was due to his general xenophobia, and once Gran assured him that, in the event of a war, he would fight for England without a moment's hesitation, Oates took his hand. 'With that, the closed book was opened, and from that moment, Oates and I were the best of friends',[12] Gran recalled. Bowers did a lot to reconcile the two playing Wilson's usual role of Christian arbitrator. Sharing a tent was obviously a way of getting to know a man intimately, very fast, and an Antarctic journey made enough demands on one's physical and mental powers without the additional problem of human conflicts.

Scott gives us a detailed picture of the daily – or rather, the nightly – routine on the march. 'We turn out of our sleeping bags about 9 p.m. Somewhere about 11.30 I shout to the Soldier, "How are things?" There is a response suggesting readiness and soon after figures are busy amongst sledges and ponies. It is chilling work for the fingers and not too warm for the feet. The rugs come off the animals, the harness is put on, tents and camp equipment are loaded on the sledges, nosebags filled for the next halt; one by one the animals are taken off the picketing rope and yoked to the sledge. Oates watches his animal warily, reluctant to keep such a nervous creature standing in the traces. If one is prompt one feels impatient and fretful whilst watching one's tardy fellows. Wilson and Meares hang about ready to help with odds and ends. Still we wait: the picketing lines must be gathered up, a few pony puttees need adjustment, a party has been slow striking their tent. With numbed fingers on our horse's bridle and the animal striving to turn its head from the wind one feels resentful.'[13]

Scott's account, apart from bringing to life the detail of the work, is riddled with the nervous irritation which men feel under great strain. At last, the caravan starts, some ponies steadily, some with a rush. 'Finneskoe[14] give poor foothold . . . and for a minute or two drivers have difficulty in maintaining the pace on their feet. Movement is warming, and in ten minutes the column has settled itself to steady marching . . . As the end of the half march approaches I get out my whistle. Then at a shrill blast Bowers wheels slightly to the left, his tent mates lead still farther out to get the distance right for the picket lines . . . [which] are run across at right angles to the line of our advance and secured to the two sledges at each end. In a few minutes ponies are on the lines covered, tents are up again, and cookers going.'[15]

Meanwhile the dog drivers, who were left behind for a long cold wait at the previous camp to give the ponies a head start, had been coming up behind and generally arrived at the lunch camp immediately after the horses. It is a telling fact that the dogs had to be held back to keep pace with the ponies, and that at the end of the second march, the dogs could be left simply to curl up in the snow, while snow walls had to be dug for the ponies – a precious expenditure of energy for men already tired and anxious to get to the warmth of tent and supper.

The dogs could be devils, however. On Tuesday, 14 February, Wilson noticed that 'Weary Willie, led by Gran, foundered just as Meares with his team of dogs was passing. The whole team turned into wolves like a wink and made for the horse as it lay in the snow and were all on top of it in a moment notwithstanding all that Meares could do to check them. They knew at once, as they always do, that the horse was done and easy prey, Gran and Meares both broke their sticks on the dogs' heads and the horse kicked and bit at them, they were at last driven off, but not before the poor beast of a horse had been pretty severely bitten.'[16] After lunch they made only three-quarters of a mile before abandoning the march. Weary Willie, covered with blood, and looking very sick, simply could not go on, and small wonder.

The next day he managed seven and a half miles, but he was giving out, and so were some of the others. They were thin and very hungry; their rations were unsatisfactory, and the autumn temperatures and winds were beyond their strength. Their hunger was well understood by Wilson. 'I think their compressed fodder isn't very feeding for them. While we were all asleep today, [one horse] ate his hobble, then got to a bale of fodder, and then got to one of our canvas tanks of biscuit and ate a lot of them . . . [he also] ate a whole cloth puttee the other day and has eaten endless head ropes and his picketing line. Now he is on a steel wire.'[17]

Scott's comment on the attack on Weary Willie was that 'the incident is deplorable and the blame widespread. I find Weary Willie's load was much heavier than the other ponies. I blame myself for not supervising these matters more effectively and for allowing Weary Willie to get so far behind.' Whether or not Oates was to blame in any way is impossible to judge. What is certain is that Scott and Oates had been irritating each other at various times. When average daily marches were well below ten miles, Scott had recorded, 'I consulted Oates as to distance and he cheerfully proposed 15 miles for the day! This piqued me somewhat'.[18] Oates's sardonic sense of humour was not likely to be appreciated by Scott, in whom an earnest seriousness and jangling nerves were fighting a continual battle on the march.

At 79° 2½' South, they made a large depot, called One Ton because of the amount of stores it contained. Scott now proposed turning back. Oates disagreed. His plan would be to despatch Weary Willie, who seemed virtually finished, and then march further on with the remaining horses, making a depot further south.

'I have had more than enough of this cruelty to animals,' was Scott's reply, 'and I'm not going to defy my feelings for the sake of a few days' march.'

'I'm afraid you'll regret, it, sir,' said Oates in the end.

'Regret it or not, my dear Oates,' Scott answered, 'I've made up my mind, like a Christian.'[19]

This exchange, witnessed by Gran, was a most crucial moment in expedition planning. Oates's impulse was more frighteningly, more deadly accurate than he could possibly have guessed. If One Ton Depot had been moved even a bare eleven miles further south, the whole outcome of Scott's expedition could have been very different.

Scott's reaction to this argument appears in his diary. 'The Soldier takes a gloomy view of everything, but I've come to see that this is characteristic of him. In spite of it he pays every attention to the weaker horses . . . all is well with us except the condition of the ponies. The more I see of the matter the more certain I am that we must save all the ponies to get better value out of them next year. It would have been ridiculous to have worked some out this year as the Soldier wished. Even now I feel we went too far with the first three.'[20] As he paused before starting the journey back to Cape Evans, Scott remarked how a spell of cold weather

142

had caused a lot of frostbite – even to the usually immune Bowers. And 'Oates's nose is always on the point of being frostbitten . . . I have been wondering how I shall stick the summit again, this cold spell gives ideas'.[21]

He soon seems to have put such thoughts behind him and decided to make for base with all speed. Base would have, for the time being, to be Hut Point, for the fifteen miles or so separating it from Cape Evans was at the moment open sea, and would only freeze up again towards the end of March. Scott was anxious to get back to hear of Campbell's party, who would have been deposited on King Edward VII Land by now. The *Terra Nova*, returning from this task, would bring news of them. Scott therefore decided to hasten back with the dog teams, accompanied by Meares, Wilson and Cherry-Garrard, leaving Oates, Bowers and Gran to plod back in their own time with the five exhausted ponies. Scott made excellent time with his dogs – completing the 130-mile journey in four days. It took the pony party more than twice as long.

The pony journey back was companionable, but not without its irritations. Often the ponies would kick over the walls which men had sweated to build for their protection. 'One cannot be angry with the silly beggars – Titus says a horse has practically no reasoning power, the thing to do is simply to throw up another wall and keep on at it.'[22] Bowers was very worried that they would lose Weary Willie 'but I took hope from the fact that Titus, who is usually pretty pessimistic, had not yet given up hopes of getting him back alive'. However, Oates did not believe that the three ponies who had been sent back earlier would survive, and had bet Gran a biscuit that Blucher would not make it. Now they came across a cairn with a fodder bale on the top, with a note from Evans recording Blossom's death. Another cairn a few miles away bore witness to the fact that Blucher, too, had succumbed.

Bowers recorded the frequent mirages that they experienced on this part of the journey. Small waves of crust called *sastrugi*, only a foot or so high and easy enough to walk over, looked like immense ridges. Some old horse droppings, distorted by the trick of light, could seem to be a herd of cattle on the horizon. At one stage they thought they had caught up with the dog-team, but the dark object in the snow ahead turned out to be a biscuit tin.

On 25 February, Safety Camp at last appeared, and once the animals saw it they never stopped. Wilson and Meares were there to welcome them, having come back out from Hut Point.

The news they brought was a great shock. At Hut Point Scott had found a letter from Campbell. In the Bay of Whales, about 500 miles away across the Ross Sea, he had come across Amundsen setting up his camp. They exchanged courtesies and Amundsen invited Campbell to share his site (King Edward's Land having proved inaccessible) but Campbell was not disposed to fraternize and had accordingly declined. He and his party disembarked instead at Cape Adare, and the ship brought his letter back to Hut Point before leaving for New Zealand. The ship also disembarked two ponies, Hackenschmidt and Jehu at Cape Evans. Campbell had decided he could not use them. They had to be swum ashore at Cape Evans and were resuscitated after this ordeal with half a bottle of brandy apiece.

The implications of Amundsen's arrival were clear and Wilson was not slow to see them. If Amundsen was lucky with his dogs, thought Wilson, 'he will probably reach the Pole this year, earlier than we can, for not only will he travel much faster with dogs and expert ski-runners then we shall with ponies, but he will be able to start earlier than we can as we don't want to expose the ponies to any October temperatures'.[23] Scott set his jaw in the face of the news and declared that 'the proper, as well as the wiser, course for us is to proceed exactly as though this had not happened'.[24] In some senses, his reaction is understandable and indeed admirable – it shows his integrity and fortitude. To reorganize hastily in the face of Amundsen's challenge might well be the height of folly. Scott had aims other than to be first at the Pole. And from the time that Amundsen's plans became known it must have been clear that he was almost certain to get there first. So Scott's refusal to acknowledge the race was, within the traditional British canon of behaviour, both graceful and gritty. Unfortunately, both he and most of his men still wanted, in their heart of hearts, to win.

The arrival of the news about Amundsen seems to have made Scott rather defensively a prisoner of his plans and preconceptions. He does not seem to accept the implications of events on the depot-laying journey: the rapid deterioration of the ponies, the speed of the dogs, the way the men got so easily frostbitten in a cold spell. What is more, though he considered the sledging rations for the men were satisfactory, he had not yet seen what a difference the exhausting business of man-hauling would make in its claims on stamina. There had been no man-hauling during the depot-laying journey.

As for the life line of depots, he had decided to spare the ponies any further suffering rather than push on and establish a depot as far south as possible. It was almost as if the problem of getting to the Pole, and the awful uncertainty about who would get there first, distracted him from the much more important consideration of how the Polar party was to get back. Scott's decision to try and ignore Amundsen's challenge, and

144

his virtual refusal to discuss it, meant also that he undertook a great personal burden of emotional and mental strain. Suppressed anger and anxiety are not good for anybody, least of all a man to whom leadership might sometimes seem a martyrdom. In the war of nerves, too, Amundsen was bound to win.

However, Scott had to conquer his nerves and organize the business of getting the remaining men, dogs and ponies back to Hut Point from Safety Camp. He was not in a good temper. 'Except for our tent camp routine is slack. Shall have to tell people that we are out on business, not picnicking.'[25] A blizzard held them up for two days, and had a disastrous effect on the ponies. 'The ravages of the blizzard became evident. The animals were terribly emaciated, and Weary Willie was in a pitiable condition.' Scott was anxious to get back to Hut Point and shelter as soon as possible, and decided to send the dogs first and then the ponies. Alas, Weary Willie collapsed almost at once, even though he had no load to pull. Scott decided to stay behind to nurse him with Oates and Gran, and sent Bowers, Crean and Cherry-Garrard on ahead with the other ponies. Wilson and Meares had already started with the dogs.

Wilson had great misgivings about the state of the sea-ice which they had to cross to reach Hut Point. It was developing sinister thaw-pools and he 'didn't believe that the sea ice would still be safe . . . without making a very big detour round the Cape Armitage thaw pool – and this point I urged – but I was overruled'.[26] Scott did, however, tell Wilson he was to use his initiative if trouble threatened. (An unusual concession in an expedition run by the British Navy.) Wilson soon came across 'an area broken up by fine thread-like cracks evidently quite fresh . . . we stopped to consider and found that the cracks in the ice we were on were actually working up and down about an inch with the rise and fall of the swell. . . I knew we must get off it at once in case the tide turned in the next half hour, when each crack would open up into a wide lead of open water and we should find ourselves on an isolated floe.'[27]

Wilson accordingly made a sharp right-angled turn – across the path of the pony party who were following only half a mile away – and scrambled up off the treacherous ice onto the reassuring rocks. This would leave half a mile of rock to cross before reaching the hut – the sledges being carried by hand and the dogs led in couples. 'A very long job', as Wilson remarked, but certainly better than finding one's party adrift on an ice floe. He now scrambled back to the edge of the ice to try and improve the path for the ponies, whom he assumed would have followed him. He must have been appalled at what he saw.

'They were miles out . . . still trying to reach Hut Point by the sea ice round Cape Armitage thaw pool, and on the ice which was showing a working crack every 30 paces. I couldn't understand how Scott could do such a thing.'[28] Of course, it wasn't Scott, but Bowers who was leading the pony party; Bowers who despite his many excellences was very inexperienced on ice. Bowers had been puzzled by the dogs' sudden right turn. 'Unfortunately the dogs misunderstood their orders and, instead of piloting us, dashed off on their own. We saw them in the distance in the direction of the old seal crack. Having crossed this they wheeled to the right in the direction of Cape Armitage and disappeared into a black indefinite mist, which seemed to pervade everything in that direction.'[29]

So Bowers, following Scott's orders, pushed on across the cracking sea ice with animals so tired as to need frequent stops. Eventually, a moving crack persuaded him to turn back, and camp on the safer ice near the shore. Poor Bowers: it was a menacing scene. 'We could see nothing owing to a black mist . . . it was a beastly march back: dark, gloomy and depressing.' He took the party as near the barrier edge as they could manage, and camped on what he considered to be safe old ice. The ponies could go no further; they were exhausted. As for the men, they were so numbed that when Bowers made the cocoa with curry-powder by mistake, Crean did not even notice. Two hours later Bowers awoke, made uneasy by a strange noise, and leapt out of the tent, to find his party marooned on a bobbing ice floe, with black tongues of water everywhere, and nothing solid as far as the eye could see. 'The floe on which we were had split right under our picketing line and cut poor Guts's wall in half. Guts himself had gone, and a dark streak of water alone showed the place where the ice had opened under him.'[30]

At about the same time as Guts plunged to his death in the icy water, Weary Willie gave up the ghost, despite the unremitting care of Oates, Scott and Gran. 'It is hard to have got him back so far only for this. It is clear that these blizzards are terrible for the poor animals', wrote Scott. 'It makes a late start *necessary for next year* . . . Now every effort must be bent on saving the remaining animals, and it will be good luck if we get four back to Cape Evans or even three.'[31] His sense of foreboding was amply justified the following day, when he found open water right up to the Barrier edge. Wilson and Meares, clambering round by the rocks, joined him and there was a council of war. In the midst of this they espied a solitary figure approaching, which turned out to be Crean, who had left Bowers and Cherry-Garrard on the floe with the three remaining ponies and sledges and jumped from floe to floe to get back with the news. There were now six men present and only three sleeping bags, so Wilson, Gran and Meares were sent back to Hut Point to deal with the

28. With Birdie Bowers and Mrs Scott on board the *Terra Nova*. 'The visitors and women are a great nuisance as we can't get really dirty.' (L. E. G. Oates).

27. The *Terra Nova* taking on coal at Cardiff.

29. Oates on board the *Terra Nova* with the ponies on the upper deck. 'The ponies fitted in splendidly and were very good, not giving the slightest trouble. . . . Scott was kind enough to say he was pleased. I only pray we don't have heavy weather going South, or there is bound to be trouble.'

30. Landing the ponies. Oates is in the background wearing a white shirt and leaning on the rail.

31. Cherry-Garrard with his pony, *Michael*, about whom he commented, 'Life was a constant source of wonder to him.'

32. Harnessing *Michael*. Cherry-Garrard is at the pony's head, and Oates is standing by the sledge. 'Dear old Titus, unperturbable as ever; never hasty, never angry, but soothing the animal, and determined to get the best out of most unpromising material in his endeavour to do his simple duty.' (T. Griffith Taylor)

dogs and their sledge. Oates and Crean stayed with Scott to try and effect a rescue.

Meanwhile, Bowers and Cherry-Garrard were waiting on the ice with their ponies and sledges. They had managed to get quite close to the shore by jumping their ponies across narrow cracks, and using the sledge as a bridge. They could easily have saved their own skins. But because Bowers was determined to save the sledges and above all the ponies, so he and Cherry-Garrard stayed put, fed the ponies, and tried to ignore the attentions of a pack of killer whales who had turned up, attracted no doubt by the bait of the drowned pony, Guts Skua gulls also settled down to wait nearby, obviously regarding the beleaguered party as certain carrion. 'It resolved itself into a question of speed, whether the wind or Captain Scott would reach us first.'[32]

Scott's party got a line to Bowers and Cherry-Garrard and ordered them ashore. 'What about the ponies and sledges?' asked Bowers. 'I don't care a damn about the ponies and sledges,' answered Scott. 'It's you I want, and I am going to see you safe here up on the Barrier before I do anything else.'[33] So they came ashore – to a profusely emotional welcome from Scott. 'He had been blaming himself for our deaths', commented Bowers, 'and here we were very much alive.'[34] Next they set about salvaging the sledges and the gear, which took most of the night. The ponies, however, presented a great problem. To get them ashore was virtually impossible across a gap of blue ice, with a steep drop down from the floe. The men dug madly, trying to build a causeway for the animals, but in the end Scott ordered them to stop, as a black lane of water opened up between the ponies and their rescuers.

After a brief pause for a few hours' exhausted sleep, they awoke to find that the ponies on their floe had drifted about a mile away. All agreed to one last attempt to get them ashore by jumping them from floe to floe. Scott's diary completes the saga. 'We found it easy enough to get down to the poor animals . . . I discovered what I thought a practicable way to land a pony but the others meanwhile, a little overwrought, tried to leap Punch over a gap. The poor beast fell in; eventually we had to kill him – it was awful.'[35] Oates had to kill the struggling pony in the water with an ice pick. 'We saved one pony, for a time I thought we should get both, but Bowers' poor animal slipped at a jump and plunged into the water: we dragged him out onto some brash ice – killer whales all about us in an intense state of excitement.[36] Scott ordered Oates and Bowers up onto the land but they stayed, still trying to get the horse to rise. 'He's done,' said Oates. 'We'll never get him up alive'.

Bowers was in a state of great anguish, for Uncle Bill was his own pony.

147

'I said, "I can't leave him to be eaten alive by those whales." There was a pick lying up on the floe. Titus said, "I shall be sick if I have to kill another horse like I did the last". I had no intention that anybody should kill my own horse but myself, and getting the pick I struck where Titus told me. I made sure of my job before we ran up and jumped the opening in the Barrier, carrying a blood-stained pick-axe instead of leading the pony I had almost considered safe. . . We returned to our old camp that night (2 March) with Nobby, the only one saved of the five that left One Ton Depot.'[37]

Scott was desolate. 'The events of the past 48 hours bid fair to wreck the Expedition.'[38] He considered that he had lost the best of his pony transport, and that since dogs and motors were a disappointment, disaster threatened. He ended his account of the affair with a buried quotation. 'Everything out of joint with the loss of the ponies.' He may not consciously have thought of Hamlet, but it is tempting to do so:

> The time is out of joint
> O cursed spite
> That ever I was born to set it right

In some ways Scott resembles Hamlet, not least in his lacerating sensitivity and the paralyzing conviction that he is fortune's fool.

Wilson evolved for himself a much more Christian interpretation of events. 'I firmly believe that the whole train of what looked so like a series of petty mistakes and accidents was a beautiful prearranged plan in which each one of us took exactly the moves and no others that an Almighty hand intended each of us to take . . . the whole thing was just a beautiful piece of education on a very impressive scale.'[39] Scott and Wilson, both intellectuals, resorted to an account of events which dispersed and absolved individual human guilt. To be the tennis-ball of fate, or in the palm of an Almighty hand, is obviously to be beyond blame for events. Oates, who had never been much of a man for metaphysics, was still bitter when he looked back on the experience six months later. 'We lost 6 ponies including mine (Punch) which was a long way the best pony we had I was very upset the more so as I think he could have been saved if Scott had not been fussing to the extent he was, this pony was one of the ones drowned, the loss of the ponies was Scott's fault entirely.'

After the débâcle, a sad little party made their way to Hut Point. The hut had originally been built by Scott's 1902 expedition and used as a workroom (the company had lived on the ship, which was frozen into the sea-ice). Shackleton's *Nimrod* expedition had been forced to use it in

1907, and when the *Terra Nova* party had first visited it a few months previously, Scott had been appalled at the state in which it had been left. 'Everyone was disgusted with the offensive condition in which the hut had been left by the latest occupants – boxes full of excrement were found near the provisions and filth of a similar description was thick under the verandah and even in the corners of the hut itself. It's extraordinary to think that people could have lived in such a horrible manner and with such absence of regard for those to follow. It seems evident that in no case can we inhabit our old hut.'[40] A broken window had let in the blizzards of three years, but the gentler Wilson reckoned it 'only wanted cleaning out to be quite habitable.'[41] He was proved right, for Atkinson, returning early from the depot-laying journey because of an injured heel had set to and, together with Crean, left behind as his assistant, got the place habitable in a very short time.

It was lucky that they did, for Hut Point was to be their home for many weeks whilst they waited for the sea-ice to freeze over and pave their way back to Cape Evans, where the scientists had been working away steadily all the time. The curve of coastline linking Hut Point and Cape Evans had never been negotiated owing to great ice falls covering the lower slopes of Mount Erebus. They had to wait for the onset of winter when the sea would freeze: there was simply no other way to get there. Scott thought a crossing would be feasible in under three weeks – around 21 March. However, it was nearly a month after that before conditions were right. Till then, camping out in the *Discovery* hut was a challenge to everybody's ingenuity. 'It was wonderful what the rubbish tip yielded up,' wrote Cherry-Garrard, 'Bricks to build a blubber stove, a sheet of iron to put over the top of it, a length of stove piping to form a chimney. Somehow somebody made cement, and built the bricks together . . . an old door made a cook's table, old cases turned upside down made seats . . . at night we cleared the floor space and spread our bags.'[42] Oates spent some time seeing to the two remaining ponies, Jimmy Pigg and Nobby, but by and large he found the spell in the *Discovery* hut 'not a very exciting time.'

Evans, however, looked back on the time with genial amusement, remembering that Oates was full of 'Robinson Crusoe genius'.[43] At Hut Point they lived a good deal off seal meat, and took it in turns to cook. '[Oates], Meares and Debenham were first class cooks, and they were always content to serve up the "hoosh" or seal fry in a very British fashion. Their efforts were much appreciated. Others in their endeavours were not so successful, and one day when some "fancy dish" was being served up by a "crank" cook, Oates deliberately stood within earshot of the company and said in a loud voice: "Some of our party, who rather fancy themselves as cooks, quite spoil the meals by messing up the food in their attempts to produce original dishes." The hint was taken, and we had no more aspirants for Paris restaurant cooking.'[44]

On 4 March Griffith-Taylor's geographical party arrived at the hut, which made a total of sixteen souls in rather spartan conditions. Scott was already growing impatient, but the sea was extraordinarily slow to freeze owing to high winds. Overcrowded, and with some of the season's failures and conflicts still in the air, the hut became less and less tolerable to him. In mid-April he risked it and dashed across the new ice with an advanced party, which included Bowers. They were lucky, and reached Cape Evans safely, where their comrades turned out to greet them. 'Ponting's face was a study as he ran up', wrote Bowers. 'He failed to recognise any of us and stopped dead with a blank look – as he admitted afterwards, he thought it was the Norwegian expedition for the space of a moment.'

'Inside [the Hut] looked tremendous, and we looked at our grimy selves in a glass for the first time for three months; no wonder Ponting did not recognise the ruffians. He photographed a group of us. We ate heartily and had hot baths and generally civilised ourselves. I have since concluded that the hut is the finest place in the Southern Hemisphere, but then I could not shake down to it at once. I hankered for a sleeping-bag out in the snow, or for the blubbery atmosphere of Hut Point. I expect that the truth of the matter was that all my special pals, Bill, Cherry, Titus and Atch, had been left behind.'[45]

Bower's 'special pals' duly joined him on 21 April, and the expedition, now all re-united with the exception of Campbell's party (which was to winter in their own hut at Cape Adare) settled down to the monotony and rigours of an Antarctic winter. Oates found that one pony, Hackenschmidt, who had been swum ashore at Cape Evans after being returned by Campbell, had died. There seemed to be no reason for his death. Some unkind souls reckoned he had died out of cussedness. But probably the shock of being swum ashore was too great and he found it impossible to recover properly.

This left ten ponies, including the two which had survived the depot-laying journey, to nurse through the winter. Unfortunately, as was to become all too apparent, some of these survivors were to prove even more cussed than Hackenschmidt, and vented their ill-temper on their masters rather than themselves. Christopher was one such devil, and Jehu was practically falling to pieces with old age and debility. Oates's feelings must have been very bitter as he surveyed his charges.

At least the ponies were comfortably accommodated, for in Oates's absence, Anton, with the help of Lashly, had refined the furnishing of the stables. Neat stalls were now arranged along the whole length of the lean to, with soundly-boarded sides and the front well covered with tin sheet to defeat the 'cribbers' (ponies who gnawed at their mangers). Scott surveyed the work with a sigh 'to think of the stalls that must now remain empty.'[46] On his return, Oates reorganized the stable, making bigger stalls, as the ten surviving ponies would benefit, in terms of space, from the demise of their fellows. Almost immediately Scott allotted the ponies for exercise – a job which sounds straightforward and leisurely, like taking a dog for a walk. In fact it could prove both exhausting and irritating, as the normally patient and tolerant Wilson records.

'Today took horse out and a nuisance he was. Having had no exercise for 3 days and feeling the breeze very much with his new, and at present thin, coat, and wanting to go back every minute of the two hours he was out he played all sorts of pranks. His favourite game is first to shake his head when he thinks you are off your guard; this hits you either in the chest or in the face or in the stomach, and then he tries to rear, comes down with straight forelegs on your feet, which are by this time just in the right place, and then you see his heels somewhere over your left shoulder. The only thing to do is to hold him tight by his head with a stiff arm, so that one is out of reach of his head and his legs . . . One hasn't very much control over the animals really as they have no bits, and one merely hangs on to a halter or a headstall. Some of them . . . seem to have learned every trick a horse ever knew. The comfort is that they all give up these tricks when they have been in harness with a loaded sledge on the Barrier for a few days . . . None of the horses are ever hit whatever they do, and some of them are beginning to understand it a little for it is a change to them evidently. They all seem to have been ill-treated all their lives up till now.'[47]

Apart from occasional horse-exercising, the men kept fit, while there was still light (for the light was gradually waning and would soon disappear entirely) by playing football. Oates was an enthusiastic participant, and whenever he was captain, always chose big, burly Petty Officer Evans first. 'Go on, Taff, break 'em up!' Oates would exhort and receive a Welsh 'Right O Sir' in reply as Taff set off to demolish the opposition. On 6 May, however, Oates strained a tendon in the back of his leg. So no doubt football was over for a while and Oates limped back to the stables where, as Scott observed, he never spared himself. 'Oates's whole heart is in the ponies. He is really devoted to their care, and I believe will produce them in the best possible form for the sledging season. Opening out the stores, installing a blubber stove, has kept *him* busy, whilst his satellite, Anton, is ever at work in the stables – an excellent little man.'[48]

Notes and references
1 R. F. Scott, diary, 24 January 1911.
2 *Ibid.,* 27 January 1911.
3 *Ibid.,* 28 January 1911
4 *Ibid.,* 30 January 1911.
5 *Ibid .,* 31 January 1911.
6 Oates is referring here to one of the great dangers of Antarctic travel – frostbite. When in the intense cold the circulation to exposed parts of the body is altered and in extreme cases that part will 'die'. First the skin turns a pale yellow colour and gradually goes blue. The unthawing process is extremely painful. In the second stage blisters appear and the fluid itself may freeze. The pain is intense. In the third stage gangrene sets in and amputation is the only cure.
7 R. F. Scott, *op. cit.,* 3 February 1911.
8 *Ibid.*
9 A. Cherry-Garrard, *The Worst Journey in the World,* p.113.
10 *Ibid.*
11 H. R. Bowers, diary.
12 Tryggve Gran, *Fra Tjuagutt til Sydpolfarer,* p. 240.
13 R. F. Scott, *op. cit.,* 10 February 1911.
14 Finneskoe. These were boots made of reindeer skin and lined with dried sedge to absorb moisture and insulate the feet, worn during the day for both marching and skiing. It was essential that they were dried at night along with the day socks. Night socks had to be worn in the sleeping bag to give protection against frostbite.
15 R. F. Scott, *op. cit.,* 10 February 1911.
16 E. A. Wilson, diary, 14 February 1911.
17 *Ibid.,* 15 February 1911.
18 R. F. Scott, diary, 14 February 1911.
19 Quoted by Roland Huntford in *Scott and Amundsen,* p. 367.
20 R. F. Scott, diary, 15 February 1911.
21 *Ibid .,* 17 February 1911.
22 Quoted by A. Cherry-Garrard, *op. cit.,* pp. 117-23, from a letter written by H. R. Bowers, *The Return of the Pony Party from One Ton Depot.*
23 E. A. Wilson, diary, 22 February 1911.
24 R. F. Scott, diary, 22 February 1911.
25 *Ibid.*
26 E. A. Wilson, diary, 28 February 1911.

27 *Ibid.*

28 *Ibid.*

29 Quoted by A. Cherry-Garrard, *op. cit.*, pp. 138-45, from a letter written by H. R. Bowers to his home.

30 *Ibid.*

31 R. F. Scott, diary, 1 March 1911.

32 H. R. Bowers, *op. cit.*

33 *Ibid.*

34 *Ibid.*

35 R. F. Scott, diary, 3 March 1911.

36 *Ibid.*

37 H. R. Bowers, *op. cit.*

38 R. F. Scott, diary, 2 March 1911.

39 E. A. Wilson, diary, 28 February 1911.

40 R. F. Scott, diary, 15 January 1911.

41 E. A. Wilson, diary, 27 January 1911.

42 A. Cherry-Garrard, *op.cit.*, p. 158.

43 Commander Evans, *My Recollections of a Gallant Comrade*, a booklet reprinted from *Strand Magazine*, December 1913.

44 *Ibid.*

45 H. R. Bowers quoted by A. Cherry-Garrard, *op. cit.*, p173.

46 R.F. Scott, diary, 13 April 1911.

47 E. A. Wilson, diary, 29 September 1911.

48 R. F. Scott, diary, 28 April 1911.

9

Winter at Cape Evans

By 13 May 1911, the whole wintering party was complete: twenty-five men who were to spend five months crowded together in a hut 50 ft long, 25 ft wide, and 8 ft to the eaves. It was built of several thicknesses of tongued and grooved boards, with an insulating layer of dried seaweed, quilted in sackcloth, in between. The roof was double boarded, also insulated with seaweed quilting, and covered with rubberoid, and the floor also double-boarded and insulated in the same way, and covered with linoleum.

To keep out draughts, volcanic sand was piled up around the base of the walls. There were two double windows, and at the west end, two doors and a small lobby, which housed the acetylene gas plant which fuelled the lighting system. The lobby led to a further area, a sort of covered alleyway built of boxes of stores (unopened crates of stores were stacked outside). Men coming in from outdoors would shake the snow off their boots and outer clothes in this alley. One had to pass through three doors in order to enter the hut, and so the draughts and heatloss of an opening door was cut down to a minimum.

Inside, the hut was divided by a shelved wall (for storage) into two large rooms, perpetuating, at this remote corner of the world, the British class structure. There was the Mess Deck, where nine men lived and ate, warmed by the cook's galley. The officers' quarters or Wardroom was dominated by a long table. Against the far sides of this room were open cubicles with sleeping bunks (iron-frame spring beds with wool mattresses). There was not much privacy. Scott had a 6 ft square area curtained off where he could be found working at his linoleum-covered collapsible table, whilst sledge chronometers ticked around him. 'Fur mittens, fur boots, woollen undergarments, draped the walls. His old navy great-coat was his bedspread. "It is twenty-three years old and I confess an affection for it." Under the bed, as if he was a transient visitor to the region, was a brown leather suit case, labelled. Around him at eye level were photographs of his wife and son, his mother, sister, and nieces. His books were by Hardy and Galsworthy, and the little Browning volume.'¹

Ponting had his own darkroom, 6 by 8 ft, with a sink, developing dishes, and a small carbide gas plant which generated his own lighting supply, independent of the hut. He had built and equipped his darkroom with great care, and slept as well as worked in it. 'This room was always kept spotlessly clean and neat, for though I cannot claim excessive orderliness in other respects to be one of my redeeming points, yet in matters photographic untidiness is abhorrent to me.'² Next to the darkroom was Atkinson's laboratory with a bench littered with microscopes, test tubes, etc for his work as a parasitologist and adjoining his area was 'Simpson's Corner' where the physicist held court, and tinkered with his various machines. 'Clockwork ticked everywhere. There were barometers, thermometers, thermographs, and a bewildering array of other scientific apparatus; and there were rows of electric batteries, and a petrol engine for running the dynamo which charged them.'³ Simpson's most extraordinary machine was Dine's Anemometer, an instrument which recorded each separate gust of wind by means of a vane attached to a 2-inch pipe which projected several feet above the roof. 'When blizzards raged,' Ponting recalled, 'the sighing and moaning and utterly unearthly sounds emitted by this tube at night were most depressing.'⁴

Opposite Simpson's bench was Wilson's corner, where he could be seen, from 5 a.m. onwards, reading, writing, and working at his sketches and watercolours. Nelson and Day shared a cubicle which was ornamented with many of the comforts of civilization, and Debenham, Griffith-Taylor and Gran, another. Gran begged a spare curtain from Ponting's darkroom, and hung it on a wire across the entrance to their cubicle. 'Whereupon Oates, scorning privacy and such "effeminate luxury" as he characterized this fitment, compared their cubicle to an "opium den" a "ladies' boudoir" and various other things expressive of his contempt. To these jibes the tenants listened with grins of delight, and retorted that he needn't be envious because he hadn't got the only curtain in the Antarctic for himself.'⁵

Oates, of course, scorned curtains. The bunk where he slept was conspicuous for its spartan simplicity: a pipe or two, a tin of baccy, a pair of socks, and various odd bits of harness and horse-tackle graced his corner. His only pin-up was a small portrait of Napoleon. He shared a large cubicle with Cherry-Garrard, Bowers, Meares and Atkinson, and it was known as 'The Tenements' because of its bare appearance. Debenham and Griffith-Taylor declared war on The Tenements and since scrapping was not allowed, the war had to be verbal. 'Griff was formidable opponent,' Debenham recalled, 'but he could never get a rise out of the Soldier, who was always imperturbable. "Poor old Griff", he would say as the disgruntled Griff threw himself noisily into his bunk – "Poor old Griff. Not a bad fellow," – pause – "but he's a bit *mouldy*". To which Griff would mutter a reply about "brutal and licentious soldiers".'[6]

Another of Oates's opponents in the verbal war was Birdie Bowers, who shared his cubicle. Bowers would wake up in the morning with a luxurious yawn, and then enquire. 'How's the hay this morning, Farmer?' There would be a long pause and then a crushing – and probably unprintable – reply. The Tenement dwellers saw themselves as true patriots, their creed was 'Down with Science, Sentiment and the Fair Sex'. In fact Oates provided a sociological definition for their community when he declared that the expedition was divided into 'gentlemen' and 'scientists'. Griffith-Taylor hit back when at the Midwinter Dinner he began a speech: 'Gentlemen . . . and non-scientists'.

The Australians were fond of provoking their chauvinistic opponents by discussing the hidebound traditions of the British Army, or the desirability of women's suffrage. In revenge Oates and Co. would invent all kinds of slanders concerning colonials, foreigners and scientists. An Australian visiting London, declared Atkinson, had been heard to remark, 'Change and decay in all around I see, except, O Lord, except in me'. The Tenement dwellers would often carol this in unison to drown any progressive political broadcasts from 'The Opium Den'. When the provocations became intolerable, a good-humoured physical assault would occasionally break out, despite the rules. 'Tonight Oates, Captain in a smart cavalry regiment, has been "scrapping" over chairs and tables with Debenham, a young Australian student', Scott recorded in his diary on Sunday, 14 May, by way of illustrating the 'general cordiality of the relations which exist among our people . . . there are no strained relations in this hut, and nothing more emphatically evident than the universally amicable spirit which is shown on all occasions'.[7]

This harmony was something almost all members remarked on, including Oates. 'We got on very well together and there was none of the quarrelling which usually accompanies a winter where a number of men are confined together in a dark hut.' Debenham attributed this air of harmony to 'the genius of Scott in exercising just the right amount of discipline with a minimum of formality, and even more to the character of Dr Wilson'.[8] It may be said that Scott was at his best in the hut during the long Antarctic winter, when inaction was inevitable and had to be accepted, when there were ample chances for him to take an interest in the work of the scientists, to exercise his considerable intellectual gifts with books and conversation, and to fraternize with both officers and men in an environment which was free from the strains, dangers and responsibilities of sledge travel.

At the end of this winter, he wrote to his wife that 'I am quite on my feet now . . . I feel mentally and physically fit for the work'.[9] In the early stages of the expedition, he admitted, 'I had lost confidence in myself',[10] but somehow the winter restored his sense of self-command. Even Gran, who had earlier provoked Scott's wrath and contempt, recalled that during the winter they were 'like a family of friends', and that he never heard a bad word while he was in the Antarctic. 'So, it couldn't have been better.'[11] This harmony in the hut was not maintained without effort, obviously, but no one indulged his irritation or negative impulses, and all destructive thoughts were thoroughly suppressed in the interests of the common good and a happy community. No mean achievement for men who had been through periods of hostility and impatience with each other.

Perhaps Wilson's contribution was the most important. Scott always listened to him, often deferred to his judgement, and felt that 'there is no member of our party so universally esteemed. He stands very high in the scale of human beings.'[12] Wilson was an excellent source of oil for troubled waters, and the man to whom everybody (including Scott) took their problems. 'Grievances there are bound to be and disagreements', Wilson wrote to his wife, 'but as long as everyone can keep them from boiling over I think we can rightly say that we have been extraordinarily free from any want of unity.'[13] Though Wilson was revered by his comrades, he was never treated with kid gloves. Oates and he forged their friendship in the most full-blooded scraps on the *Terra Nova*, and continued to bait each other at every opportunity. Oates liked a drink, and Wilson guarded the brandy, which was to be used for medicinal purposes only. Oates was always trying to think up ways of getting his hands on it, and on Napoleon's birthday he had proposed that a toast should be drunk in his honour. Wilson declared that this was merely an excuse for a drink – at which Oates complained that the medical faculty were so grudging with the brandy because they were saving it up for themselves.

One day Oates asked Atkinson what ailments might qualify for a prescription of brandy, and learnt that among other things, convulsive fits usually merited a dram or two. 'H'm. I saw a cat having a fit once', mused Oates, and walked away thoughtfully. Days later, when Wilson and some others were shovelling snow, Oates walked up to them and threw a most credible fit at Wilson's feet. The fit was rich in circumstantial detail repoduced from memories of the cat. Wilson's companions were instantly alarmed, but he simply leaned on his spade without any appearance of concern. 'Poor old Soldier's having a fit', he remarked. 'Rub some snow down the back of his neck: he'll soon get over it!'[14] and returned smilingly to his work.

Despite all this romping and teasing, the winter was not primarily a time for rest and relaxation. Only the evening hours were strictly speaking recreational. Every man had his work to occupy him, and if he had not, he would be wise to invent some. For Scott took a most emphatic interest in the work of his men. He was constantly watching them and assessing them and into his diary went not only details of their discoveries which intrigued him, but his own impressions of their abilities, energies and moral fibre. Scott drove himself remorselessly, and judged his men by the same rigorous standards he set himself. He was quick to be impressed but also alert for any signs of laziness, and when Gran was given a dressing-down on this subject, Wilson took him to one side and advised him never to look unemployed when Scott was about. If necessary, Wilson suggested, he should lace and re-lace his boots, giving the impression of industry.

Cherry-Garrard busied himself most usefully during the winter by resuscitating a journal called *The South Polar Times* which had sprung into being on Scott's *Discovery* Expedition. It contained articles, stories, poems, many of Wilson's beautiful drawings and a 'Letters from Readers' section. Oates wrote to the *South Polar Times*, a mock complaint about the conduct of some evening lectures which Scott had instituted. There were three of these lectures per week, and everyone in turn spoke about his special subject: Wilson about zoology, Atkinson on scurvy, Evans on Polar surveying, Wright on glaciology, Bowers on Polar clothing, Nelson on biology, Debenham on volcanoes, and so forth. Oates took up his pen to bring to the Editor's notice the 'regrettable direction' in which the lectures were tending.

'The lecturer shouts out the wildest theories. In a recent lecture, a harmless horticulturalist, by name Mendel, was dragged in and his small research mercilessly torn to pieces, built together again, and exaggerated until the gentle monk appeared to have attempted the solution of life itself. Had the refined cleric attended the lecture in spirit, I am convinced that he would have earnestly wished that he had never handled a pot of earth or a trowel in his life . . . A most painful scene was enacted the other night. Two heated scientists were seen shouting and hurling personal abuse at one another . . . Sir, I ask you to bring the full weight of your influential paper to bear, in order that these lectures may be carried on in a calmer and more dignified manner.'[15]

On 17 May it was Oates's turn to hold the floor. His subject was 'Horse Management' or rather, 'Horse Mismanagement', and almost the whole company turned out to hear what he had to say, for the idea of the normally silent Dragoon launching into public utterance was intriguing. He confounded all expectation by giving a most accomplished performance, and one moreover, which was not devoid of humour. He was, it was recalled, the only lecturer who made his audience laugh as well as informing them. He explained the plan of feeding the ponies 'soft' during the winter, and hardening them up in the spring. Grass and hay, he explained, were short on nutritive value, relative to their bulk. Oates showed how chaff, hot bran mash with oilcake or boiled oats, could be fed to the animals in winter – adding more of the greasy, energy-producing oil-cake and oats as spring approached. He also attacked the problem of training. However, he was known to object strongly to the length of the scientific lectures, and he wanted to fend off what he knew would be a tide of facetious questions at the end. (Just as he loved to tease the scientists by asking them silly time-wasting questions and treating them to his absurd theories.) So he finished his lecture with an anecdote.

'When I was a subaltern,' he recalled, 'I attended a lecture on the management of horses given by a veterinary surgeon. There were a number of farmers present. They asked a lot of foolish questions, and eventually the vet lost his temper. One farmer asked him, "What sort of grass-seeds were best to sow a tennis-lawn with?" The vet, now quite furious, replied, "Gentlemen, I am a veterinary surgeon, not a bally gardener".' Amidst laughter and applause Oates coyly informed his audience that they were to hear more from him another time, for, 'I have been fortunate in securing another night'.[16]

His second lecture expanded points raised by his first, and ended with yet another story. Oates recalled having been at a sophisticated dinner party, when a young lady arrived extremely late, and in a positive froth of embarrassment and apology. It was, she explained, the cab-horse: he wouldn't get on at all. 'Ah, perhaps he was a jibber', suggested her hostess. 'Oh, no,' smiled the damsel, all unknowing, 'he was a bugger. I heard the cabby say so several times.'[17]

The routine of evening lectures was enlivened occasionally by Ponting, who showed slides of his travels in Japan. The beauties of its landscape – and incidentally its womenfolk – were amply, and tastefully, illustrated. Such treats were most welcome and eagerly anticipated. 'Coming to the pictures tonight, dearie?' Oates would enquire to Meares.

(He often called Meares 'dearie' and Atkinson was sometimes known as 'Jane' – though the origins of this nickname remain shrouded in mystery.) Meares became Oates's inseparable companion during the winter months.

Though Meares had been responsible for buying the ponies, Oates never held it against him. For with his curious, enigmatic life of travelling about and exploring, his rejection of polite society, his scruffy unshaven appearance and his indignant individualism, Meares was very much a man after Oates's heart. They spent many an hour together at the blubber stove in the stable, Oates wearing his ancient balaclava and smoking his pipe as he helped Meares to prepare dog-pemmican out of seal meat. (They made about eight hundredweight of it.) They swapped stories, for they had both been involved in the Boer War. (Meares had served in the Scottish Horse as a trooper, and finally as a sergeant.) They also made a few piquant remarks about the travel arrangements of the present expedition. The photograph of them taken at the blubber stove was at a moment when Meares had just said that he reckoned Scott should buy a shilling book on transport. Scott overheard this remark, and was not pleased.

'Meares is a nice chap, very quiet and has travelled in Tibet, China and Siberia and is very interesting', was Oates's verdict. Wilson, in a letter home, remarked the 'Meares and Oates, the Dragoon, are just the finest men one could hope to meet'.[18] Oates's stable was not the only place where a private chat was possible. Ponting recalled a memorable talk he had had with Oates and Nelson in his darkroom. 'The point was raised as to what a man should do if he were to break down on the Polar Journey, thereby becoming a burden to others. Oates unhesitatingly and emphatically expressed the opinion that there was only one possible course – self-sacrifice. He thought that a pistol should be carried, and that "if anyone breaks down he should have the privilege of using it".'[19]

For Oates, being out in the stable was not just a convenient escape from society, and a place for dark thoughts. The ponies continued to give cause for anxiety. They had colic and parasites, and Bones, one of the best ponies, frightened his masters by a dramatic and sudden illness, including violent spasms of pain. He deteriorated fast, until he was lying stretched out at full length on the floor, 'twitching very horribly with the pain and from time to time raising his head and even scrambling to his feet when it grew intense'.[20] Oates gave him opium pills, heated sacks were placed on him, and Oates and Crean (who had been exercising the pony when it first became ill) could do no more than watch over him, hope and wait.

Scott visited him throughout the night, in a state of high anxiety for 'we cannot afford to lose a single pony – the margin of safety has already been far overstepped . . . we must keep all the animals alive or greatly risk failure'.[21] At around 3 a.m., the crisis seemed past. The horse took a drink, and Scott went to bed, much relieved. The next day the pony passed a ball of semi-fermented hay covered with mucus and containing tape worms, with a strip of the lining of the intestine attached to it. Oates thought a good many of the ponies might have worms and they considered means of worming them. The very next day Chinaman went off his feed and lay down twice. 'What on earth is it that is disturbing these poor beasts?'[22] wondered Scott.

He was desperately anxious about the ponies. On 8 May he had presented his plans for the Polar journey, which reflected his change of heart over transport. 'I'm afraid we can place but little reliance on our dog teams,' he wrote in his diary, reflecting 'ruefully on the provision of our transport. Well, one must suffer for errors of judgement.' He told his men that he had no faith in the dogs' ability to reach the Beardmore Glacier (despite their excellent performance on the return from the depot-laying journey). Of the motors, one lay at the bottom of the sea and the other two were plagued with minor faults and obviously could not be relied upon. Ponies were, therefore, the prime method of transport, and the point where they were to be killed was not yet decided. From then on it would have to be man-hauling. The men would probably have to pull their own sledges for the 10,000 ft climb up the Glacier onto the Polar Plateau. From the point at which the last ponies would most likely be killed, on or around the foot of the Beardmore Glacier, it meant a 1000 mile journey of man-hauling for the final Polar party – which was to be four men.

Bowers was pleased, looking forward to doing 'that plateau with man-haulage in these days of the supposed decadence of the British race.'[23] Wilson's only comment was mild disappointment that the late return of the Polar party (it was scheduled for 27 March) would mean that they would miss the ship, and therefore be unable to send letters home. The Polar party would have to return late because they would be forced to start late – 3 November – owing to the vulnerability of their ponies to the low spring temperatures.

The men's own human vulnerability to the low temperatures they would encounter on the return journey was another matter. So far, a gruelling journey in Antarctica in the later month of March, just as the winter was setting in, had never been attempted. Even if they had known of the suffering it would entail, most of them would gladly have embraced the experience, so thoroughly had their society bred in them a belief in manly indifference to rigours, and a contempt for the easy way, the super-soft refinements of civilization.

As Midwinter Day (22 June) drew near, the storms rampaged around Cape Evans, and the winds shrieked and howled in the pipe of Simpson's Anemometer. The hut fairly shook at times, and the party prepared a feast to celebrate the darkest point of the year. It was the equivalent of Christmas Day. Champagne replaced cocoa, and Clissold the cook quite excelled himself. Midwinter dinner began at 7 p.m., with seal soup as an entrée, and ended much later with liqueurs. They drank to the success of the expedition, and then everyone was called on to speak, working round the table clockwise, like the port. Fairly early in the proceedings Scott was 'obliged to request the omission of compliments', though he was obviously pleased that the scientists appreciated his support and interest.

Bowers, when his turn came, said he could not make a speech, but he had something to show them, whereupon four seamen entered with an enormous Christmas tree, made of pieces of ski-stick with penguin feather foliage. It bore flaming candles and crackers, and there was a toy for everyone. The presents had been prepared long before by Wilson's sister-in-law, and Oates got a present most suitable to his tastes, for the child is father of the man, and never since childhood had he been able to resist the pleasures of a popgun. He immediately embarked on an orgy of homicide, saying, 'If you want to please me very much, you will fall down when I shoot you',[26] to each of his intended victims.

Ponting's magic lantern was produced and displayed a scintillating show of some of his best slides. Then the table was put back for snap-dragon and a brew of milk punch, in which they drank the health of Campbell's party (having their own celebration in their hut at Cape Adare), and the crew of the *Terra Nova*. 'By this time,' Scott confided, 'the effect of stimulating liquid refreshment on men so long accustomed to a simple life became apparent. Our biologist had retired to bed, the silent Soldier bubbled with humour and insisted on dancing with Anton.'[24] Keohane grew Irish and politically argumentative while Clissold sat in a benign torpor, only rousing himself to give vent to an occasional 'whoop' or hiccup. At last the party began to fade away, and Debenham recalled that Oates 'showed signs of unsteadiness of leg and speech, and Wilson looked after him. When we all went out to say goodnight to the Antarctic, Oates insisted on putting on all his blizzard-proof clothing, though we told him it was a calm starry night even if the temperature was in the minus forties.

'Wilson guided him out, and when they had been out for nearly a quarter of an hour instead of three minutes, I took out balaclava and gloves for Wilson in my excess of zeal. I found Oates resisting all Wilson's attempts to get him in, and explaining at length that he had made a "marvelloush dishcovery, that the Milky Way wasn't a lot of shtarsh, it was jusht a frozhen Aurora". Oates stopped his dissertation and as we went back to the hut he resumed his ordinary walk and normal speech as he hissed in my ear, Curse you, Deb, another five minutes and I'd have got him frostbitten".'[25] Wilson's resistance to frostbite was a fact of which he was, in his humble way, quite proud, and it was very much an ambition of Oates's to bring the good doctor down to the level of the rest of suffering humanity.

With the midwinter solstice passed, thought turned with increasing energy to the challenge of the coming season. But one journey was made in the very depths of winter: Wilson, Bowers and Cherry-Garrard made a horrifying trip to Cape Crozier in search of Emperor penguins' eggs at a certain stage of development, to further research into embryology. They returned five weeks later with the vital eggs, having suffered beyond words. Their ordeal was later described by Cherry-Garrard in *The Worst Journey in the World*. When they staggered in, emaciated, unshaven and wild-eyed, they found they could not describe the horrors they had experienced. 'I for one', reported Cherry-Garrard, 'had come to that point of suffering at which I did not really care if only I could die without much pain. They talk of the heroism of dying – they little know – it would be so easy to die, a dose of morphia, a friendly crevasse, and blissful sleep The trouble is to go on . . . It was the darkness that did it. I don't believe minus seventy temperatures would be bad in daylight . . .'[26]

Ponting's reaction to their ordeal was thoroughly typical of his age. 'We all [ought] to be thankful that our race produces such men, for the thirst for science is insatiable, and Britain has ever been foremost in the van of those who have not hesitated if need be to sacrifice all for it.'[27] It is doubtful whether a historian of science would support this view, bearing in mind the suspicion science has constantly aroused in Britain, and the ostracism it long had to endure from academic institutions, but nevertheless Ponting's admiration of his colleagues is understandable.

Scott likewise heaped laurels on their heads. 'That they should have persisted in their efforts in spite of every adversity for five weeks is heroic', he commented. But he was also acutely interested in the way each man had stood up to the ordeal. 'I have had several little chats with Wilson on the happenings of the journey. He says there is no doubt that Cherry-Garrard felt the conditions most severely . . . a propos, we both conclude that it is the younger people that have the worse time.'[28]

This must have been most encouraging for Scott, who on 6 June 1911 celebrated his forty-sixth birthday with a celebration dinner with many toasts, and an atmosphere of good-fellowship. 'They are boys, all of them', Scott wrote, from the benign heights of his newly acquired middle age, 'but such excellent good-natured ones . . .' Though Gran considered that Scott was not a fatherly man (and Gran himself had had ample demonstration of the fact), Scott certainly did enjoy patronizing the younger men of the expedition, much as a feudal knight must have watched over his squire. Knowing that the younger men went to pieces more quickly and felt the cold more must have been immensely reassuring.

'Felt very young, sang and cheered', Scott wrote on 25 August, to celebrate the return of the sun. They welcomed it with champagne. 'We were reminded of a frosty morning in England – everything sparkled and the air had the same crisp feel.' Everyone felt different. Even the animals 'went half dotty over it', as Evans put it, and the superstitious little Russian groom was soon grinning broadly. (Anton was convinced that the *Aurora Australis* which could be seen in those latitudes, was caused by spirits, and he attempted to propitiate them by leaving his precious cigarettes – his most valued possession – out in the snow.)

Scott, with his customary responsive ardour, positively basked in happiness and optimism. The trials, setbacks and mortifying reflections of the past year were forgotten; Amundsen's trespass briefly shrugged off. He looked forward rapturously to a successful season and the conquest of the Pole. Scott's fluctuations of mood, and his joy at the return of the sun, show him at his most simple and elemental. We all feel revived and cheered by the appearance of the sun – a relic of the days in the caves when we depended absolutely on its light and warmth. Scott's scientific interests, and his sentimentality towards animals show the modern man. But fundamentally he seemed to be in touch with an ancient world: his sensitivity to weather, which could plunge him into deepest gloom or the most infectious glee; his instinctive soul (Scott trusted his instincts and listened to his heart – not necessarily desirable characteristics in an Antarctic explorer, though undoubtedly lovably human); his impulse to prove his strength and manhood; and above all his sense of powerlessness of human struggles in the face of an implacable fate – in all these ways he seems in a curious sense to be more like an ancient Greek than a modern naval captain.

The sun rose again in the north, but all minds were now fixed on the south. Oates's second lecture on horse management, on 11 August, was full of practical tips for the men who would be leading their ponies across the Barrier. First he reassured them that a good horse manager was 'not born but made', then informed them that a horse has no reasoning power at all, only memory. He warned that it was counter-productive to shout at a horse or cry 'Whoa!' to a bucking one. 'I know', said Oates, 'because I have done it.' The great thing was to be firm and quiet – especially as horses are excitable, and their memory warns them of events to come. Therefore, he advised that when in camp and preparing for the day's march, they should remove the ponies' rugs only at the last minute. He then discussed improvements for the coming journey – in nose-bags, picketing lines, and rugs, and went on to outline the problem of snowblindness and snow shoes. Many solutions to the problem of snow-blindness were swapped around. As for the snow shoes, over which Oates and Scott had disagreed on the depot-laying journey, Scott records that the discussion cleared the air a good deal. Scott concluded that two types of shoe were needed: a sort of stiff bag over the hoof for hard surfaces, and a larger one 'on the grating or racquet principle'[39] for soft snow.

At about this time Scott assigned the ten horses to the men who were to lead them, as follows: Bowers – Victor, Wilson – Nobby, Atkinson – Jehu, Wright – Chinaman, Cherry-Garrard – Michael, Petty Officer Evans – Snatcher, Crean – Bones, Keohane – Jimmy Pigg, Oates – Christopher, Scott – Snippets. The idea was for the new masters to take charge of their beasts and exercise them often, so as to get to know them as well as possible. Oates was increasing their feed and exercise to build them up for the Polar journey, and their high spirits and bad habits were noted by Scott.

'The ponies are very fit but inclined to be troublesome: the quiet beasts develop tricks without rhyme or reason. Chinaman kicks and squeals at night . . . Victor and Snippets are confirmed wind-suckers. They are at it all the time when the manger-board is in place, but it is taken down immediately after feeding time, and then they can only seek vainly for something to catch hold of with their teeth. Bones has taken to kicking at night for no imaginable reason. He hammers away at the back of his stall merrily; we have covered the boards with several layers of sack, so that the noise is cured, if not the habit.'[30] There was good news about the ponies' parasites. Oates had got rid of them by washing the ponies with a tobacco infusion. And the beasts were certainly pleased at the return of daylight, so much so that they often bolted while being exer-cised and galloped off with tails and heels flung high.

On 21 August three broke away. 'Nothing but high spirits, there is no vice in the animals', Scott moralized, 'but I fear we are going to have trouble with sledges and snow-shoes.'[31] Watching Oates trying to harness

Christopher up to a sledge, Scott may well have begun to see the force of Oates's argument against snow shoes. For Christopher was a fiend. 'Certainly', commented Oates, 'one wants the temper of an archangel to get on with a swine like him.'[32] Soon enough Scott realized that 'as soon as a sledge comes into the programme he is seized with the very demon of viciousness, and bites and kicks with every intent to do injury'.[33] It always took four men to harness him up to a sledge, for he had to have one foreleg tied up to incapacitate him. He was still unmanageable even on three legs, however, and usually had in the end to be thrown down (cast) before being harnessed. Bowers was often one of those who struggled with him, and he did not enjoy the experience. 'Three times we downed him and he got up and threw us about, with all four of us hanging on like grim death. He nearly had me under him once, he seems fearfully strong . . . he gets more cunning each time, and if he does not succeed in biting or kicking one of us before long it won't be his fault.'[34]

An incident during one of these preparatory exercise sessions illustrates Christopher's character very well. 'He was going along quietly with Oates when a dog frightened him: he flung up his head, twitched the rope out of Oates's hands and dashed away. It was not a question of blind fright, as immediately after gaining freedom he set about most systematically to get rid of his load. At first he gave sudden twists, and in this manner succeeded in dislodging two bales of hay; then he caught sight of other sledges and dashed for them. They could scarcely get out of his way in time; his intention was evident all through, to dash his load against some other pony and sledge and so free himself of it. He ran for Bowers two or three times with this design, then made for Keohane, never going off far and dashing inward with teeth bared and heels flying all over the place.

'By this time some people were gathering round, and first one and then another succeeded in clambering on to the sledge as it flew by, till Oates, Bowers, Nelson and Atkinson were all sitting on it. He tried to rid himself of this human burden as he had the hay bales and succeeded in dislodging Atkinson with violence, but the remainder dug their heels into the snow and finally the little brute was tired out. Even then he tried to savage anyone approaching his leading line, and it was some time before Oates could get hold of it. Such is the tale of Christopher. I am exceedingly glad there are not more ponies like him.'[35] Wilson was glad that 'we have such an excellent man as the Inniskilling Dragoon to manage these beasts. We should be in great trouble without him'.[36]

Other ponies caused dismay in different ways. Atkinson reported that his pony Jehu was too weak to pull a load. Jehu was a 'weedily built

166

animal'. Oates's care during the winter had improved him a great deal, but on 6 October Scott 'had a look at Jehu and became convinced that he is useless; he is much too weak to pull a load'. (In fact, Jehu performed nobly, covering almost 150 miles before having to be shot.) Chinaman was 'rather a doubtful quantity' and James Pigg 'not a tower of strength'. Scott was at last beginning to understand Oates's pessimistic assessment of the ponies. But he consoled himself by noting that 'six of the animals at least are in splendid condition: Victor, Snippets, Christopher, Nobby and Bones are as fit as ponies could be and are naturally strong, well shaped animals whilst little Michael, though not so shapely, is as strong as he will ever be.'[37] Scott was obviously keeping his fingers crossed.

Wilson's assessment of the ponies was very damning. 'I am afraid the string of ponies which we have were not chosen under the best possible conditions at Vladivostock. The chooser was not very knowledgeable about horses . . . he was handicapped also by being told to get white ones if possible, which must have reduced his selection enormously . . . We really have very few decent horses amongst the whole lot, and several of them are as old as the hills and have passed a life of ill-treatment, hard work and poor food.'[38]

The ponies, of course, were not the only consideration. Atkinson gave a lecture on scurvy of which the cause was then unknown. The symptoms were familiar enough: mental depression, debility, loss of consciousness, livid patches, pains in the leg-bones, spongy gums, swellings. Scott had had direct experience of it on the *Discovery* expedition. We now know that scurvy is caused by vitamin deficiency but of course Scott and his contemporaries were ignorant of the existence of vitamins, and Atkinson's attempts to suggest a cause of scurvy make poignant reading. 'He holds the first cause to be tainted food, but secondary or contributary causes may be even more potent in developing the disease. Damp, cold, over-exertion, bad air, bad light, in fact any condition exceptional to normal healthy existence.' They knew that fresh vegetables were curative, 'lime juice only useful if regularly taken'. At Cape Evans, lime juice was a regular part of the diet but it was not thought important enough (or perhaps practicable) to take it on the sledging journeys. 'It is certain we shall not have the disease here,' commented Scott, 'But one cannot foresee equally certain avoidance in the southern journey to come. All one can do is take every possible precaution'.[39] But the lime juice, alas, was left behind on the shelf at Cape Evans, its importance unperceived, its vitamins as yet unidentified.

During September, Scott made 'a remarkably pleasant and instructive little spring journey',[45] man-hauling with Bowers, Simpson and Petty

Officer Evans, to the Ferrar Glacier. Some stakes had been placed there the previous autumn, and now a trip to inspect them would indicate the glacier's rate of flow. (It had moved 30 ft in 7½ months.) Each man pulled the equivalent of 180 lbs a distance of 175 miles, in low temperatures (−40°F at the glacier) and they experienced poor surfaces and some frostbites. It was a good rehearsal for the Polar journey. Bowers enjoyed it enormously, and it probably confirmed Scott's admiration for him and his conviction of Bowers's indispensability. 'He is a positive wonder; I never met such a sledge traveller.'[40] Petty Officer Evans, a *Discovery* veteran, was also fairly sure of a place in Scott's heart. His rugged physique was impressive and during the winter Scott had observed his tireless mending and making of equipment. In particular, Evans had perfected an excellent new snow boot for the men. During the spring journey he performed well, and it is likely that Scott decided that he could ill do without Bowers or Evans on a final sprint to the Pole.

Many of the men who would be on the Polar sledging party must, at this stage, have been speculating on their chances of being in the last party of four who would go on to the Pole. (The others on the outward journey would return at intervals as supporting parties.) Wilson, otherworldly though he was, wondered if he would get to the Pole. 'May I be there!' he prayed. 'With so many young bloods in the heyday of youth and strength beyond my own I feel there will be a most difficult task in making choice towards the end *and* a universal lack of selfishness and self-seeking.' Saintly Wilson always hoped for the best from his fellow-humans.

Realistic Oates was mulling over the matter. He was also suffering an increasing attack of nerves. On his shoulders rested Scott's ambitions. Should the ponies fail, Scott would not get to the Pole. His responsibilities were enormous, the ponies were crocks, and continuing battles with Scott had left him defensive and hurt. However, he too speculated on his chances. 'We hope to start up the Beardmore Glacier three tents of four men each and I am in Scott's tent. Whether this means I am going in the final party or not I don't know but I think I have a fairish chance that is if Scott and I don't fall out. It will be pretty tough having four months [with him], he fusses dreadfully.'

Then his thoughts turned to the competition. 'I wonder how the Norwegians have got on this winter I expect they have had a pretty rough time, if they are not all drowned I expect they have started for the Pole by this time and have a jolly good chance of getting there if their dogs are good and they use them properly, from what I see I think it would not be difficult to get to the Pole provided you have proper transport but with the rubbish we have it will be jolly difficult and means a lot of hard work.' His responsibilities were becoming all too clear.

On 24 October he wrote, 'the motors were to have left today and to have kept in front of us but after going about 200 yards they came to a full stop, they are tinkering away at them and hope to get away tomorrow. The fact of the motors not getting off is I think pretty serious as they would have relieved the ponies of a lot of weight. We started the winter with 10 ponies and have 10 now and they are very fat and well but they are without exception the greatest lot of crocks I have ever seen that were seriously meant for use, four are lame now and another only wants a days hard work to be lame too.'

He was at this time angry and resentful at the magnitude of his task – the way that his work had been undermined at the outset by the incompetence of the pony-buyers. He had no idea how the ponies would perform and to make matters worse, Scott was still trying to delude himself about their condition. 'I am of course very annoyed', Oates fumed, 'as it is perfectly wretched starting off with a lot of cripples and Scott won't believe how bad they are, he thinks I am always making them out worse than they are. Scott has put two or three people's backs up lately and Meares, who looks after the dogs . . . had a regular row with him, myself I dislike Scott intensely and would chuck the whole thing if it was not that we are a British Expedition and must beat those Norwegians. Scott has always been very civil to me and I have the reputation of getting on well with him but the fact of the matter is he is not straight, it is himself first the rest nowhere and when he has got all he can out of you it is shift for yourself . . . I must knock off for a minute as I am getting very hungry and must get something to eat I may then feel a little more kindly to Scott.'

His attack on Scott is qualified by some kind of sardonic semi-humorous apologetic afterthought, as if he feels his anger is running away with him. It is clear that at this point in the expedition Oates feared that the pony transport would founder, throwing the whole enterprise into disarray and leaving him looking very foolish. There is also the unspoken fear that Scott would blame him for such a disaster, for if Scott refused to believe the ponies were awful crocks, then their manager must be held responsible for any failure. Oates seems to have felt he was in an impossible position, and Scott's lack of judgement (in sending Meares to buy the ponies) had put him there. His shrewd comments on Amundsen's chances show his suspicions that ponies were the wrong form of transport for the Antarctic in any case. He must at times have wondered what he was doing there at all.

It was not the first time Oates's discontent with a superior officer had boiled up into resentment and anger. In the army, some of his superiors had excited his contempt. But his reaction against Scott was stronger than any previously recorded feelings, no doubt because of the claustrophobia of the situation, the burden of his responsibilities, and the fact that there was so much at risk. But in the best of circumstances, it is unlikely that Oates would have taken to Scott in any hearty way.

Oates was a soldier and a gentleman through and through. He believed in simple and straighforward solutions to problems, and in a regular, decent life devoid of much intellectual engagement. He spoke his mind – when he felt free to do so. Scott was a man of considerable intellect and, above all, delicate sensibility. Literary, emotional, unpredictable, given to melancholy moods and bouts of fussing, his sensibility was his enemy. Conscious of the need to prove his manhood, in an age when manhood welcomed physical exertion, he punished himself by arduous marches and by enduring pain in a spirit of gladness.

Oates was free from such masochistic episodes. He did not need to prove his manhood to himself, to a wife, or anyone else. He probably never gave it a thought. When Oates said that Scott was not 'straight' this is surely what he must have meant – that he could never get Scott to see the issues so clearly as he, Oates, experienced them. Scott's reactions were veiled by a complex web of intellectual assumptions, moralistic fervour and paralyzing self-consciousness. Scott clearly liked Oates a great deal, valued him and appreciated him. But Scott got on Oates's nerves, and Oates's feelings, at this stage at least, were sunk into sourness.

Notes and references

1 Reginald Pound, *Scott of the Antarctic*, p. 240.
2 H. G. Ponting, *The Great White South*, p. 124.
3 *Ibid.*, p. 126.
4 *Ibid.*, p. 127.
5 *Ibid.*,p.129.
6 From a record of a conversation between G. Seaver and F. Debenham, February 1929.
7 R. F. Scott, diary, 14 May 1911.
8 Professor Frank Debenham, *An Expedition in Harmony*.
9 Quoted by E. Huxley in *Scott of the Antarctic*, p. 235.
10 *Ibid.*
11 *Ibid.*, p. 232.
12 R. F. Scott, diary, 31 May 1911.

13 E. A. Wilson, letter to his wife.
14 From conversation between Frank Debenham and Sue Limb.
15 L. E. G. Oates writing in the *South Polar Times*.
16 Commander Evans, *My Recollections of a Gallant Comrade*.
17 From conversations between Frank Debenham and Sue Limb.
18 E. A. Wilson, letter to his wife.
19 H. G. Ponting, *The Great White South*, p. 288.
20 R. F. Scott, diary, 14 July 1911.
21 *Ibid.*
22 *Ibid.*, 16 July 1911.
23 Quoted by Frank Debenham, diary, 8 May 1911.
24 R. F. Scott, diary, 22 June 1911.
25 Professor Frank Debenham, *An Expedition in Harmony*.
26 A. Cherry-Garrard, *The Worst Journey in the World*, p. 237.
27 H. G. Ponting, *The Great White South*, p. 156.
28 R. F. Scott, diary, 6 August 1911.
29 *Ibid.*, 11 August 1911.
30 *Ibid.*, 11 August 1911.
31 *Ibid.*, 21 August 1911.
32 L. E. G. Oates, diary, 30 November 1911.
33 R. F. Scott, diary, 13 October 1911.
34 H. R. Bowers, diary, quote by A. Cherry-Garrard, *op. cit.*, p. 328.
35 R. F. Scott, diary, 13 October 1911.
36 E. A. Wilson, diary, 13 October 1911.
37 R. F. Scott, diary, 6 October 1911.
38 E. A. Wilson, diary, 15 October 1911.
39 R. F. Scott, diary, 14 August 1911.
40 *Ibid.*, 1 October 1911.

10

To the Pole

Towards the end of October, Oates added his last few thoughts to his letter home. 'If you get this without hearing of the return of the Polar party and I happen to be in the party, there is no cause for anxiety as the only dangerous part of the journey is the ascent of the glacier and you will have heard if we get up that safely, the coming back is not nearly so bad.' Oates here shared his leader's delusion about the return journey. Of course coming back, in the mundane experience of day-to-day living, usually is easier than outward journeys. And Oates was also keen to reassure his mother.

The boredom of the Antarctic winter, and the fact that those on the final Polar party would be condemned to another one on their return (having missed the ship) provoked in him a moment of nostalgia for home and his loved ones. 'Please give my love to all the family. I often wonder how Lilian and Eric are getting on in their new house and if Violet has got fixed up and settled with yet. I have half a mind to see Scott and tell him I must go home on the ship but it would be a pity to spoil my chances of being on the final party especially as the regiment and perhaps the whole army would be pleased if I was at the Pole.'[1]

For two days their departure was delayed, while a blizzard raged, but on 31 October Scott recorded that, 'the blizzard has blown itself out this morning and this afternoon the sun was shining and the wind is dropping. The future is in the lap of the gods: I can think of nothing left undone to deserve success'. Scott characteristically viewed this moment portentously, with a Greek sense of it all as cosmic theatre. Oates's observations anticipated farce. 'I expect there will be a bit of a circus getting off tomorrow as most people have been very remiss about exercising their ponies and they are full of beans.' At the end of his letter, however, he does have time for a moment of sombre reflection. 'If anything should happen to me on this trip, which I don't think likely, ask for my notebook. I have written instructions on the fly leaf that it is to be sent to you but please remember that when a man is having a hard time he says hard things about other people which he would regret afterwards.' Oates's hard comments about Scott are vital to an understanding of the situation. His regrets are no less important.

Just before they started for the Pole, Scott wrote to Mrs Oates: 'There is a possibility that your son may not return to England this year. Under these circumstances, I think you may be glad to have a word of him from a companion, the more as he has rendered very great service to the Expedition. I really don't know what our party of sailor and scientific men would have done without him, we might have kept our ponies alive but we certainly should not have had them in such fit and promising condition for the journey which is to come. Everything depends on the successful work of these animals and your son kindly took charge of them, their feeding, their housing, and their exercise, besides personally leading the least tractable of them. To this really great service his welcome personality is a great addition, he has been and remains one of the most popular and cheery members of our small community. Also in spite of the troubles and responsibilities of his fractious animals I think he has enjoyed himself very much. He seems to be in excellent spirits and he is certainly in excellent health.

The future, whether we remain here for a second season, is very uncertain but if we remain I shall hope your son will continue with the party. I realise how keen a soldier he is and that it will not do for him to drop out of the running but if all goes well I hope the War Office will recognize his very unusual services and abilities. I think it will as there was evident pleasure at his inclusion in the party. Meanwhile it is a pleasure to tell you how well he is and how popular with the exceedingly diverse set of men with whom he is living.'[2]

On 1 November, the main Polar party set out. The motors, back in action, had gone ahead under Teddy Evans's leadership. Jehu, the most ancient pony, and Jimmy Pigg, also in an advanced stage of decrepitude, had started early, coaxed along by Atkinson and Keohane. The rest of the ponies started full of life, and in some cases, mischief. Christopher set off in his usual style – galloping off on three legs (with his foreleg still tied up), his sledge careering wildly about behind him. 'Dear old Titus', wrote Griffith Taylor, who was amongst the Cape Evans party who cheered him off, 'that was my last memory of him. Imperturbable as ever: never hasty, never angry, but soothing that vicious animal.'[3] Christopher completed his first march having been 'bucking and kicking the whole way. For the present there is no end to his devilment, and the great consideration is how to safeguard Oates'.[4]

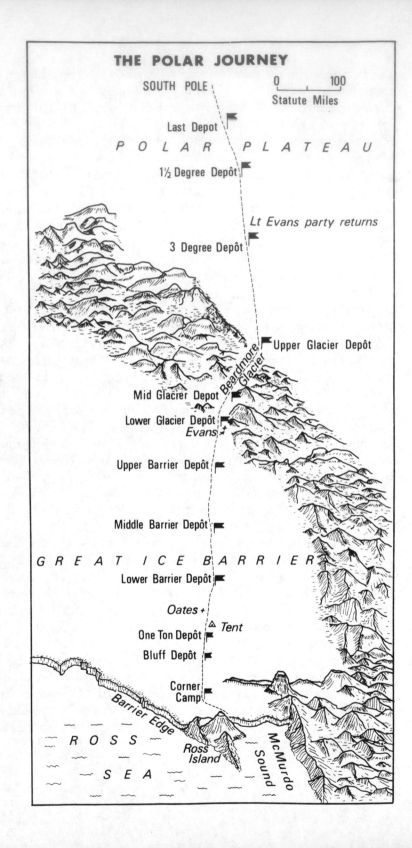

THE POLAR JOURNEY

SOUTH POLE

Last Depot

P O L A R   P L A T E A U

1½ Degree Depôt

Lt Evans party returns

3 Degree Depôt

Upper Glacier Depôt

Beardmore Glacier

Mid Glacier Depot

Lower Glacier Depôt
Evans

Upper Barrier Depôt

Middle Barrier Depôt

G R E A T   I C E   B A R R I E R

Lower Barrier Depôt

Oates +

△ Tent

One Ton Depôt

Bluff Depôt

Corner Camp

Barrier Edge

R O S S

Ross Island

McMurdo Sound

S E A

0   100
Statute Miles

At Hut Point, Scott realized he had left the Union Flag behind – the flag presented to him by Queen Alexandra, which was to fly at the South Pole. Gran was sent back on ski to fetch it. So a Norwegian carried the British flag its first few miles to the Pole. Scott accepted the flag with a smile. 'An irony of fate', he remarked – obviously aware of his journey as a saga involving irony and fate, even though it had hardly begun. For a few hours Ponting was kept very busy recording the beginnings of this saga, but then he, and Gran, went back to Cape Evans. Gran was not expected to compete with his fellow Norwegians.

The plan was to average ten miles a day from Hut Point to One Ton Depot with the horses lightly laden (the motors, it was hoped, would do the donkey work). The dog teams would be on hand, carrying fodder for the ponies. From One Ton to the bottom of the Beardmore Glacier, a daily average of thirteen miles would be necessary to carry twenty-four weekly units of food for four men each to the foot of the glacier. This was 369 miles, the first stage of the journey, and at the end of it the ponies would be shot. The routine for this part of the journey was again to march at night.

Only fourteen miles out from Hut Point, however, they came upon the signs of a not altogether unexpected disaster. One of the motors was finished. The big end of the number 2 cylinder of Day's motor had broken, and the motor itself was already drifted up, presenting a melancholy air. Notes had been left explaining the problem, and it was evident that despite the trials in Norway and Switzerland, the engines were not fitted to working in the Antarctic climate. Cherry-Garrard felt that 'Scott had set his heart upon the success of the motors . . . at the back of his mind, I feel sure, was the wish to abolish the cruelty which the use of ponies and dogs necessarily entails'.[5] At the same time, Scott had clearly realized that the motors were not yet beyond the experimental stage. The second motor managed to travel fifty miles, to just beyond Corner Camp, before seizing up. No motor-driven machine had travelled on the Barrier before, and useful experience had been gained. All the same, the motors' direct contribution to Scott's journey had been almost negligible. The motor men took to manhauling as their machines gave out, and camped further down the line to wait for Scott and the ponies to catch them up.

The ponies were divided into different teams, according to speed, and the slowest given a head start. The dogs, performing well under Meares, had started later and on 7 November, when Scott was tentbound in a blizzard, they turned up in camp, apparently unconcerned at the conditions. Meares's arrival gave Oates a chance for a bit of a growl. He recorded in his diary that they both damned the motors. 'Three motors at £1000 each, 19 ponies at £5 each, 32 dogs at 30/– each. If Scott fails to get to the Pole he jolly well deserves it.' [6]

It was beginning to dawn on Scott that his experience with the dogs on the *Discovery* expedition had been misleading. 'It is satisfactory to find the dogs will pull the loads and can be driven to face such a wind as we have had. It shows that they ought to be able to help us a good deal',[7] he commented, and confessed to Cherry-Garrard that he thought that on the *Discovery* expedition, they had done everything wrong with their dogs. It was unfortunately too late to make the most of this lesson.

Meanwhile, the ponies were performing well. Scott was impressed and recorded that 'even Oates is pleased'. When blizzards struck, the high walls sheltered the ponies and their new rugs were also a great improvement. Scott celebrated this as 'a direct result of our experience last year, and it is good to feel that we reaped some reward for that disastrous journey'.[8] On 8 November Oates recorded in his diary 'had great trouble with Christopher. He seems to get worse instead of better. Scott told me today he was very pleased with the way the ponies were going and was kind enough to say he owed me a lot for the trouble I had taken. I must say the ponies are going now better than I expected'. All the same, Scott's euphoria did not last long. Blizzards soon began to tell on the ponies' condition. Scott conjectured that it was the exceeding fineness of the snow particles, which penetrated the ponies' coats, then melted and ran away, carrying off the animals' vital heat. 'Also, no doubt, it harasses the animals by the bombardment of the flying particles on tender places such as nostrils, eyes, and to a lesser extent ears.'[9] Jehu and Chinaman were giving cause for concern. 'Poor ancient little beggar,' Bowers brooded over Chinaman, 'he ought to be a pensioner instead of finishing his days on a job of this sort. Jehu looks pretty rocky, too.'[10] But when the wind eased and their rugs were stripped away, both Chinaman and Jehu 'had a skittish little run'.

Scott was constantly on the watch for such encouraging signs, making a host of detailed observations in his diary as to the progress of each horse. At the midday (or rather midnight) halt for lunch, both men and beasts had a chance for a breather – except for Oates. For once mad Christopher had been harnessed (a procedure still demanding the cunning and brute strength of four men) he would hurtle off into the distance with Oates clinging on like grim death to the bridle, and stopping him was impossible until a full day's march had been accomplished – usually ten to thirteen miles. This meant, of course, that Oates went without his midmarch rest and snack, which must gradually have eroded his stamina.

Scott's diary shows, at this time, how heavily he relied on Oates. On

12 November there was a debate about Chinaman's fitness. 'The Soldier thinks Chinaman will last a good many days yet, which is an extraordinary confession of hope for him.' The next day, Scott's tensions broke out. 'I am anxious about these beasts – very anxious, they are not the ponies they ought to have been, and if they pull through well, all the thanks will be due to Oates.' Oates's own diary entries hover between hope and scepticism. 'Scott seems pleased with the way the ponies are going . . . if only these wretched old cripples of ours can stick it and we get all the stuff to the glacier I think we shall do the trick . . . I hope that after this trip I never have to do with such a bad lot of horses again . . . Meares said he was surprised how well the ponies were going which is rather amusing considering he was responsible for buying the old screws.'[12]

Scott's anxiety boiled over now and again into direct conflict. 'Scott had a breeze up with Bowers when we got in about the loads on the various sledges', Oates recorded. 'He is I think beginning to realise what wretched crocks the ponies are.' Bowers wrote that 'he accused me of putting upon his three horses to save his own. He went through the weights in detail after our meal and, after a certain amount of argument, decided to carry on as we were going.' Forgiving little Bowers added that he could 'quite understand his feelings'. He was not the only victim of Scott's tension. 'Had words with Scott when he arrived', remarked Oates, 'he is a very difficult man to get on with.'

Progress, however slow, was made. On 15 November they reached One Ton Depot, 130 miles from Hut Point. There they found a note from Teddy Evans saying that he and the motor party had gone on ahead, man-hauling, and would await the main party at 80 ° 30' S. This was the moment for a prolonged council of war. Scott called Oates and Bowers into his tent after supper was finished. They decided to pause for a day or two to rest the ponies, and then push on at an average of thirteen miles a day. Oates thought the ponies would get to the glacier, but admitted they had lost condition much more quickly than he had expected. 'Personally I am much more hopeful', wrote Scott. 'I think that a good many of the beasts are actually in better form than when they started, and that there is no need to be alarmed about the remainder, always excepting the weak ones which we have always regarded with doubt.'[13]

At this meeting Scott made it clear that the ponies would all be shot at the foot of the Beardmore Glacier, and no attempt would be made to take them up it. 'This was a great relief, commented Cherry - Garrard, 'for the crevassed state of the lower reaches of the glacier as described by Shackleton led us to believe that the attempt was suicidal . . . I am sure that in this kind of uncertainty the mental strain on the leader of a party is less than on his men . . . Scott probably was always of the opinion that it would not be worthwhile taking ponies on the glacier. The pony leaders, however, only knew that the possibility was ahead of them.'[14] It was apparently only in formal councils of war that Scott would reveal the plans which he had been arguing over in solitude. The men had to wait until then, bear the uncertainty with fortitude and, if they disagreed, to do so with great tact and delicacy, for as Debenham observed, Scott had been trained to regard discipline and obedience as vital.

Obediently, therefore, Scott's men moved out again onto the march. By now the work was done with a silent, automatic sense of routine. In the early days there were jolly conversations around the primus. They discussed literature, with Scott providing reminiscences about Barrie and Galsworthy, and joking that Max Beerbohm, on being told he looked like Scott, had grown a beard. But about three weeks out, the University of the Ice faded away and from then onwards it was often that whole days passed without conversation beyond the routine 'Camp ho! All ready? Pack up! Spell ho!' Each man was left alone with his own thoughts, and in Scott's case the progress of the ponies was his uppermost concern.

'The weakness of breeding and age is showing itself already', he wrote on 17 November, and on the next day, 'the ponies are not pulling well . . . Oates gives Chinaman at least three days. This is slightly inspiriting, but how much better it would have been to have had ten really reliable beasts!' The next day, they came across 'a real bad surface . . . ponies sinking in very deep. The result is about to finish Jehu. He was terribly done on getting in tonight'.[15] Oates found time for a moment's ironical satisfaction. 'Scott realises now what awful cripples our ponies are', he observed, 'and carries a face like a tired sea boot in consequence.'[16]

Scott found a moment for a brief note to his wife, which revealed the extent of his realization. 'Just a note from the Barrier to say that I love you. . . Everything is going pretty well for the present, though we had a bad scare about the condition of the ponies last week. The animals are not well selected. I knew this in New Zealand, though I didn't tell you. That they are going well now and bidding fair to carry us through the first stage of our journey is due entirely to Oates. He is another treasure.'[17]

Generous, indeed, lavish with his praise at times, Scott found it hard to face up to his own mistakes and inadequacies. His instinct for concealment had been made very clear in an earlier letter to his wife. He had lamented how, until arriving in the Antarctic, he had lost confidence in himself. 'I don't know if it was noticed by others consciously, but it was acted on unconsciously, as a dozen incidents in my memory remind me.

33. The shore party, October 1911. Left to right, standing: Griffith Taylor, Cherry-Garrard, Day, Nelson, Lieutenant 'Teddy' Evans, Oates, Atkinson, Scott, Wright, Keohane, Gran, Lashley, Hooper, Forde, Anton (in front). Left to right, sitting: Bowers, Meares, Debenham, Wilson, Simpson, Petty Officer Evans, Crean. Fifty-three years later, Debenham became instrumental in the initial plans for this book.

34. Oates at the stable door. 'An unwavering strength of purpose was written on Oates's firm face; and his sturdy frame was a foundation on which Scot largely built his hopes later — in the great final effort.'

(H. Ponting)

35. 'The Tenements.' Left to right: Cherry-Garrard (below), Bowers, Oates, Meares, Atkinson (below). Their creed was 'down with Science, Sentiment and the Fair Sex.'

36. Meares and Oates in the stables. At the moment when this photograph was taken, Meares had just said he thought Scott should buy a shilling book on transport. Scott unfortunately overheard.

Had I been what I am now, many things would have been avoided. I can trace these things to myself very clearly and can only hope that others do not.'[18] Poor Scott. He could not face a sense of his own weakness. That makes it very hard ever to learn from mistakes (which Scott did manage) or, more important, ever to feel secure in one's real powers. Once a man has faced the worst in himself, he can begin to believe in himself. Scott seems somehow very lonely in his self-protecting authoritarianism – full of affectionate and admiring impulses for men whom, in some cases, he had already alienated.

On 24 November, Jehu was shot, about 150 miles from the glacier. He had, however, covered almost the same distance since leaving Hut Point. Considering he was 'the crockiest of crocks' it was a great achievement, with all credit due to Oates and, of course, to Jehu himself. 'Gave Jehu the bullet on getting into camp', wrote Oates, in an uncharacteristic burst of feeling, 'it is a brutal killing these poor ponies. The sad part is that Jehu had plenty of march left in him, but the dogs have to have food, and forage is running short.'[19] The dogs, having carried the ponies' fodder, were now to feast on the ponies themselves. It was indeed a gory and upsetting business.

Bowers tried hard to justify it to himself. 'A year's care and good feeding, three weeks' work with good treatment, a reasonable load and a good ration, and then a painless end. If anybody can call that cruel I can not understand or agree with them.'[20] Bowers marshalled his arguments with the rather hollow bravura tone of a man trying to fight off an overwhelming, and weakening, emotion. His turn would come. His pony would be shot, too. In the meantime Jehu was cut up and fed to the dogs. Meares reported he had had plenty of fat on him and no doubt the dogs found him tasty. Later the men ate their share of ponymeat, and immediately felt the benefit, for having spent three weeks on sledging rations they were already, as yet without being aware of it, suffering vitamin deficiency.

As they caught up with the motor-party, now man-hauling, Day and Hooper turned back northwards to Cape Evans carrying a note from Scott to Simpson. 'My dear Simpson, This goes with Day and Hooper now returning. We are making fair progress and the ponies doing fairly well. I hope we shall get to the glacier without difficulty, but to make sure I am carrying the dog-teams farther than I intended at first – the teams may be late returning, unfit for work or non-existent. – R. Scott.' They plodded on, with bad surfaces and bad light making the going very slow. The whole landscape was blotted out with thick mist for days on end. The ponies were gradually tiring and 'a tired animal makes a tired man, I find'.[21] The monotony of travelling on the Barrier was deadly. 'It was always rather dismal to walk over the great snow plain when the sky and surface merge in one pall of dead whiteness', wrote Scott, taking pleasure only in good company.

On 28 November, Chinaman was shot. 'He was a game little devil', commented Oates, 'and must have been a goodish kind of pony 15 years ago.'[22] Scott noted that they were now less than ninety miles from the glacier, and there was enough forage left for seven more marches with the ponies. The next day the weather cleared and a scintillating sight met their eyes. 'Right on top of us were the triple peaks of Mount Markham . . . after some 300 miles of bleak, monotonous Barrier it was a wonderful sight indeed.' Cherry-Garrard went on to remark on how depressed they had become during the bad weather. 'The mental strain on those responsible was very great in those early stages.'[23] This, of course, included Oates. But the sight of the mountains, and the sunshine, worked wonders. 'Altogether things look much better and everyone is in excellent spirits',[24] reported Scott.

They added a little pony-meat to their hoosh and found it good eating. These 'hooshes' or stews were their basic daily meal. They were made with dried meat, pemmican, to which several extras could be added: biscuit, curry powder, cocoa or raisins. But the fresh pony-meat did them most good. The surviving ponies did well on their last few marches. They outlasted the forage. On 2 December, Scott decided 'against some opinion' (Oates's, no doubt) that Christopher should be shot. 'Less regret goes with him than with the others, in remembrance of all the trouble he gave at the outset, and the unsatisfactory way he has behaved of late.'

Christopher's death was dramatic. 'He was the only pony who did not die instantaneously', wrote Cherry-Garrard. 'Perhaps Oates was not so calm as usual, for Chris was his own horse though such a brute. Just as Oates fired he moved, and charged into the camp with a bullet in his head. He was caught with difficulty, nearly giving Keohane a bad bite, led back and finished. We were well rid of him.'[25] As Christopher was gone, Oates was now at leisure, and need fear no longer the hoof or teeth of his old enemy. Scott offered him a roving commission to watch over the animals, but he preferred to lead one, so Scott handed over Snippets and went roving himself on ski, photographing the ponies as he went.

Scott was still wishing that a good snow-shoe for ponies could have been devised. 'Nobby was tried in snow-shoes this morning, and came along splendidly in them for about four miles, then the wretched affairs racked and had to be taken off. There is no doubt that these snow-shoes are the thing for the ponies.' Scott's solution may have been a good one, but perhaps totally impractical. It was certainly cultural: adapting a natural creature by artificial aids to cope with life in a hostile environment. The smug dogs, curled up in their snow-holes, or fleeting lightly over the surfaces, needed no such adaptation. Nature had already done the work.

The next pony to die was Victor – Bowers's special friend. He had to be shot because forage was short – a sad expedient since he was still going very well, and some fodder had been jettisoned at One Ton to give the animals lighter loads to pull. Bowers recorded his anguish in his diary. 'It seemed an awful pity to have to shoot a great stong animal, and it seemed like an irony of fate to me, as I had been downed for over-provisioning the ponies with needless excess of food, and the drastic reductions had been made against my strenuous opposition to the last. It is poor satisfaction to know that I was right now that my poor horse is dead. Good old Victor! He has always had a biscuit out of my ration, and he ate his last before the bullet sent him to his rest.'[26]

As each pony was killed, men and dogs ate the meat ravenously. 'We have all taken to horse meat', wrote Scott, 'and are so well fed that hunger isn't thought of.' Oates ate his pony hoosh that night in Scott's tent (changing with Cherry-Garrard). Such changes were routine, but men who went into Scott's tent were obviously being sized up. Scott was also keeping a keen eye on the weather, and grumbling about it, often. 'The whole weather conditions seem thoroughly disturbed, and if they continue so when we are on the Glacier, we shall be very awkwardly placed. It is really time the luck turned in our favour – we have too little of it.'[27] White floury blizzards and drifting snow made progress difficult at times.

On 4 December they could clearly see the ice-rounded, boulder-strewn Mount Hope and the gateway to the Glacier, and Scott calculated that another march should take them there. He also praised the ponies, saying that they must have been fitter than Shackleton's animals, since they had lasted so well, 'and indeed there isn't a doubt they would go many miles yet if food allowed'. They were also of course wanted for food themselves – this time Michael was sacrificed to the hungry, yelping dogs – who, Scott records, were 'simply splendid'. Michael had been a highly strung, spirited animal, often consumed with the fidgets on off-days. 'Life was a constant source of wonder to him', said Cherry-Garrard, his sorrowing master. Michael's time for wonder was at an end. The dogs ate him, and over the camp a raging, howling blizzard broke.

It was a full-blown Antarctic blizzard, with very fine, powdery snow that stuck to everything in the high temperatures 'One cannot see the next tent, let alone the land', commented Scott. 'What on earth does such weather mean at this time of the year? It is more than our share of ill-fortune.' He tormented himself with the thought that if this blizzard was the result of 'exceptional local conditions', his party might be stuck helpless while 'others go smilingly forward in the sunshine.'[28] He was not the only one to have such thoughts. 'I think we shall get to the Pole now,' wrote Oates, 'but I think there is a very good chance of the Norskies getting there before us.'[29]

As the blizzard raged, the ponies drooped. Scott flung himself into a dramatic melancholy. 'The ponies look utterly desolate. Oh! but this is too crushing, and we are only 12 miles from the Glacier. A hopeless feeling descends on one and is hard to fight off.' Bowers confines himself to a simple – and very effective catalogue of wetness. 'We are wet through, our tents are wet, our bags which are our life to us, are wet; the poor ponies are soaked and shivering far more than they would be ordinarily in a temperature fifty degrees lower. Our sledges – the parts that are dug out – are wet, our food is wet, everything on and around and about us is the same. The warmth of our bodies has formed a snow bath for each of us to lie in . . . This idleness when one is simply jumping to go on is bad enough for most, but it must be worse for Captain Scott. I feel glad he has Dr Bill [Wilson] in his tent, there is always something so reassuring about Bill, he comes out best in adversity.'[30] Scott's depression had evidently been noticed by Bowers.

On 7 December the storm persisted. One more small feed remained for the ponies, and more seriously, the men had to start their summit rations, which they were not officially due to broach until the party was on the Glacier. Scott tried to teach himself resignation, but it was a hard lesson to learn in the face of what he found totally unprecedented weather for December – usually the finest month. He paints a picture of deadly languor. 'To be here watching the mottled green walls of our tent, the glistening wet bamboos, bedraggled sopping socks and loose articles dangling in the middle, to hear the everlasting patter of the falling snow and the ceaseless rattle of the fluttering canvas . . . add the stress of sighted failure to our whole plan, and anyone must find the circumstances unenviable.'

Whilst Scott and the others were languishing in the tent, Oates was more often than not out in the full blast of the blizzard. He had continually to turn out to save his little animals being snowed up; they lost condition with a rapidity that was dreadful to observe . . . whenever one peeped out of the tent there was Oates, wet to the skin, trying to keep life in his charges'.[31] On 9 December the blizzard ended. 'Poor Oates had suffered as much as the ponies', recalled Evans. 'He had felt that every time he re-entered his tent [which was also Captain Scott's] he took in more wet snow and helped to increase the general discomfort. This being the case when he went out to the ponies he stopped out, and kept his vigil crouching behind a drifted-up pony wall. We could not help laughing at him, after the blizzared, when he wrung the icy water out of his clothing. His personal bag was in a dreadful state. The sodden tobacco had discoloured everything, and as he squeezed his spare socks and gloves a stream of nicotine-stained water flowed out.

'I am unable to reproduce his observations on the subject – they were dry, picturesque, and to the point, and even our bluejackets, who were none too particular about language, looked at Oates with undisguised astonishment at the length and variety of his emergency vocabulary.' The laughter soon faded, however, as the conditions of the resumed march became clear. 'The ponies could hardly move, sunk up to their bellies, and finally lay down. They had to be driven, lashed on. It was a grim business',[32] Cherry-Garrard lamented. The last day of pony-haulage was probably the worst, and it must have been with some relief that Oates put a bullet in his remaining charges. Their sufferings were over, but it had been a painful struggle, and this was a gruesome end. They called it Shambles Camp.

'Well! I congratulate you, Titus!' beamed Wilson to Oates, as they stood in the shadow of Mount Hope.

'And I thank you, Titus',[33] said Scott. Thanks to Oates's care, the ponies had reached the glacier. Though he did not know it, Oates had probably earned his place in the Polar party.

On 4 December, when he had first seen the approaches to the Polar Plateau, Oates had remarked, 'saw several enormous glaciers coming down between the mountains, and some of the chasms which stopped Shackleton. And now one is here one can realise what a wonderful journey his was and the daring which prompted him to strike up the Glacier instead of following the coast line'.[34] Following in Shackleton's footsteps, the party now depoted four sledges and some personal gear, and regrouped as three four-man teams, each team pulling about 500 lbs. Scott's team included Oates, Wilson and Petty Officer Evans. Team II consisted of Lieutenant Evans, Atkinson, Wright, Lashley, and Team III, Bowers, Cherry-Garrard, Crean, and Keohane. Evans and Lashley in Team II had already been man-hauling since the breakdown of the motors, a distance of over 300 miles, and were understandably more tired than the other two. Scott and Wilson were both glad that now the man-hauling would begin. 'Thank God the horses are now all done with and we begin the heavier work ourselves',[35] wrote Wilson. Scott, anxious about the fitness of Team II, celebrated his own. 'It is a very serious business if the men are going to crock up. As for myself, I never felt fitter and my party can easily hold its own. Petty Officer Evans, of course, is a tower of strength but Oates and Wilson are doing splendidly also.'[36]

Those who were newcomers to man-hauling were astonished at the rigours of the work. They had to pull 200 lbs per man uphill to the Polar Plateau at 10,000 ft – a journey of 120 miles. Bowers, never one to complain, indeed a most stoical and devoted workman, and of great physical strength, described man-hauling as 'the most back-breaking work I have ever come up against . . . The starting was worse than the pulling as it required from ten to fifteen desperate jerks on the harness to move the sledge at all . . . I have never pulled so hard, or so nearly crushed my inside into my backbone by the everlasting jerking with all my strength on the canvas band round my unfortunate tummy.'

The Beardmore Glacier was covered in a thick layer of soft snow from the recent blizzard, so whereas Shackleton travelled often upon blue ice, Scott's sledges and their men were struggling and floundering in deep drifts. 'It seems an extraordinary difference in fortune, and at every step S's luck becomes more evident', commented Scott petulantly. The soft surfaces, and the hidden danger of lurking crevasses, made the use of ski almost essential, but Scott commented that his 'tiresome fellow-countrymen [are] too prejudiced to have prepared themselves for the event'. In fact, he must share some of the blame – after all, he had not organized a systematic ski-school either. In the long months before the Pole journey, Gran, the ski expert had been left with little to do (hence Wilson's advice about tying and re-tying his shoelaces). If ski-techniques were fumbling and primitive, snow blindness was also rife. Oates suffered from it, as did Wilson, Petty Officer Evans, Bowers, Keohane, and Lashley. 'I had a rotten afternoon with snow-glare, streaming eyes and at times nearly blind . . . was awake for nearly six hours with pain',[37] recorded Wilson. The party was also suffering from cracked, sore and bleeding lips, and scabby, blistered faces – the effects of sunburn. On 16 December, when they had been travelling on the glacier for a week, Scott remarked, 'certainly dogs could have come up as far as this'. It must have been a mortifying reflection.

A certain amount of rivalry between the three sledges was inevitable, for of the twelve men present only four, including Scott, could be chosen to travel the last leg to the Pole. (Scott, although selecting the team, might not necessarily include himself in the party). Two other parties of four men each would have to turn back for home with the Pole unseen – an unglamorous and ignominious role to play. Teddy Evans's sledge fell behind at times – possibly because of defective runners, possibly because of the party's considerable fatigue. Yet Evans was an extremely competitive person, very keen to impress Scott. He was not one to give up. When they struggled, he would exert himself feverishly to try and regain momentum. Wilson was probably least affected by the spirit of rivalry; though he, too, was keen to be chosen, he had a kind of Christian fatalism to underpin his self-control. 'If the end comes to me here or hereabouts', he wrote, 'there will be no great time for Ory [his wife] to sorrow. All will be as it is meant to be.'[38] Wilson took the opportunity of every halt to do a little sketching. Apart from his own keen interest in the landscape, he had a page of notes from Griffith-Taylor requesting observations about geological phenomena. As for Oates, he contented himself with a keen interest in the distance covered, and was always asking what the sledgemeter showed. After several hellish days of deep snow and wallowing sledges, on 19 December they at last found some blue ice. Bowers thought 'it was like walking over cucumber frames,' and they made great progress: twenty-three miles instead of the recent average of eight to ten miles in the 'damnably dismal' days. 'That's not bad going on the hard high road,' conceded Oates.

But Oates had confided to his diary, 'my feet are giving me a lot of trouble. They have been continually wet since leaving Hut Point and now walking along this hard ice in frozen crampons has made rather hay of them, still they are not the worst in the outfit by a long chalk.'[39] Scott fell into two large ice-cracks and later Petty Officer Evans cut his hand while mending a sledge – a cut which refused to heal. But everyone was prone to cuts, knocks and bruises, and the blisters and snowblindness. On 21 December, when Scott had to tell four men to start back, there was really nothing to choose between any of them. 'I dreaded this necessity of choosing – nothing could be more heartrending,' he lamented. Atkinson, Wright, Cherry-Garrard and Keohane were the ones who had to go.

They were all disappointed, 'poor Wright rather bitterly, I fear,' remarked Scott. Wright was indeed. 'Too wild to write more tonight', he concluded his diary entry. Cherry-Garrard, though disappointed, was perhaps not terribly surprised, for he was young, extremely myopic, and not the strongest of men. Wilson consoled him by telling him it was a toss-up whether he or Oates should go on. This may have been a kind fiction to reassure the young man. In view of Oates's final selection for the Polar party, it rather looks like it. Atkinson, however, told Cherry-Garrard that he was sure Oates did not want to go on. He was limping: partly because his feet were deteriorating, and partly because his old thigh wound from the Boer War was giving him trouble.

One of the symptoms of scurvy is that scar tissue from old wounds begins to dissolve. It is possible that Oates's limping from his war wound was the vaguest first symptom of scurvy. Pains in the leg bones are often the first signs. Teddy Evans collapsed with scurvy a few weeks later and nearly died. By the time Scott's party had reached the top of the glacier they must have been suffering from vitamin deficiency. The sledging ration per man per day was 20 gm (0.7 oz) tea, 454 gm (1lb) biscuits, 24 gm (0.8oz) cocoa, 340 gm (12 oz) pemmican, 56.75 gm (2 oz) butter and 85.13 gm (3 oz) sugar – a total of 980 gm (2 lbs 3 oz) which produced 4430 calories. A healthy man doing manual work in a temperate climate needs about 3600 calories per day. Scott's gruelling man-hauling made much greater demands. His party probably burned up 5500 calories each, every day. They were therefore suffering from malnutrition.

Of course, Scott was not told that Oates was feeling slightly below par, or that perhaps he was none too keen on going on. The conspiracy of stoicism kept such important facts hidden. These men had been brought up to believe that physical weakness was something to be ashamed of, that it was there to be overcome, that making an issue of one's malaises was feeble and womanish (rather like being inoculated against smallpox). Scott himself had immense physical stamina, and his men constantly strove to equal him. Some, no doubt, out of a desire to do him proud, others perhaps to show him they were as tough as he was – a kind of tacit competitiveness he encouraged. 'I am exceedingly fit and can go with the best of them', he asserted. But beyond it all, the moral dimension of Scott's expedition is inescapable. If you felt weak, you kept quiet about it. Suffering in silence was all part of the business of being an English Gentleman. Oates had ever been one of the most silent of them. Also he probably wanted to go on, believing that he had a sporting chance and that sheer guts would pull him through all right.

Before the supporting party turned back, there was one more march – an epic one, with Scott going flat out, fast and furious, as he did whenever possible. 'Scott was fairly wound up', wrote Bowers, 'and went on and on.' As a result of this exertion, over bad terrain pitted with crevasses (into which they all fell at times, dangling occasionally at the length of their harness straps), they finally camped at 85 °S. They had got out of the valley and away from the fog and crevasses. They were nearly out onto the plateau. The supporting party must have felt great regret. Their job was to struggle off down the glacier again, leaving their comrades to strike off towards the unknown. Cherry-Garrard gave Wilson his pyjamas and a bag of tobacco as a Christmas present for Scott.

Before they left, Scott instructed Atkinson to bring the dogs out later in the season to meet the Polar party on its way back, if Meares should have returned to civilization in the ship. There was every chance that Meares would do so. He and Scott had not got on well. Scott also knew that the dogs had performed more and more impressively. It obviously would be encouraging to tired men as they struggled back towards Cape Evans, to know that a frisky team of dogs, pulling a load of provisions, was on its way to meet them. Scott seems to have been unnerved by slight glimpses of the small margins of error for the return journey – such as the enormous 120-mile gap separating Mid Barrier Depot from One Ton – and by what he considered had been extraordinarily bad luck as regards weather. The dogs were to be his safety-net.

The eight men who travelled on south had two sledges and were pulling 190lbs per man: twelve weeks' supply of oil and food. Scott's party was unchanged: Wilson, Oates, and Petty Officer Evans. Teddy Evans's party consisted of Bowers, Lashley and Crean. The route was still uphill – and would remain so for another sixteen days until they reached their maximum altitude of 10,570 ft. After that there was a slight slope down the plateau to the Pole – a distance, from the Glacier, of 300 miles.

They were not entirely free of crevasses after all, as Lashley demonstrated. He celebrated his forty-fourth birthday by plunging down one. 'The thing was fifty feet deep and eight feed wide. Rather a ghastly sight when dangling in one's harness',[40] he admitted. Lashley was a West Countryman, of pure and healthy habits, a 'tough old sportsman' in Bowers's view. Crean, his messmate, was an Irishman who called himself 'The Wild Man of Borneo' – a man of mighty courage and no respecter of persons. It was going to be difficult for Scott to choose his last three companions.

For a while, however, there was no need. Christmas Day first, and they celebrated their white Christmas with an exhausting, and splendid, 15-mile march. It was another of Scott's blockbusters. Bowers recorded their exertions. 'My breath kept fogging my glasses, and our windproofs got oppressively warm and altogether things were pretty rotten. At last [Scott] stopped and we found we had done 14 miles. He said, "What about fifteen miles for Christmas Day?" so we gladly went on – anything definite is better than indefinite trudging.' Even Bowers, so often described as 'indefatigable' shows signs here of weariness.

In camp that night, they were rewarded for their efforts. Teddy Evans had kept a large piece of pony meat and the two tents shared it. 'The Soldier was delighted when we handed the meat over as a Christmas present – Oates was a tremendous meat-eater. We all fancied one thing more than another, but the Soldier's hankering was always after meat. A beefsteak is what he wished for most.'[41] Perhaps pony meat was an acceptable substitute, especially since it was thickened by ground biscuit, and followed by another hoosh of chocolate, cocoa, sugar, biscuit, and raisins, thickened with arrowroot; 2½ sq. ins. each of plum duff, a mug of cocoa, four caramels and four pieces of crystallized ginger. 'Could not hardly move', Lashley commented, and Scott remarked next day that perhaps they found themselves 'a little slow after plum pudding'.

Scott was not relaxed, despite the celebrations. Bowers broke the hypsometer (an instrument for determining altitude) and when he reported it, 'got an unusual outburst of wrath in consequence, in fact my name is mud at present. It is rather sad to get into the dirt tub with one's leader at this juncture, but accidents will happen'.[42] The strains of leadership were beginning to tell, as Scott confessed. 'I find it is very tiring and worrying.' The constant need for vigilance, and the responsibility for decisions, must have been most taxing – especially since he maintained the strict naval tradition of the loneliness of command.

Scott's anxieties also manifested themselves in the contest, now fairly naked, between the two remaining teams. Men who had got so far were obviously keen, maybe even desperate, to go on to the Pole – except perhaps Oates. 'The back tendon of my right leg feels as if it had been stretched about 4 inches. I hope to goodness it is not going to give trouble,' he wrote on 26 December, and, suffering himself, he watched the struggles of Evans's team with compassion. 'Scott is very annoyed about the other team's sledge. They must have had a cruel time this week . . . they had a dreadfully heavy day arriving in camp ¾ hour after us . . . Poor devils, they are having a cruel time of it. They have a lighter load than us, but their sledge must have something the matter with it.'[43]

Scott's reaction was more impatient. He, too, saw the possibility that something was wrong with Evans's sledge. 'I have told them plainly that they must wrestle with the trouble and get it right for themselves . . . they have not managed well for themselves.'[44] Evans and Lashley, of course, had been manhauling for 300 miles longer than anyone else – since the breakdown of the motors. Evans was also in the early stages of scurvy. If Scott's attitude seems unsympathetic, it must be said that often people who arouse one's guilt are treated badly. Scott must have known that he was going to send back Evans, Lashley and Crean, long before the official decision was broadcast. Sending men back at such a stage seems very hard – like a rejection. A sensitive man such as Scott could easily have fallen into the habit of persecuting his victims. It would make a change from persecuting himself, and besides, he had to gird up his resolution and tell them they had to go back.

On New Year's Eve the teams halted for half a day's repair work, stripping down their 12-foot sledges, removing the worn runners and replacing them with new 10 ft runners, giving a new, lighter sledge. The seamen busied themselves with this work, while the five officers gathered in Scott's tent for a long talk. Evans records that a most unusual thing happened – 'Oates took the lead in the conversation. He told us all about his home and his horses; he described his life with his regiment at Mhow, and we were amused that he shared a bungalow with a subaltern who was not of his own troop . . . so it was not then his business to shake him up if he "slacked it in the mornings"! He gave the most interesting descriptions of the polo teams in India; he told us of the shooting-trips he had made; he described the pig-sticking, and told us how the NCOs of his regiment were allowed and encouraged to get leave for shooting expeditions. He described their regimental life, and we were delighted at the efficiency and splendid goodfellowship that he had convinced us prevailed in the regiment he was so proud of and loved so well.

'He talked on and on, and his big, kind, brown eyes sparkled as he recalled little boyish escapades at Eton. He made us all laugh by telling us about an examination of a subaltern for the rank of captain. Oates was then one of the Board. A rather nervous major was interrogating the candidate, who was a magnificent athlete, but who had not really worked up for his examination. They wanted to pass the young officer as he was such an asset to the regiment, but he was not up to the examination standard by a long way, and the major could get nothing out of him. Suddenly, to the surprise of everyone, the candidate patted the major on the shoulder with the remark, "It's all right, old chap; you needn't be so nervous or shy about your questions!"

'Oates talked for some hours. At length Captain Scott reached out and affectionately seized him in the way that was itself characteristic of our leader, and said, "You funny old thing, you have quite come out of your shell, Soldier. Do you know, we have all sat here talking for nearly four hours?" ' Evans recalled that on this New Year's Eve 'we warmed to each other in a way that we had never though of, quite oblivious to cold, hardship, scant rations, or the great monotony of sledge hauling'.[45] Certainly Oates gave his comrades a glimpse of his whole character and background: his place in a quintessentially English tradition. The hunting, the shooting, and the horses, the effortless security, the indifference towards, even contempt for, the details of rank and the minutiae of regulations. Oates revealed himself as the perfect Tory anarchist.

But what is most significant is that Oates should talk so freely and so personally in Scott's tent. Several of his comrades remarked on it. It was as if for the first time in Scott's presence Oates had fundamentally relaxed. In earlier days, when worries over the ponies preoccupied him, he would not have managed to shake off his anxieties and be so expansive. Perhaps, once the last pony had been shot at Shambles Camp, an enormous sense of relief had flooded over him. The tensions of responsibility, and the resentments over incompetence, must have faded away, and with them, surely, the worst of his irritation with Scott.

The next day, back on the march, Evans's team abandoned their skis – on Scott's orders – and marched on foot. Scott's team meanwhile kept theirs. Scott gave no reason for this somewhat strange decision, even recording in his diary that it was 'a plod for the foot people and pretty easy going for us'. Was he attempting to make it easier to send them back by tiring them out on the last few days' march? Was he conducting an experiment? Certainly Scott's mind seems sometimes to have worked in a mysterious way, and on many levels and at varying degrees of consciousness. The next day he went to their tent to perform the dreaded deed: to tell them that it was his team, not theirs, which was going on the Pole, and that they were going back. As he stepped inside, Crean happened to be coughing. 'You've got a bad cold, Crean,' said Scott. 'I understand a half-sung song, sir', Crean cannily replied. In truth they must all have been expecting it – except perhaps Evans, who as second-in-command might well have cherished hopes.

But there was a remarkable sting in the tail of Scott's message, tough as it already was. He wanted Bowers to leave Evans's tent, join his own party and play his part in a five-man assault on the Pole. Evans, Lashley and Crean were to make the 600 miles or so back to Cape Evans as best they could, one man short. This was an extraordinary decision, quite overturning all expectation. Evans agreed, probably too shocked to think it all out properly, certainly too proud to object lest he look small, and moreover too well-trained as a naval officer to resist an order even if it were disguised as a request.

It was the moment at which, given retrospect, all was balanced in the scales. If Evans had resisted the plan, might disaster have been avoided? Even if Scott had listened in a more relaxed way to advice from his fellows he would still, by the force of his intellect and will-power, have made out an excellent case for a five-man Polar party. Scott was good at marshalling arguments and an eloquent and persuasive talker. But in fact the selection of his final party rested not so much on arguments as on emotion. He was truly great of heart. His spontaneous seizing of Oates on New Year's Eve, that 'You funny old thing, you have quite come out of your shell, Soldier!' – is utterly typical of the way Scott took to people.

And once he had taken to them, like a terrier, he was very reluctant to let them go.

Wilson was in many ways an obvious choice. He had been Scott's companion on his previous Farthest South in 1902. He was a medical man, a spiritual prop and stay, a peacemaker, and physically very fit. And he had an unchallengable place in Scott's heart. On all possible grounds, his place was with the Polar party. Bowers had made himself indispensible and was obviously a tireless worker and a strong traveller, buoyed up by a cheery temperament and an overtly expressive faith. He, too, was an excellent choice.

But over Petty Officer Evans and over Oates there hung many unanswered questions. Evans was the largest man of the party, a strong-as-an-ox, salt-of-the-earth type. But he had in recent years become something of a drinker, and Wilson was not confident of his ability to perform well under stress. In fact, just before Atkinson's return, he and Wilson had agreed that, of the seamen, Lashley was the best fitted, mentally and physically, to go on to the Pole. But Lashley did not have a place in Scott's heart. Taff Evans did. He had been with Scott on the *Discovery* and they had fallen down crevasses together. His sheer bulk inspired confidence, in the way that appearances often deceive. Scott, with a touching sensitivity to the requirements of British Liberalism, wanted a member of the Lower Deck -- the Working Class -- to be at the Pole. And Taff Evans was the man he wanted there.

As for Oates -- his selection could easily be accounted for. He was a soldier: Scott wanted the army to be represented at the Pole. (In fact Scott seems to have been a little too conscious of his comrades as representatives rather than hard travellers.) Oates had, also, patently, earned his place by his tireless and self-sacrificing work with the ponies. But under the obvious reasons for his selection lies a deeper enigma. Since mid-December his feet had been giving him trouble. His old war wound was hurting. Atkinson had guessed he wasn't feeling fit enough and didn't want to go on. During the pony marches earlier, he had always had to march non-stop with the wicked Christopher and missed his rest at lunch -- day after day, week after week. During the four-day blizzard he had spent hour upon hour out in the snow, seeing to the horses. He had been harder worked than his fellows. He had had less rest and shelter. Now he was tired.

Of course none of this was said. Oates had always enjoyed sailing close to danger. This present journey had long since ceased to be enjoyable, but he was prepared to play the endurance game. All the same, it was a strange letter that he penned to his mother on 3 January 1912.

Dear Mother,

I have been selected to go on to the Pole with Scott as you have seen by
the papers. I am of course delighted but I am sorry I shall not be home
for another year as we shall miss the ship. We shall get to the Pole
alright. We are now within 50 miles of Shackleton's Farthest South.

It is pretty cold up here (9500 feet) and the work has been very
heavy but it is easier now as we can ski . . . I am very fit indeed and
have lost condition less than anyone else almost. I hope the
alterations at Gestingthorpe have been carried out, I mean the
archway between Violet's and my room and my gear in the room
opposite the bathroom, it will be nice in there as I can have a fire at

night better than in my old one. My clothes I left in the ship for returning to Lyttleton in will be in a fearful state from damp I am afraid so I have enclosed a list of things I should like sent out for me if you will, also I enclose a note for Brujum it is about the filly.

Can you please also send me ½ doz books so I can start working for my major's exam on the way home, these things should be addressed to the Terra Nova at Lyttleton. What a lot we shall have to talk about when I get back – God bless you and keep you well until I come home.

L. E. G. Oates

PS.

4th – Waiting in the tent for hoosh. We get plenty of food and as soon as we start back we have plenty in the depots. Please give my love to Violet Lilian and Eric. . .

I am afraid the letter I wrote to you from the hut was full of grumbles but I was very anxious about starting off with those ponies.

There follows a list of clothing he would like sent out. He also ordered some tobacco, cigarettes and a big box of caramel creams.

This letter is a brave attempt to rally his own spirits and reassure his mother about his fitness, even though two weeks earlier when he had said goodbye to Atkinson he had given the impression of a man 'who knew he was done – his face showed him to be and the way he went along'.[46] He reassures himself, too, about the food rations and the waiting depots (which were to loom larger and larger in their expectations as the Polar party returned). But the letter lapses uncontrollably into a yearning celebration of the world he had left: his manor house, the crackling fire, his vital, breezy single sister and his poised, elegant married one, his younger brother and their conspiracies in horseflesh.

Just as he talked suddenly and rapturously about his life at home (in Scott's tent on New Year's Eve), now he seems desperate to conjure it up in detail. He makes his list of things he would like sent as if by organizing for a future, there will be one – as a major, perhaps. But the poignant undertones of his mood emerge all too clearly in his awkward-elegant apology, by proxy, to Scott for his 'grumbles' and above all, in the way he signs himself off: 'God bless you and keep you well until I come home.' Oates had never before indulged himself in more than the slightly brusque 'Yours affectionately'. It is the only time God is ever mentioned in any of his letters. It is as if he senses that human agencies may not, any longer, be enough.

Scott had not yet sensed the real shadow, for Oates, of his increasing exhaustion and pain. He was buoyed up on high hopes. 'The excitement was intense', Teddy Evans recalled. 'It was obvious that with five fit men – the Pole being only 145 miles away – the achievement was merely a matter of ten or eleven days' good sledging.' Evans and his party made their farewells and it was a touching scene, 'Oates being far more affected than any other of the Southern Party. He handed me a letter for his mother, and told me to write and let his people know how fit and happy he was. His last words were words of consolation at our not going forward, and thanks for our undertaking the return journey short-handed.

'I'm afraid, Teddy, you won't have much of a slope going back, but old Christopher is waiting to be eaten on the Barrier when you get there.'[47] They waved goodbye. Crean wept: Irish tears in the snow, and even hard-bitten old Lashley was affected. They cheered, and then turned northwards towards Cape Evans, carrying a message from Scott that the dogs were to be brought out to meet the returning Polar party between 82 ° and 83°S – a good deal further south than previously envisaged. Misgivings filled the air, as well as cheers.

Soon there was fuel for the misgivings. Cooking for five took considerably longer than cooking for four. And Bowers, who had been in Teddy Evans's team when the ski had been jettisoned, was having to plod along on his stumpy legs and keep up with his mates on their ski. On 6 January, Scott decided that the whole party would leave their ski and continue on foot as the surface was too much cut up for ski and they reckoned would remain so. They were wrong, and next day, had to go back and fetch them. With ski or without, it was heavy going, with strong head winds, a whirling blizzard one day that made steering impossible, and slow progress.

Scott consoled himself by celebrating his companions. 'Oates had his invaluable period with the ponies; now he is a foot slogger and goes hard the whole time, does his share of camp work, and stands the hardship as well as any of us. I would not like to be without him either. So our five people are perhaps as happily selected as it is possible to imagine.'[48] Scott had a way, when feeling good, of polishing away at his happiness like Aladdin, in the hopes, no doubt, of the arrival of some genie to bestow climactic success. 'It is wonderful to think that two long marches would land us at the Pole,' he wrote on 15 January. But the abyss was beneath him. 'The only appalling possibility is the sight of the Norwegian flag forestalling ours.' They must all have known it would, of course: they were all too intelligent, or too sceptical to think otherwise – except for Evans. Evans, with his touching faith in his captain, and his bar-room dismissals of all challenges to the British world of roast beef, plum pudding and manhauling; Evans alone probably still believed in the fairytale that the British flag would be flying there first. On this day, Oates confided, 'my pemmican must have disagreed with me at breakfast, for coming along I felt very depressed and homesick'.[49]

The next day brought an end to their uncertainties. 'About the second half of the march Bowers's sharp eyes detected what he thought was a cairn: he was uneasy about it . . . Half an hour later he detected a dark speck ahead. Soon we knew that this could not be a natural snow feature. We marched on, found that it was a black flag tied to a sledge bearer; nearby the remains of a camp; sledge tracks and ski tracks going and coming and the clear trace of dogs' paws – many dogs. This told us the whole story. The Norwegians have forestalled us and are first at the Pole. It is a terrible disappointment, and I am very sorry for my loyal companions. Many thoughts come and much discussion have we had. Tomorrow we must march on to the Pole and then hasten home with all the speed we can compass.'[50]

'We are not a very happy party tonight', Oates reported from the tent on that dismal evening. 'We have picked up the Norskies' tracks pointing straight there. Scott is taking his defeat much better than I expected.'[51]'

On 18 January, they found the Norwegians' last southerly camp, with its tent, Norwegian flags and various pieces of broken and unwanted gear. There was a letter from Amundsen.

Dear Captain Scott,
As you are probably the first to reach this area after us, I will ask you kindly to forward this letter to King Haakon VII. If you can use any of the articles left in the tent please do not hesitate to do so.
With kind regards I wish you a safe return.
Yours truly

Roald Amundsen

The request to forward the letter may simply have been a precaution on Amundsen's part against a mishap of some kind. It certainly had a humiliating effect. The dispirited British party marched onwards for a couple of miles towards the spot which they had calculated to be the exact geographical Pole. (In fact they were a mile or two away, as was Amundsen's tent.) Here they built a cairn and Scott recorded: 'Put up our poor slighted Union Jacks, and photographed ourselves – mighty cold work, all of it . . . The Pole,' continued Scott in his diary. 'Yes, but under very different circumstances from those expected . . . Great God! This is an awful place and terrible enough for us to have laboured to it without the reward of priority.'[52] Wilson commented, 'A very bitter day'. Only Oates had some words of appreciation for Amundsen.

'I must say that man must have had his head screwed on right. The gear they left was in excellent order and they seem to have had a comfortable trip with their dog teams very different from our wretched man-hauling.'[53] Wilson and Bowers, for all their Christian piety, seem to have had to struggle much harder for a charitable reaction. Bowers rejoiced that 'we have done it by good British man-haulage. That is the traditional British sledging method and this is the greatest journey done by man'.[54] Wilson conceded that Amundsen had 'beaten us in so far as he made a race out of it'.[55] Oates was the only one of the party with the magnanimity – and the complete lack of delusion – to call a spade a spade. They had what would have been a celebratory meal with a small stick of chocolate as a treat. It was some slight consolation to a most demoralized party. 'Now for the run home and a desperate struggle,' wrote Scott. 'I wonder if we can do it.'

It did not start too badly. The wind was behind them: they hoisted a sail. But they could not hoist their hearts. 'One of my big toes has turned black.' Oates wrote. 'I hope it is not going to lame me for marching.'[56] Evans had lost his cheeriness, and Scott observed, 'I don't like the easy way in which Oates and Evans get frostbitten.' He didn't like the weather, either. 'Is the weather breaking up? If so, God help us . . .' Still, it held. And they were lucky in being able to find and follow their tracks: a sure way of keeping on course. On 31 January, Bowers picked up his jettisoned ski – 'my dear old ski'. His affection for his ski is understandable. They meant an end to the intolerable, jolting march he had been forced to make for so long. Around this time Oates also found the pipe which he had dropped on the way out. Comforted by this, he relaxed enough to confess to Wilson about his black toe. But despite the toe, they were making good marches of around sixteen or seventeen miles a day.

Now serious ailments plagued them. All Evans's fingernails were coming off, 'very raw and sore' commented Wilson. 'Titus' toes are blackening and his nose and cheeks are dead yellow . . . Evans' fingers suppurating, nose very bad and rotten looking.' Wilson himself strained a tendon in his right leg, and on 2 February Scott had a nasty fall on the point of his shoulder. Little flaws in the organization ate away at their confidence. On 7 February they discovered that a whole day's biscuit ration was missing. Scott, who described it as a 'panic', recorded that Bowers was 'dreadfully disturbed'. As stores officer, Bowers must have felt responsible. He made no more entries in his diary, in which his cheerfulness had persisted so long.

'We are in rather a nasty hole tonight', Oates reported on 12 February. 'Got among bad crevasses and pressure, all blue ice. We struggled in this chaos until about 9 p.m. when we were absolutely done, and camped on some ice between crevasses.' They were lost on the way down the Beardmore Glacier – desperate to find their depot, with only one meal left. Next day, thick fog threatened to add to their torments, but briefly the fog lifted and Wilson spotted the cairn. Scott said it was 'the worst experience of the trip and gave a horrid feeling of insecurity.'[57] But there was worse in store. Though they were all weakening, Evans was giving 'serious anxiety. This morning he suddenly disclosed a huge blister on his foot. It delayed us on the march, when he had to have his crampon re-adjusted. Sometimes I fear he is going from bad to worse . . . He is hungry and so is Wilson . . . We can't risk opening out our food again, and as cook at present I am serving something under full allowance.'[58]

By now they were all suffering from malnutrition with its uneasy effects of mental dislocation. 'It is an extraordinary thing about Evans', wrote Oates, 'he has lost his guts and behaves like an old woman or worse.'[59] Scott agreed. 'Evans has nearly broken down in brain, we think. He is absolutely changed from his normal self-reliant self . . . perhaps all may be well if we can get to our depot tomorrow fairly early, but it is anxious work with the sick man.' Oates had little hope. 'Evans is quite worn out with the work and how he is going to do the 400 odd miles we have still to do I don't know',[60] he reported, and added a day later, 'Camp at 8.15 owing to poor Evans having a partial collapse. He first had to get out of his harness and hold onto the sledge and later said he could not go on. If he does not get by tomorrow God knows how we are going to get him home. We could not possibly carry him on the sledge.'[61]

Again and again the party was delayed, as Evans, becoming more con-fused, lagged behind.

His ski shoes came adrift, so he had to get out of harness to fix them. They were, as Scott put it, 'in a desperate pass . . . with a sick man on our hands at such a distance from home'. On 18 February Oates's diary entry was bleak indeed. 'Twice Evans had to get out of his harness – the second time for good.' Again, Evans had claimed that his ski shoes were wearing loose, and asked Bowers for a piece of string to fix them. 'I cautioned him to come on as quickly as he could', said Scott, 'and he answered cheerfully as I thought. We had to push on, and the remain-der of us were forced to pull very hard, sweating heavily. They camped for lunch, expecting Evans to catch them up, but there was no sign of him.

'After lunch', Oates wrote, 'as Evans was not up we went back on ski for him, Scott and I leading and we found him on his hands and knees in a most pitiable condition.' Evans's clothing was disarranged, his hands uncovered and frostbitten, and there was a wild look in his eyes. Scott, deeply shocked, asked him what was the matter. Evans mumbled that he didn't know, but he thought he must have fainted. 'He was unable to walk', Oates recorded, 'and the other three went back for the empty sledge and we brought him into the tent where he died at 12.30 a.m.'[62]

No doubt dreadfully shocked, his companions tried to make sense of events. 'On discussing the symptoms', wrote Scott, 'we think he began to get weaker just before we reached the Pole, and that his downward path was accelerated first by the shock of his frostbitten fingers, and later by falls during rough travelling on the glacier, further by his loss of all confidence in himself. Wilson thinks it certain he must have injured his brain by a fall.' Wilson's diagnosis was supported more than sixty years later by Dr A. F. Rogers, M.D., who concluded after many years of research that Evans's death was due to a 'slowly developing cerebral lesion of the central nervous system',[63] to which his restricted diet had contributed. In other words, Evans had scurvy, which led to an increased fragility of the blood vessels. In his condition, a minor head injury could result in a slowly developing brain haemorrhage 'It is a terrible thing to lose a companion in this way', commented Scott, 'but calm reflection shows that there could not have been a better ending to the terrible anxieties of the past week.'[64]

Shocked by Evans's death, and yet, in a sense relieved, for 'the absence of poor Evans is a help' – especially over rations – they sledged on hurriedly to Shambles Camp. Horsemeat in plenty awaited them there. 'We have had a fine supper,' wrote Scott 'to be followed by others such, and so continue to more plentiful era if we can keep good marches up. New life seems to come with greater food almost immediately.'[65] For a brief spell, Scott was optimistic. 'It is perhaps premature to be anxious about covering distance. In all other respects things are improving. We have our sleeping-bags spread on the sledge and they are drying, but, above all, we have our full measure of food again. Tonight we had a sort of stew fry of pemmican and hoosh, and voted it the best hoosh we ever had on a sledge journey. The absence of poor Evans is a help to the commissariat, but if he had been here in a fit state we might have got along faster.'[66]

These brief rays of hope soon paled and disappeared. Surfaces were dreadful and they floundered along, bogged down and struggling desperately, only achieving pitiful marches of four or five miles at times. 'We can't go on like this,' Scott commented. To make matters worse they wandered off their tracks and nearly missed a food depot and the life-sustaining horsemeat. To men so exhausted and debilitated, who had dragged their wretched sledge by now hundreds of miles, such scares must have been a desperate drain on their nervous energy. They were on the edge of starvation. 'We want more food and especially fat . . . We talk of little but food, except after meals.'

Temperatures were dropping very low. On the night of 27 February it was -40°F and on 1 March, - 41.5°F. 'The light airs come from the north and keep us horribly cold.' On 2 March they reached the long-awaited Middle Barrier Depot. Their supply of oil had only just lasted thus far and now to their horror they discovered a shortage of oil in this depot. The leather washers on the oil cans had perished, and some oil had evaporated. A shortage of fuel would mean cold food, and not enough heat even for a cup of tea or cocoa, at a later stage. 'With the most rigid economy,' wrote Scott, 'it can scarce carry us to the next depot on this surface' (71 miles away).

On the same day, to double misfortune upon misfortune, 'Titus Oates disclosed his feet, the toes showing very bad indeed, evidently bitten by the late temperatures.' Of course, Oates had been only too aware of his problem. His feet had now been giving him trouble for over two months, but for as long as he could, Oates had kept his problem hidden. Now concealment had become impossible. 'It fell below − 40 in the night', Scott reported, 'and this morning it took 1½ hours to get our foot gear on . . . In spite of strong wind and full sail we have only done 5½ miles. We are in a *very* queer street since there is no doubt we cannot do the extra marches and feel the cold horribly.'[67]

Temperatures were now regularly down to - 40°F. The autumn was closing in with a vengeance, and the surface so atrocious that the marches rarely rose above four or five miles a day. 'God help us, we can't keep up this pulling, that is certain. Amongst ourselves we are unendingly cheerful, but what each man feels in his heart I can only guess.' Each morning it took longer and longer for them to put their footgear on, especially Oates, whose feet were now swollen. Oates had stopped keeping his diary on 24 February with the entry, 'Dug up Christopher's head for food but it was rotten'. Christopher, that swine, who had given Oates so many bruises and received so much patient care in return, had played his last dirty trick.

Scott was living in terror of another cold spell. 'I fear that Oates at least would weather such an event very poorly. Providence to our aid!'[68] The shortage of food and fuel plagued them. 'We went to bed on a cup of cocoa and pemmican solid with the chill off . . . we pretend to prefer the pemmican this way . . . The result is telling on us all, but mainly on Oates, whose feet are in a wretched condition. One swelled up tremendously last night and he is very lame this morning . . . the poor Soldier is nearly done. It is pathetic enough because we can do nothing for him: more hot food might do a little, but only a little, I fear.' Wilson did his best to dress Oates's feet and keep his spirits up.

On 6 March, 'poor Oates is unable to pull, sits on the sledge when we are track-searching – he is wonderfully plucky as his feet must be giving him great pain. He makes no complaint, but his spirits only come up in spurts now, and he grows more silent in the tent.' Terrible surfaces and general exhaustion were making the sledge 'as heavy as lead'. For the first time, Scott makes Oates's awful dilemma clear. 'If we were all fit I should have hopes of getting through, but the poor Soldier has become a terrible hindrance, though he does his utmost and suffers much I fear.'

Oates's physical suffering was in itself quite horrifying. By now gangrene had set in and the pain must have been intolerable. He was totally exhausted, as indeed were the others. By 10 March it is clear that Scott has given up hope for himself. 'I should like to keep the track to the end.' Oates, too, would have liked to keep the track to the end, but to add to his physical torture was a moral one. Without him, the other three would undoubtedly get on faster. Without him, they might have a chance. Unable to pull, sitting miserably on the sledge during the halts, he found himself playing a dreaded role. Evans had played it before: he recognized all its sickening, humiliating details.

'Poor Titus is the greatest handicap,' Scott lamented on 10 March. 'He keeps us waiting in the morning until we have partly lost the warming effect of our good breakfast, when the only wise policy is to be up and away, and once again at lunch. Poor chap! it is too pathetic to watch him; one cannot but try to cheer him up.' Wilson had tried to do exactly that, the very same morning, when Oates asked him if he had a chance. Wilson replied that he didn't know. 'In point of fact he has none', wrote Scott. The next day the crisis seemed nearer. 'Titus Oates is very near the end, one feels. What we or he will do, God only knows. We discussed the matter after lunch: he is a brave fine fellow and understands the situation, but he practically asked for advice. Nothing could be said but to urge him to march as long as possible. One satisfactory result to this discussion: I practically ordered Wilson to hand over the means of ending our troubles to us, so that any one of us may know how to do so.' There was no revolver, which Oates had told Ponting should be taken on such trips, and which he might have used. He received instead thirty opium tablets. Not a soldierly solution.

Still the urge to survive, and a kind of obstinate defiance of death provoked him to limp on. The temperature was now down to -43°F. Oates's comrades were themselves faltering. Wilson got so horribly chilled on 14 March that he could not get off his ski for some time. They all felt deadly cold. 'Must fight it out to the last biscuit,' Scott wrote. A fierce, life-destroying wind came shrieking down on them from the heart of a gathering Antarctic winter. 'No idea there could be temperatures like this at this time of year with such winds', Scott observed. He clearly felt that fate had dealt him a truly disastrous hand. And on 'Friday March 16 – or 17 – lost track of dates' he had to report: 'Tragedy all along the line'.

On 15 March, Oates said he could go no further, and suggested they should leave him in his sleeping bag. They could not face doing so and urged him to march on. 'In spite of its awful nature for him he struggled on . . . At night he was worse and we knew that the end had come.' Oates knew he needed death. It was mercilessly clear. He was slowing the others up at every step. It took him almost two hours to get his foot-gear on. With advanced frostbite on hands and feet, he must have felt as if he had severe burns. Intense pain simply paralyzed him: the simplest actions took hours to perform. Bravely he had struggled on, hoping to make it, but his comrades' plight was now crucial. He was their problem. He was nothing but a hindrance to them. He had to die.

But how? The revolver might have been the right way. The opium was somehow wrong; it was cheating on nature. He had dodged small-pox inoculation, protested against 'wretched hospitals' and vowed never to be caught in one again, and was not the man to take such a way out. Medicines were for women and hypochondriacs. Now it was clear that sheer will-power would not get him through, that his strength was only a mortal man's, his time was up. And since death was coming too slowly for him, he simply got up and went out to meet it.

'He was a brave soul. This was the end. He slept through the night before last, hoping not to wake, but he woke in the morning – yesterday. It was blowing a blizzard. He said, 'I am just going outside and I may be some time.' He went out into the blizzard and we have not seen him since.' Out went Oates into the cold, and disappeared into a white and pitiless world: the kingdom of the chaste and the brave.

Notes and references

1 He continues this theme in his eight page letter written between 24 and 28 October 1911. 'Scott wants me to stay on here another year but I shall clear out if I get back in time for the ship which I hope to goodness will be the case, it will only be a small party to remain next year. Scott pretends at present he is going to stay but I bet myself a fiver he clears out, that is if he gets to the Pole, if he does not and some decent transport animals come down in the ship I have promised him I will stay to help him have another try but between you and me I think if he fails this time he will have had a pretty good stomach full.'

2 R. F. Scott, letter to Caroline Oates, October 1911.

3 T. Griffith Taylor, With Scott, *The Silver Lining*, p. 325.
4 R. F. Scott, diary, 1 November 1911.
5 A. Cherry-Garrard, *The Worst Journey in the World*, p. 321.
6 L.E.G. Oates, diary, 7 November 1911.
7 R. F. Scott, diary, 5 November 1911.
8 *Ibid.*
9 *Ibid.*
10 H. R. Bowers, quoted by A. Cherry-Garrard, *op. cit.*, p. 325.
11 R. F. Scott, diary, 13 November 1911.
12 L. E. G. Oates, diary, 12 November 1911
13 R. F. Scott, diary, 15 November 1911.
14 A. Cherry-Garrard, *op.cit., p. 328.*
15 R. F. Scott, diary, 19 November 1911.
16 L. E. G. Oates, diary, 18 November 1911.
17 R. F. Scott, letter to Kathleen Scott, 24 November 1911.
18 *Ibid.*, 28 October 1911.
19 L. E. G. Oates, diary, 24 November 1911.
20 H. R. Bowers, quoted by A. Cherry-Garrard, *op. cit.*, p. 335.
21 R. F. Scott, diary, 27 November 1911.
22 L. E. G. Oates, diary, 28 November 1911.
23 A. Cherry-Garrard, *op.cit.*, p. 337.
24 R. F. Scott, diary, 29 November 1911.
25 A. Cherry-Garrard, *op.cit.*, p. 339.
26 H. R. Bowers, quoted by A.Cherry-Garrard, *op. cit.*, p. 340.
27 R. F. Scott, diary, 3 December 1911.
28 *Ibid.*, 5 December 1911.
29 L. E. G. Oates, diary, 29 November 1911.
30 H. R. Bowers, diary, 8 December 1911.
31 Commander Evans, *My Recollections of a Gallant Comrade.*
32 A. Cherry-Garrard, *op. cit.*, p. 348.
33 *Ibid.*, 349.
34 L. E. G. Oates, diary, 4 December 1911.
35 E. A. Wilson, diary, 9 December 1911. In the same entry, '*Nobby* had all my five biscuits last night and this morning, and by the time we camped I was ravenously hungry.'
36 R. F. Scott, diary, 10 December 1911.
37 E. A. Wilson, diary, 17 December 1911.
38 *Ibid.*
39 L. E. G. Oates, diary, 19 December 1911.
40 W. Lashly, diary, 25 December 1911.
41 Commander Evans, *op. cit.*

42 H. R. Bowers, diary, 27 December 1911.

43 L. E. G. Oates, diary, 28 and 30 December 1911.

44 R. F. Scott, diary, 28 December 1911.

45 Commander Evans, *op.cit.*

46 E. L. Atkinson, quoted by A. Cherry-Garrard, diary, 4 April 1912.

47 Commander Evans, *op. cit.*

48 R. F. Scott, diary, 8 January 1912.

49 L. E. G. Oates, diary, 15 January 1912.

50 R. F. Scott, diary,16 January 1912.

51 L. E. G. Oates, diary, 16 January 1912.

52 R. F. Scott, diary, 17 January 1912.

53 L. E. G. Oates, 18 January 1912.

54 H. R. Bowers, letter to his mother, 17 January 1912.

55 E. A.Wilson, diary, 17 January 1912.

56 L. E. G. Oates, diary, 25 January 1912.

57 R. F. Scott, diary, 13 February 1912.

58 *Ibid.*, 14 February 1912

59 L. E. G. Oates, diary, undated.

60 *Ibid.*, 15 February 1912.

61 *Ibid.*, 16 February 1912.

62 *Ibid.*, 18 February 1912.

63 A. F. Rogers, *The Death of Chief Petty Officer Evans.*

64 R. F. Scott, 17 February 1912.

65 *Ibid.*, 18 February 1912.

66 *Ibid.*, 19 February 1912.

67 *Ibid.*, 2 March 1912.

68 *Ibid.*, 4 March 1912.

11

Hero or Victim?

Oates had lived in obscurity When he died, he became the world's property: a dead hero, his name a touchstone for certain values, his death an
example which thrills the imagination. Scott began the work of turning
his tent-mate into a legend. Only a few hours after Oates walked out, to
disappear for ever, Scott wrote: 'Should this be found I want these facts
recorded. Oates's last thoughts were of his mother, but immediately
before he took pride in thinking that his regiment would be pleased at
the bold way in which he met his death. We can testify to his bravery.
He has borne intense suffering for weeks without complaint, and to the
very end was able and willing to discuss outside subjects. He did not –
would not – give up hope till the very end. He was a brave soul . . . We
knew that poor Oates was walking to his death, but though we tried to
dissuade him, we knew it was the act of a brave man and an English
gentleman. We all hope to meet the end in a similar spirit, and assuredly
the end is not far.'[1]

Scott's own end is too well known to need detailed rehearsal here. He,
Bowers and Wilson died of starvation and exhaustion two weeks later in
their tent, held up by a blizzard only eleven miles from One Ton Depot.
Cherry-Garrard made a fatally hesitant journey towards them with the
dogs. He had been at One Ton Depot for six days, from 4 to 10 March,
but did not press on to meet the returning Polar Party due to the scarcity
of food for the dogs, his clear orders not to go further south and also out
of a very reasonable fear of missing Scott's party en route. They were at
the time only 65 miles away – three days' journey with dogs. This
haunted Cherry-Garrard for the rest of his life. The party at Cape Evans
gradually realized that their comrades were not going to return, and spent
a sombre last winter in the hut with its empty bunks. Led now by
Atkinson, they set out in the spring to search for the bodies. They found
Scott's tent on 12 November, 1912. Petty Officer Williamson described
the awful moment when Scott's tent was first glimpsed.

'Mr Wright came towards us and said it was the Polar Party, but how many he could not say. It was a great blow to us, and I must own I shed a few tears and I know the others did the same . . . I did not go over for quite a good time, for I felt I could not look on this most pitiable scene. But when at last I made up my mind I saw a most ghastly sight. Three sleeping-bags with frozen bodies inside them. The one in the middle I recognized as Captain Scott, our most brave and kind-hearted leader . . . [his] face and hands looked to me like old alabaster. His face was very pinched and his hands, I should say, had been terribly frostbitten. Never again in my life do I want to behold the sight we have just seen.'[2]

The search party did not move the bodies, but after removing the note-books, last letters and so on, simply took the bamboos of the tent away, and the tent itself covered them. A cairn was built over the spot and a rough cross erected. Then, said Cherry-Garrard, 'we go on to see if we can find Titus Oates's body, and so give it what burial we can. We start in about an hour, and I for one shall be glad to leave this place'.[3] Oates's body was never found. They found his sleeping-bag and footgear, though. 'One of the finneskoe was slit down the front as far as the leather beckets, evidently to get his bad foot into it.'[4] Near the spot where Oates walked to his death the party built a cairn and left the message: 'Hereabouts died a very gallant gentleman, Captain L. E. G. Oates of the Inniskilling Dragoons. In March 1912, returning from the Pole, he walked willingly to his death in a blizzard to try and save his comrades beset by hardship.'

At 2.30 a.m. on 12 February, 1913 (three months later), the *Terra Nova* 'crept like a phantom ship' into the little harbour of Oamaru, New Zealand. She came skulking back in this way because the relatives of the dead had to be told before the news became public. Also press contracts had to be honoured. A boat was lowered and Atkinson and Pennell landed, to send the telegrams. On board the *Terra Nova*, the survivors waited. 'At dawn the next morning, with white ensign at half-mast, we crept through Lyttleton Heads. How different it was from the day we left and yet how much the same: as though we had dreamed some horrible nightmare and could scarcely believe we were not dreaming still. The Harbour-Master came out in the tug and with him Atkinson and Pennell. "Come down here a minute", said Atkinson . . . "It's made a tremendous impression. I had no idea it would make so much", he said. We landed to find the Empire – almost the civilised world – in mourning.'[5]

Cables had been sent with the aim of informing the families before the news broke. But Mrs Oates was in London at the family flat in Evelyn Mansions, and missed the cable. Oates's elder sister Lilian (by now the

206

proud mother of a baby daughter, Sheila) was walking down a London street when she saw a newspaper placard announcing the tragic loss of Scott and the Polar party. Caroline Oates had two grandchildren to console her in her grief – for Bryan was also by now a parent: the father of a year-old son, Edward. But for Caroline Oates, the blow of her son's death was perhaps the bitterest experience of her life. Every night she slept in the bedroom he had used. In her handbag she kept one of his regimental epaulettes, and there were always fresh flowers under his portrait. Others shared her sense of loss.

Black-bordered letters flooded Gestingthorpe from every corner of the world. The most poignant came from Edward Wilson, who had written it in Oates's own notebook shortly after Oates's death. 'Dear Mrs Oates, This is a sad end to our undertaking. Your son died a very noble death, God knows. I have never seen or heard of such courage as he showed from first to last with his feet both badly frostbitten – never a word or a sign of complaint or of the pain – he was a great example. Dear Mrs Oates, he asked me at the end, to see you and to give you this diary of his. You, he told me, are the only woman he has ever loved. Now I am in the same can and I can no longer hope to see either you or my beloved wife or my mother or father – the end is close upon us, but these diaries will be found and this note will reach you some day.

'. . . If ever a man died like a noble soul and in a Christian spirit your son did. Our whole journey's record is clean and though disastrous – has no shadow over it. He died like a man and a soldier without a word of regret or complaint except that he hadn't written to you at the last, but the cold has been intense and I fear we have all of us left writing close until it is almost too late to attempt anything but the most scrappy notes. God comfort you in your loss.'[6] None of the other letters had so far to travel, but many came from people who had known Oates well and loved him dearly. His Inniskilling comrades wrote rapturously of him. 'I don't suppose that even you realised how much he was always loved and admired by every officer and man in the regiment', wrote Tim Gibson. 'I have just been talking to two of my servants who were in the regiment with him, one of them simply wept like a child.' Fergus Nixon declared, 'I have really lost my greatest friend'. Mabel Deighton, the wife of Oates's kennel master in India, wrote: 'My husband is proud he did serve him and often while serving him he said he never had a master to equal him in every way'. William King, to whom Oates had written from the Antarctic, and had sent his regards to the 'missus' whom they used to bore with their yarns about hunting and shooting, simply could not take in the news. It was 'difficult to realise, as it all happened so far away, and

Punch, or the *London Charivari*, 19 February 1913

I often think that someday he will come sailing home to tell us about what he did, and all the wonderful things he saw'. Major Richardson of the 13th Hussars provides the most characteristically sporting of the tributes. 'I was so sorry to hear about poor Oates, I did not know him well, but I do know that he was a right fellow to hounds, and other things generally follow.'

Oates's regiment, still in India, received the news with stunned disbelief. 'At a time when we were expecting word of Captain Scott's expedition after a long period of silence, and sanguine of their success, the news of the loss of the entire party of five who were selected for the final dash to the Pole, including our brave comrade Captain L. E. G. Oates, comes as a crushing blow to us all',[7] lamented the editorial of the journal of the 6th (Inniskilling) Dragoons, and confided that 'for hours we hoped there was a mistake somewhere, but as cablegram after cablegram came in from all sources, a distinct gloom was noticeable throughout the regiment'.[8]

Telegrams of condolence flew, to the bereaved families, to the regiment, to the Geographical Society – cables and letters from King George V, Queen Alexandra, the other crowned heads of Europe. All the Geographical and Philosophical Societies in the world, it seemed, from the Society of Naturalists, Odessa, to the Lima Geographical Society, were moved to respond. The news went around the globe like an electric shock, and to everyone it seemed that there was something about Oates's death in particular that was quite extraordinary. Sergeant-Major Williams, a former Inniskilling Dragoon, recalled, 'I was in London on the 12th of February, the day the news first became generally known, and everybody was talking of Captain Oates, in train and tram and tube one heard it, and I sitting and knowing him so well simply swelled with pride, and had difficulty in restraining myself from joining in every conversation I heard'.[9]

The press pounced on the story, and for days little else could find space as whole editions of some newspapers were given over to the expedition.[10] 'The Great Victory,' sang *The Observer*. 'Five Men of Deathless Glory,' answered the *Daily Mirror*, echoed by the *Primitive Methodist*'s leader, 'We Glory in Our Dead'. But perhaps it was paradoxically, a Belgium newspaper, *Le Temps*, which expressed most simply and eloquently what Oates's death meant to his contemporaries. In the course of a tribute entitled 'Un Gentleman', *Le Temps* asserted that 'his self-sacrifice bears the mark of that absolute self-control which an Englishman prizes above all else in the world. When the question is asked, What is a true gentleman? our neighbours will have no need to search their history or Shakespeare. It will suffice to reply that he is the man who behaves like Captain Oates'.

Harold Owen took up this theme in *The National Weekly*, in which he expands on Oates's epitaph, 'Hereabouts died a very gallant gentleman'. He laments that the word 'gentleman' had become a vulgarized cliché, and that 'futile and unnecessary efforts have been made to enlarge its meaning by defining what a gentleman really is'. But Oates, says Owen, simply embodies it, in his way of meeting death. 'No histrionics, no fuss, not even the emotional satisfaction of a formal farewell to his companions – a hero without heroics.' Again and again the same sentiments were reiterated. 'When Captain Oates went off to die alone, that he might cease to be a burden on his companions', remarked *World's Work*, 'he reached a furthest limit of what we are told is most excellent in human nature: *Greater love hath no man than this*. Few can have made the great sacrifice under circumstances more terrible.'

Yet the *World's Work* article goes on to ask, what was it all for? And concludes that Polar exploration is unlikely to yield any commercial results, nor add much to the sum of human knowledge. Nor, it believed, was national prestige enhanced by the arrival of certain Englishmen – forestalled ones at that – at the Pole. 'But it is for the sake of the great illusion, glory . . . the greatest of mankind will always pursue great objects . . . like Captain Scott's party we are journeying in a cold world towards nothing that we know. Yet we feel better for every proof that some of us can put up with hardship, run risk, make effort, throw life away, and rise with the wings of heroism above even the most pardonable weakness. It is lives thus lost that make all life worth living.'

That paradox captures something essential about Oates's death. When strangers heard of it, their sense of being alive was enriched. On the flood tide of sorrow and admiration, memorials to Oates sprang up everywhere. His regiment established the Oates Memorial Fund with the aim of providing homes for old soldiers. Memorials were unveiled, among other places, at Eton College, the Cavalry Club, St Anne's Church, Eastbourne, Meanwood Church, and in the Parish Church, Leeds. The Navy presented his regiment with a silver statuette. In later years the Oates Memorial Library and Museum was founded at Selborne, Hampshire; schools in Leeds and South America were named after him, he was commemorated by a Masonic Lodge in South Africa and a YMCA hut in East Anglia, and part of the Antarctic continent was named Oates Land. But perhaps the most important was the brass memorial which was placed in the north wall of Gestingthorpe Church 'In affectionate remembrance by his brother officers'. Every week, almost until her dying day, Caroline

37. The tree for Midwinter Day, 22 June 1911. Oates is seated on the left. Later that evening 'the silent soldier bubbled with humour and insisted on dancing with Anton.' (R.F. Scott)

38. Attempting to rescue three ponies stranded on an ice floe during the return from the depot-laying journey. A sketch by Dr Wilson.

39. At the Pole. 'We are not a very happy party tonight. Scott is taking his defeat much better than I expected.' (L. E. G. Oates).

40. While the children at many schools were told of the 'heroism and tragic fate' of Captain Scott and his comrades, the adults paid their respects in and outside St Paul's Cathedral.

41. The silver statuette presented to the 6th (Inniskilling) Dragoons by the Royal Navy.

42. The memorial cross on Observation Hill, near Hut Point. On it are inscribed the names of Scott, Wilson, Oates, Bowers and Evans, and this line from Tennyson's *Ulysses*: 'To strive, to seek, to find and not to yield.'

43. Captain L. E. G. Oates

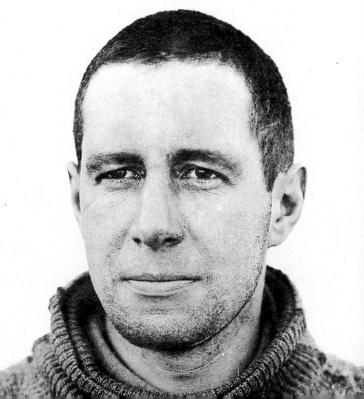

Oates would clean it. Towards the end of her life, she scarcely ever left the grounds except to go across to the church. A strong, white-haired figure in deep mourning, she kept the great brass plaque shining. On the day of its unveiling, the church was crowded by villagers, many of whom could remember their first glimpse of Oates as a serious eleven-year-old. Against their subdued clothes, the military visitors dazzled. 'A brilliant dash of colour was given by the scarlet uniforms and gold facings of the dragoon officers and by the richly gold-embroidered blue uniforms of the naval officers who had been Captain Oates's companions on the Scott Expedition'.[11] Atkinson and Meares were there, but it was Major-General Allenby[12] who gave the speech, and then six trumpeters of the Queen's Bays, standing in the porch, sounded the Last Post. His regiment also began a long-standing tradition by holding a Memorial Service each year in his honour on the Sunday nearest to 16th March.

The idiosyncratic and loving tributes of his friends contrast with the ringing rhetoric of the public voices. The national — even international — frenzy of feeling fed on whatever details could be gathered from those who had known him. Ponting told the *Daily Chronicle* of the conversation he had had with Oates in his darkroom, when Oates had declared that any one who broke down on a Polar journey should kill himself. 'And he's lived up to his ideal', said Ponting. 'To my mind it is the most touching thing of the whole tragedy.' Nansen, who had advised Scott about Polar travel, astutely commented that he thought that scurvy, not adverse weather conditions, was the chief cause of the Polar party's death. He concluded 'they set an example to the youth of coming generations of what true men are, and how men bear suffering and hardship for the cause which they have taken in hand'.[13] Above all, the feeling was that Oates and his comrades had taught

> The noblest of all lessons man can teach
> Not how to live but rather how to die.

This was a very timely lesson. The First World War, now brewing, was shortly to break out. For years England had been educating her young gentlemen in the virtues of self-sacrifice. But in the new century, British racial and cultural confidence was beginning to crack. To a nation uncertain of her values, and threatened by enemies, the example of Oates's death 'dispelled the doubt — from those frozen regions of the South there seems to come, like a trumpet call, a message: *the greatness of England still.*' One could go farther and say, *the greatness of manhood still.*[14] English manhood, thus encouraged, could face the Boche with exactly the right spirit of reckless self-sacrifice. Oates had died, it seemed, to encourage others.

Ponting's cine-film of the expedition, *90° South*, became hot property. In 1915, in response to an appeal from the Front, he gave prints of the film for the benefit of the British troops in France, and it was shown to more than 100,000 officers and men of the British Army. The Senior Chaplain to the Forces, the Reverend F. I. Anderson, wrote to Ponting, 'I cannot tell you what a tremendous delight your films are to thousands of our troops. The splendid story of Captain Scott is just the thing to cheer and encourage out here . . . the thrilling story of Oates's self-sacrifice, to try and give his friends a chance of "getting through" is one that appeals so at the present time. The intensity of its appeal is realized by the subdued hush and quiet that pervades the massed audience of troops while it is being told. We all feel we have inherited from Oates and his comrades a legacy and heritage of inestimable value in seeing through our present work.'[15] Ponting concludes his book *The Great White South* by asserting that 'twenty, fifty, a hundred, five hundred years hence, the story of the Immortal Five who perished after conquering the South Pole will inspire our youth just as it does to-day'. And as for Oates, the general feeling amongst his contemporaries was 'no one will ever dispute his heroism'.[16]

They have. On 4 June 1980 the *Guardian*'s headline screamed, 'Doubts cast on heroism of Captain Oates's walk out.' A new book, *Scott and Amundsen* by Roland Huntford suggested that Oates's act was not a spontaneous act of sublime courage, but a response to 'a day or two of silent hints' from Captain Scott. The view put forward is that Oates was a rugged survivor, not tainted with the mawkish and masochistic spirit of self-sacrifice which characterized his era and motivated his companions. So Scott had to exert moral pressure in order, cuckoo-like, to shoulder Oates out. The theory is based on a letter by Bernard Shaw, a friend of Lady Scott and of Cherry-Garrard whom he helped to write *The Worst Journey in the World*. Shaw conjectured that 'there was no getting away from the fact that Scott . . . had finally . . . to give Oates silent hints that he should go out to perish for a day or two before he did – too late [to save his companions' lives] – Poor Oates'.[17]

This compelling book is a masterpiece of iconoclasm. Indignant with the pedestal which history has accorded to Scott, Huntford seeks to substitute for it a deep hole. Not that the book is anti-heroic: it simply attempts to show that Amundsen deserves our admiration and that Scott does not. It interprets Scott's expedition as a series of catastrophic blunders from first to last, and suggests that Scott decided to lie in his tent and wait for death, trusting to the power of his poignant pen to snatch a greater victory from the jaws of defeat. In other words, Scott's posthumous glory was a literary creation, and demonstrates the British taste for death and failure rather than survival and success. Scott was the sacrificial victim, whose death affirmed jingoistic values and sent tens of thousands of young men to a meaningless death in the trenches in a spirit of sick self-sacrifice. Oates is seen as a relic of a more rational and secular age which placed more value on life than death, and who wanted to survive, but his stoical persistence did not suit Scott's death-and-glory mood. And so the 'silent hints' had to be given. Scott is also accused of falsifying the account of Oates's death to create the éclat of glorious heroism, whereas the reality was a 'poor suffering devil taking the only way out'. Scott is even accused of inventing Oates's famous last words: 'I am just going outside and I may be some time.'

Such ideas created a storm of protest. We live in a jaded, secular anti-heroic age, in which notions such as that of English manhood are more likely to arouse a satirical smile than a thrill of admiration. Nevertheless, an attempt to cut Scott down to size aroused almost universal anger and indignation. 'Leave our heroes alone', was the cry. 'Let the dead rest in peace'. It became clear how deeply embedded in the national consciousness was the need for heroes, especially Captain Scott. Sir Peter Scott, the explorer's son, spoke of 'character assassination' and a 'despicable maligning' of his father's memory. But the fury was not confined to those intimately connected with the explorers' families. The very ordinary British public wanted the patina of their heroes left intact; burnished, not tarnished, by any literary attention they might receive.

In fact Huntford was by no means the first to criticize Scott's methods, or even cast doubts on Oates's heroism. Previous biographies of Scott including those by Reginald Pound and Elspeth Huxley, have made his weaknesses and mistakes very clear. Scott himself, by the time of his death, was beginning to realize that dogs were the ideal form of Polar transport. And the *Geographical Journal*, published in March 1913, saw clearly enough the reasons for the disaster: the deterioration of Evans and Oates, the addition of a fifth man to the party of four originally intended for the Pole, the postponement of the start for a whole month because of the ponies' susceptibility to spring conditions, and above all 'the decision of Scott to rely on human haulage in preference to dogs'. The *Geographical Journal*, however, tempers these insights with its glowing appreciation of the moral example set – especially by Oates. 'Does history contain a finer picture than this young fellow, only thirty two years old – exactly the same age as Sir Philip Sidney at Zutphen – walking out of the tent in the shrieking snowstorm to give up his life for his friends?'[18]

If the *Geographical Journal* was both shrewd and sensitive, there was even in 1913 the old isolated voice of total scepticism. One B.J. of Birmingham wrote to the *Daily Sketch*, pursuing an argument about justifiable suicide: 'Captain Oates must necessarily, as an Arctic [sic] explorer, have been a very brave man. But to compare his death with the miner who steps aside from certain salvation to a horrible death, possibly to let a comrade reach daylight and happiness is quite past my comprehension . . .' B.J. was not so impressed, in Oates's case, by 'a dying man who chooses a speedy and not essentially painful death'. A debate about justifiable suicide was provoked. On one hand, the Christian prohibition was a very strong influence. On the other hand, the country was going to need heroes, and for a man to lay down his life for his friends was sublime. Most of Oates's contemporaries were thrilled and stirred by his death, but a few who did not know him demurred. Huntford was not the first to probe the dazzling myth. David Thomson in *Scott's Men* sees Oates as a listless, embittered man whose death came almost by accident. He 'cultivated a wordly indifference, as if it were gentlemanly. It leaves an odd, vulnerable dryness in his letters, not very appealing, not convincing either'.[19]

Of course it is easy now to find the hysteria of the 1913 reaction to news of the tragedy a trifle preposterous. Some of the poems topple into bathos.

> . . many a day his suffering did he hide,
>   A silent prisoner to his body pent,
>   Then, waked once more to find no message sent
> By Heav'n's kind angel, lo! he rose and cried
>   'Tarry ye here awhile, I go outside.'
>   And brave into the blizzard forth he went.[20]

The spurious archaisms of this poem identify these twentieth-century explorers with that tradition of chivalrous action dating from early mediaeval times, and culminating perhaps in the death of Sir Philip Sidney, to whom Oates is often compared. The suffocating, inflated tone of much of the celebration is slightly repellent to us nowadays. Yet, it seems, we share the feelings of our forbears, if not the excesses of their expression. Jilly Cooper, writing in *The Sunday Times* in 1974, confessed, 'I cry every time I read about Captain Oates going quietly off in the snow to die'. And there is no doubt that Mrs Cooper speaks for many. We obviously needed heroes in 1913 and still need them now. Why do we need them at all? And were Scott and Oates heroes – or Scott merely a bungler and Oates the victim of that incompetence?

We need heroes, especially heroes who are explorers, for a very simple reason. We are all travelling irrevocably towards 'that undiscovered country from whose bourn no traveller returns'. 'I runne to death, and death meets me as faste', wrote John Donne, and poets have tried for centuries to come to terms with death, our only certain destiny. Dylan Thomas urged old men to 'rage against the dying of the light', not supinely to accept it. But the death-bound poet Sylvia Plath, who committed suicide, declared that

> Dying is an Art
> Like everything else
> I do it exceptionally well.

Oates's contemporaries felt that he had died not just well but sublimely. He even pretended death didn't exist. His murmured last words, 'I am just going outside and may be some time,' refuse to acknowledge the horror of his certain end. Such defiant courage thrills those of us who hear it. Oates's note of understated nonchalance is the mark of true bravery. Real heroes do not strike attitudes. They are too busy living – or dying.

It is easy to dismiss Bernard Shaw's allegation that Scott 'had to give Oates silent hints that he should go out and perish'. Bernard Shaw was not there. He was relying on the opinions of his friend Cherry-Garrard, who was not there either. Cherry-Garrard's failure to meet his friends Wilson and Bowers, together with a conviction that Scott might not have appreciated his merits properly, left him with many painfully unresolved feelings. Cherry-Garrard had been told by Wilson, when he was about to leave with the rest of his supporting party, that the choice as to who should go on had been between him and Oates. So Cherry-Garrard's conjectures about what Scott and Oates said and did in the hours before Oates's death are not just as fragile as most conjectures are. They are complicated by the desperate turmoil of his own feelings about the event: his guilt and his mortification. They should not be taken as sufficient evidence to convict Scott of moral bullying or Oates of stubborn self-protectiveness. As for the idea of Scott's inventing Oates's last words, it is highly improbable. They are so exactly what Oates would have said: so drily non-committal. And so very different from what eloquent, emotional Scott would have invented for him. Those words have the ring of absolute authenticity.

Was Scott merely a bungler? Many of his men praised and admired him, dead and alive. Some, such as Oates, criticized him, found him hard to get on with, and subsequently regretted their harsh words. A few, such as Meares, appeared to have formed an enduring dislike of him. All this suggests – as do Scott's own words – the effect of a powerful, complex personality. Some men, having been with him on the *Discovery*, declined his invitation to join the *Terra Nova*. Others leapt at the chance. If Scott were nothing but a bungler, who could not have explored his way out of a paper bag, he could never have got away with it. His men would simply not have closed ranks in a conspiracy to protect the memory of a man who was downright incompetent and dangerous – and nothing else.

The answer to this enigma may be that Scott offered his companions – and posterity – some beliefs, values and characteristics which were at the very heart of his age. Our own society has evolved its own priorities and may now choose to dismiss patriotism, courage and self-sacrifice as impossibly old-fashioned notions. Scott's complex and charismatic character may not have been the ideal equipment for the commander of an Antarctic explorer even then, but it amounted to a personality of great human appeal. His emotional nature contributed to his mistakes. But a man of strong responses, and varying moods, is certainly more alive than a cold fish (and the fact is that Scott, even after his death, seems more alive to us than the admirable but cold Amundsen ever does). If Scott saw his actions rather self-consciously in terms of Greek myth, he was prepared to follow up the implications to the hilt. His conscious structuring of his experience was grand rather than grandiose. We may be embarrassed now by his rhetorical insistence on the greatness of the English race, but our shrinking from patriotism may in turn be an unhealthy excess.

Of course, Scott had faults – and many have pointed them out. His inflexibility, his failure to plan, his reluctance to admit weakness, his sentimentality and his resistance to advice were all evident to Oates and many others – at the time and since. But despite this, many of his officers and men loved him, lamented him and saluted the bravery and spirit which emerges from his last messages. Scott's end is a tragedy on the Shakespearean model: a truly great man who fails through a combination of his own weaknesses and the hostility of fate. To be encumbered with weaknesses and faults, and still be loved, honoured and celebrated, is a more interesting psychological and human paradox than an absolute world of black and white.

And what of Oates? He would have been amused and incredulous if he had known that his actions would be subjected to so close a scrutiny –

and that his heroism would be debated. He would have made no claims to heroism at all. We know what he thought of 'little putty heroes'. Nevertheless he is admired and celebrated as a hero by people who know nothing of his life. It is as if nothing matters except his death. But that incandescent death was not an uncharacteristic convulsion at the end of a banal and ordinary life. His friends were not surprised by it. It was what they would have expected of him. His character, his opinions, his assumptions, all prepared him for the final part he had to play. And in a sense the pattern of his life seems to lead to some extraordinary denouement.

Oates was England. The bedrock of his character was feudal: an *Otes* occupying the manor of Gestingthorpe at the time of the Domesday Book: his own simple pleasures of dog, horse, and hunt; huge open fires and the occasional drink. These sturdy patterns of life had changed little since the age of barbarism. Then, there were the Georgian resonances: his thoroughly democratic spirit, mucking in with the lads, wearing rough old clothes and absurd boots tied up with wire. His deeply rational attitudes owe much to the Age of Enlightenment. So do his dry wit, his sense of irony, and his satirical eye. His indifference to social convention and his spirited pessimism conjure up the picture of the English squire, so often described as eccentric and unorthodox.

Oates drew his strength from centuries of English history. But his own age brought new challenges – some congenial to him, some not. It brought Christian/stoical notions of service and duty. The stoicism suited Oates well. He liked to keep his mouth shut, and he welcomed hard physical work and the chance to try his strength against others. He could do without the late Victorian piety. Evangelical religion, like opiates, were for old men and women. And as for women, their growing emancipation unnerved him slightly. Like his forbears, he preferred women to keep to their own territory, and was easy only if he could regard them as an alien species. Watching one of the expedition's dogs, he remarked to Cherry-Garrard, 'Frami is just like a woman. She is always putting her head into places where she ought not to go . . . and then she screams for help when anything happens'.

The twentieth century brought other challenges to his assumptions. He baulked at the Labour Socialists of Cardiff. After all, he already treated all men as equals, and did not want to be legislated into it – or into anything else. Sophisticated medical techniques were an insult to his manhood. Growing professionalism and the importance of technical and scientific education offended his sense of the individual vigour of the amateur and the sportsman. And it is this notion of the sportsman which lies at the heart of Oates's nature. Luckily, his own age cultivated the idea of sport, more earnestly than previous eras, which had found enough justification in the enjoyment and excitement of it. All Oates's instincts were sporting ones – which means that his senses and appetites were sharply tuned towards experiences which were physically taxing, combative, fun, and held some element of risk. All this is very much in keeping with the old England. The new England with its stifling social conformity, trivial bourgeois rituals and leaden religiosity, must have become unendurable at times to such a free and sporting spirit. He belonged to an England deeper and older than that. So when strangers called him the perfect example of an English gentleman they spoke a more complex and complete truth than they knew.

His energies drove him towards several fields of action. The first was exciting sports: riding hard, sailing in the teeth of a gale, defying 120 Boers (for that, surely, was a sporting experience for him, too). They all show his taste for danger. He sought thrills, and that sense of enhanced life which comes from being a breath away from death. But there was always a cut-off point to his recklessness, later than most men's which, up until the Antarctic, had enabled him to survive. Apart from the frequent and brief forays into sport, he longed restlessly for the refreshment of travel. Egypt, India, Antarctica came as alluring new adventures to him. Oates was not the only explorer who may have been driven, to some extent, by an impatience with his society. Mary Kingsley was treated as an outcast by Victorian society because of her illegitimacy, and ended up in Africa. If your society allows you no sense of yourself you have to go out and find it – somewhere else.

Many elements combined to bring him to Antarctica: a desire to escape from social constrictions, the promise of great trials of strength, the excitement of being on the frontiers of discovery, and the sportsman's aim to be first if possible but if not, to have a thundering good time anyway. He came to this great adventure, as he had come to everything else in his life, with a striking degree of personal strength, albeit veiled by his habitual quietness. He had grown up wealthy and loved, into a man whose joy lay in the active exploration of the physical world, undisturbed by philosophical uncertainties. No wonder he was a powerful figure. He never had to struggle to assert his personality – it was simply there, as many of his companions describe – massive, unobtrusive, impossible to ignore, irresistibly attractive. Oates was his own man. He could never, in any circumstance, have been anyone else's victim.

On the way back from the Pole, he found himself suddenly, and much earlier than he might reasonably have expected (his brother and sisters all lived into their eighties) at the end of his road. To some extent, other people's blunders and misconceptions had brought him there. He certainly realized that for survival in Antarctica, Amundsen's techniques were far superior to his own expedition's methods. But there were other facts, too: the bad weather, the gradual erosion of health and spirits by the unseen enemy, scurvy: his own war-wound, which was in some way's a death blow whose final despatch had merely been delayed some eleven years. And apart from all these causes which contributed towards his end, there was his own stubborn refusal to turn back, his own sportsman's gamble to chance his luck. Before setting out on the Polar journey he had debated whether to tell Scott he wanted to go back with the ship (and would therefore have to be sent back with one of the supporting parties). Later, when Atkinson turned back, he said he felt Oates knew he was 'done' — could tell it by his face. His feet were already giving him trouble. He could have admitted his problems and turned back then. But that was not the sportsman's way.

He probably still wanted to get to the Pole. He probably still felt his luck would hold and enough sheer grit would get him there and back. His courage was Titanic — but so, alas, was his destiny. When the Norwegians' flag appeared in the snows and they knew they had lost, it was a struggle even for the overt Christians of the British party to be entirely graceful in defeat. But for Oates the sportsman it was easy. He was a good loser. And a few weeks later, when he reached the end of his time and his energies, he raised the art of losing well to sublime heights. He knew what to do, although not, for a moment, exactly how to do it. There was no revolver. Hence his question to Scott — the moment when Oates appeared to falter. 'Poor fellow, he practically asked for advice', wrote Scott. 'Nothing could be said but to urge him to march as long as he could.' In fact, Oates was probably not asking about his chances of life, but how to achieve the obviously necessary death.

He knew his time was up; he knew that, for the others, it was not, and they might have a chance if he disappeared and stopped holding them up. In some ways, his walking out might seem the logical last step for a man who had felt frustrated by his society and wanted, all his life, to be out in the cold. But that is too simple a view. It is clear from his last recorded thoughts and words, from his nostalgic last letter and his ceaseless talk, on New Year's Eve, of his regiment, his home, his horses, that he very much wanted a future. He had come as far away as possible, to a world of nothingness. And he had half-turned from its bleak embrace, longing to see again the England which, despite everything, he loved, and which he embodied.

So it must have been terribly hard to leave the tent, that last vestige of civilization; hard to leave the dreams of a future, the open fire in the manor house, the major's exams. All the same, he had gambled and lost. With a shrug, and with an offhand phrase he went – a sportsman who knew how to lose. He faced the most difficult act of all, a truly horrifying death, and he made it look easy. And because it took him two hours of painful struggling to put his footgear on, he went out to die in his socks. What more can we ask of our heroes?

1 R. F. Scott, diary, 16 or 17 March 1912.
2 Thomas Williamson, diary, 12 November 1912.
3 A. Cherry-Garrard, diary, 13 November 1912.
4 *Ibid.*, 14 November 1912.
5 A. Cherry-Garrard, *The Worst Journey in the World*, p. 573.
6 E. A.Wilson, letter to Mrs Oates, March 1912. This letter was written in Oates's diary, as was Wilson's final letter to his wife. 'Please be so good as to send pages ^54 and 55 of this book to my beloved wife addressed Mrs Ted Wilson, Westal, Cheltenham. Please do this for me Mrs Oates – my wife has real faith in God and so your son tells me have you – and so have I.'
7 *Journal of the 6th (Inniskilling) Dragoons*, February 1913.
8 *Ibid.*, D. Squadron Notes.
9 *Ibid.*, March 1913.
10 No attempt has been made to reference newspapers. The story was covered by every national, regional and local paper in the country, as well as countless foreign newspapers. For two weeks, from 11 February 1913, the story filled these papers. It was still receiving enlargement and comment in June 1913.
11 *East Anglian Daily News.*
12 Major General (later Field-Marshal Viscount) Allenby had served in the 6th (Inniskilling) Dragoons from 1882 to 1901. He was their acting commanding officer for a period during the Boer War.
13 *The Daily Mail*, 13 February 1913.
14 *The Red Triangle*, quoting Professor Cramb.
15 Quoted by H. Ponting in *The Great White South*, p. 297.
16 Prince Alexander of Teck made this comment at Eton School when unveiling the bronze of Oates (executed by Lady Kathleen Scott).
17 George Bernard Shaw, letter to Lord Kennet (second husband to Kathleen Scott), 28 February 1948.
18 *The Geographical Journal*, March 1913, p. 212.
19 David Thomson, *Scott's Men*, p. 163.
20 *The British Review*, April 1913.

Bibliography

GENERAL AND MILITARY

Amery, L. S., *The Problem of the Army*. London, Edward Arnold, 1903

Ansell, Colonel Sir Mike, *Soldier On*. London, P. Davies, 1973

Arnold-Foster, H.O., *The Army in 1906: A Policy and a Vindication*. London, John Murray, 1906

Barnett, Correlli, *Britain and Her Army: A Military, Political and Social Survey*. London, Allen Lane, The Penguin Press, 1970

Baynes, Lieutenant-Colonel J., *Morale: A Study of Men and Courage*. London, Cassell, 1967

Blacker, General Sir Cecil, and Woods, Major-General H. G., *Change and Challenge: The Story of the 5th Royal Inniskilling Dragoon Guards*.London, William Clowes, 1978

Cairnes, Captain W. E., *Social Life in the British Army*. London, J. Long, 1900

– , *The Army from Within*. London, Sands & Co., 1901

– , *The Absent-Minded War*. London, John Milner, 1900

Churchill, Winston S., *A History of the English Speaking Peoples: The Great Democracies*. London, Cassell, 1958

Cromer, Earl of, *Modern Egypt*. London, Macmillan & Co., 1908

O'Brien, Marie and Conor Cruise, *A Concise History of Ireland*. London, Thames & Hudson, 1972

Davidoff, Leonore, *The Best Circles*. London, Croom Helm, 1973

Dunlop, Colonel J. K., *The Development of the British Army 1899-1914*. London, Methuen, 1938

Evans, Major-General R., *The Story of the 5th Royal Inniskilling Dragoon Guards*. Aldershot, Gale & Polden, 1951

Farwell, Byron, *For Queen and Country: A Social History of the Victorian and Edwardian Army*. London, Allen Lane, 1981

– , *The Great Boer War*. London, Allen Lane, 1976

Girouard, Mark, *The Return to Camelot: Chivalry and the English Gentleman*. Yale University Press, 1981

Haley, A. H., *The Crawley Affair*. London, Seeley Service, 1972

Hamer, W. S., *The British Army: Civil-Military Relations 1885-1905*. Oxford, Clarendon Press, 1970

Hawkey, A., *Last Post at Mhow*. London, Jarrolds, 1969

Jackson, Major E. S., *The Inniskilling Dragoons: The Records of an Old Heavy Cavalry Regiment*. London, Arthur L. Humphreys, 1909

Journals of the 6th (Inniskilling) Dragoons 1911-1914

Kipling, Rudyard, *Stories and Poems*. London, Dent, 1970

Lawrence, T. E., *Seven Pillars of Wisdom*

Lloyd, R. A., *A Trooper in the Tins*. London, Hurst & Blackett, 1938

Moran, 1st Baron (C. M. W.), *The Anatomy of Courage*. London, Constable, 1966

O'Connor, Sir James, *History of Ireland 1798-1924 Volume II*. London, E. Arnold & Co., 1925

Coulton, G. C., *Fourscore Years*. Cambridge, University Press, 1943

Pakenham, T., *The Boer War*. London, Weidenfeld & Nicolson, 1979

Parsons, Major-General L. W., *Training the Intelligence of Officers and Men*. 1906

Pomeroy, Major the Hon. R. L., *5th Princess Charlotte of Wales' Dragoon Guards*. Edinburgh & London, W. Blackwood & Sons, 1924

Prescott-Westcar, Lieutenant-Colonel V., *Big Game, Boers and Boches*. London, Stanley Paul & Co., 1937

Prior, M., *Campaigns of a War Correspondent*. London, Edward Arnold, 1912

Regimental Historical Records, *6th Inniskilling Dragoons 1898-1914*

Richards, Frank, *Old Soldier Sahib*. London, Faber & Faber, 1936

Robertson, Field-Marshal Sir William Robert, *From Private to Field-Marshal*. London, Constable, 1921

Shelley, A. R., *The Victorian Army at Home*. London, 1977

Spiers, Edward M., *The Army and Society 1815-1914*. London, Longmans, 1980

Turner, E. S., *Gallant Gentlemen: A Portrait of the British Officer*. London, Michael Joseph, 1956

Watkins Yardley, Lieutenant-Colonel J., *With the Inniskilling Dragoons: The Record of a Cavalry Regiment During the Boer War 1899-1902*. London, Longmans, 1904

Wyndham, Horace, *Following the Drum*. London, Andrew Melrose, 1912

ANTARCTIC

Amundsen, Roald, *The South Pole*. London, John Murray, 1912

Bernacchi, L. C., *A Very Gallant Gentleman*. London, Thornton Butterworth, 1933

Brent, Peter, *Captain Scott and the Antarctic Tragedy*. London, Weidenfeld & Nicolson, 1974

British *(Terra Nova)* Antarctic Expedition, 1910-1913, *Miscellaneous Data*. London, Harrison & Sons, 1924

Cameron, Ian, *Antarctica: The Lost Continent*. London, Cassell, 1974

Cherry-Garrard, Apsley, *The Worst Journey in the World*. London, Chatto & Windus, 1965

Debenham, F., *In The Antarctic*. London, John Murray, 1952

Evans, E. R. G. R., *South With Scott*. London & Glasgow, Collins, 1921

— , 'My Recollections of a Gallant Comrade' *(Strand Magazine*, Dec. 1913)

Griffith Taylor, T., *With Scott: The Silver Lining*. London, Smith, Elder & Co., 1916

Huntford, Roland, *Scott and Amundsen*. London, Hodder & Stoughton, 1979

Huxley, E., *Scott of the Antarctic*. London, Weidenfeld & Nicolson, 1977

Kennet, Lady, *Self-Portrait of an Artist*. London, John Murray, 1949

King, H. G. R., *The Antarctic*. London, Blandford Press, 1969

Kirwan, L. P., *A History of Polar Exploration*. Harmondsworth, Penguin Books, 1962

Lashley, William, *Under Scott's Command, Lashley's Antarctic Diaries*.London, Gollancz, 1969

Markham, Sir Clements, *The Lands of Silence, A History of Arctic and Antarctic Exploration*. Cambridge, University Press, 1921

Ponting, Herbert G., *The Great White South*. London, Duckworth & Co., 1923

Pound, Reginald, *Scott of the Antarctic*. London, Cassell, 1966

Priestley, Raymond, *Antarctic Adventure: Scott's Northern Party*. London, T. Fisher Unwin, 1914

Savours, Ann, *Scott's Last Voyage: Through the Antarctic Camera of Herbert Ponting*. London, Sidgwick & Jackson, 1974

Scott's Last Expedition, arranged by Leonard Huxley. London, Smith, Elder & Co., 1913

Seaver, George, *'Birdie' Bowers of the Antarctic*. London, John Murray, 1938

— , *Scott of the Antarctic*. London, John Murray, 1940

The South Polar Times Volume III. London, Smith, Elder & Co., 1914

Wilson, Edward, *Diary of the 'Terra Nova' Expedition to the Antarctic 1910-1912*, ed. H. G. R. King. London, Blandford Press, 1972

Index

British Army *(continued)*
state of in 1899, 27
British Army of Occupation in
Egypt, 72
Broderick reforms, 65
Bromwick, Reverend, Rector
of Gestingthorpe, 19
Brooke, Lieutenant-Colonel J.
A., 41, 59, 81, 94, 95, 108
Bruce, W., 115
Bull, Captain S. C., 77, 78

Cairnes, Captain W. E., 25, 38,
59, 62
Cairo, 74, 82, 83
Campbell, V., 116, 120, 128,
155, 165
Cape Evans,
description of hut, 154–155
Cape Town, 120
Cardwell, Lord, 27
Cavalry Brigade, 3rd, 53
Cavalry Club, 210
Cavalry School, Netheravon, nr
Salisbury, 63
Cestrian, S.S., 71
Chamberlain, Joseph, 35
Chambers, Miss Florence, 39
Cherry-Garrard, A.,
edits *South Polar Times*, 158
trip to Cape Crozier, 163
on Polar journey, 173 passim
attempt to rescue Scott, 205
Chester, F., 86
Chinaman (pony), 122
shot, 180
Chivalry
in Egypt, 77
conventions in 1900, 59

Christmas celebrations
in 1910, 128
in 1911, 187
Christopher (pony), 122
vicious and capricious
nature, 166
shot, 180
Churchill, Sir W., 30, 68
Citadel in Cairo, 75
Clifden, Nellie, 58
Clissold (cook), 162
Connaught, Duke of, 60
Cook, Captain, 111
Coulton, G. C., 18
Crean, T., 136, 146
on Polar journey, 183 passim
Cromer, Lord, 68, 74, 80
Cub, *see* Horses
Curragh, the, 31, 53, 57
Curzon, Viscount, 37

Daddy, *see* Horses
Damascus, 83
Day, B., 114, 155, 175
Debenham, F., 114, 155, 175,
163
first impression of Oates,
124
lecture on volcanoes, 158
Deighton, kennel man, 103,
105
Deighton, Mrs Mabel (wife of
the above) reaction to
Oates's death, 207
Delhi, Base Hospital, 106
Denishwai, 76–81
Depot Barracks, York, 24
Derwish Zahran, 76, 79
Disraeli, B., 68

230

Owen, H., comment on Oates's death in *The National Weekly*, 210

Petit Bleu, a Belgian newspaper, 80
Pine Coffin, Major, 77, 81
Polo, 57, 82
Ponies, for Scott's expedition
  bought in Siberia, 115
  catalogue of defects, 122
  how stabled on board ship, 124
  sufferings in storm, 126, 127
  snowshoes, 136, 137, 165, 180
  walls of snow for protection, 139
  their various vices, 165
  exercised, 165
  last ponies shot, 183
Ponsonby Barracks, the Curragh, 53
Ponting, H., 150
  his darkroom, 155
  shows slides in winter, 159, 162
  records departure of Polar party, 175
  his film *90° South* shown in trenches during First World War, 212
Port Said, 74
Pound, R., 213
Prescott-Westcar, Lieutenant-Colonel V., 81

Priestley, R., 114
Prince of Wales, 53
  as Edward VII, 91

Prince of Wales's Own West Yorkshire Regiment, the 3rd Battalion, 22, 29
Punch (pony), 140
  killed, 147
Punchestown race course, 56
Putney, 263; Upper Richmond Road, 9

Quail Island, where ponies quarantined, 121

Racing, *see* Horse racing
Rawlings' house, Eton, 17, 18
Remenham Place, Henley-on-Thames, 16
Rhodes, Cecil, 34, 35
Richards, Frank, 95, 100
Rimington, Lieutenant-General Sir Michael, 49, 53, 56, 105
Roberts, Field-Marshal Lord, 37, 63
Robertson, Field-Marshal Sir William, 64
Rogers, A. F., M.D., 199
Ross, Sir James, 111

Saunterer, 62, 87, 101
Scott, Robert Falcon
  Discovery expedition, 112
  recruits *Terra Nova* staff, 113
  daily routine on depot-laying journey, 140
  celebrates his 46th birthday, 164
  affectionate nature, 189
  shyness, 129
  anxiety over ponies, 130, 137, 139, 161, 177